Leading Equity-Focused Inquiry for Continuous School Improvement

Edited by
Margaret Terry Orr

Foreword by David Imig

Teachers College Press
Teachers College, Columbia University

Published by Teachers College Press,® 1234 Amsterdam Avenue, New York, NY 10027

Front cover design by Geronna Lewis-Lyte. Illustration by Alex Eckermann / Unsplash.

Library of Congress Cataloging-in-Publication Data is available at loc.gov

ISBN 978-0-8077-8772-4 (paper)
ISBN 978-0-8077-8773-1 (hardcover)
ISBN 978-0-8077-8341-2 (ebook)

Printed on acid-free paper
Manufactured in the United States of America

Contents

Foreword

This volume brings together a collection of exciting efforts to advance work in the field of education, with a focus on continuous improvement using improvement science. Dr. Margaret Terry Orr and contributors offer a comprehensive overview of improvement science, from a foundational introduction to practical strategies for leading school and district transformation. Each chapter, written by school leaders in the New York City area, presents rich and vital examples of how we can transcend static research by focusing on the "implementation" part of school change. By extending efforts to truly understand issues within communities, neighborhoods, and schools, and by applying that knowledge to the design of effective structures and strategies, the contributors establish a pathway for school leaders to achieve true engagement and meaningful improvement in learning outcomes. That promise is exciting on its own, but this book goes further: It documents both the experiences and lessons learned from when these projects were implemented. This volume is a welcome and much-needed exegesis of some of the best efforts to implement an improvement framework in schools.

One of the most significant scholars of school leadership preparation and practice, Terry Orr, is the driving force behind this collection. She is the guru behind the redesign of the EdD program at Fordham University in NYC and a uniquely talented doctoral supervisor. Her focus on the role of leaders in schools serving marginalized students defines the spirit of this work. Terry's introduction to this book offers a primer on improvement science and the tools and principles to be used "to help America's schools get better at getting better." Subsequent chapters continue to support this theme, offering a look at ways leaders lead the transformation of schools and school districts. The final chapter provides a superb synthesis and analysis of how effective leaders lead.

Leading Equity-Focused Inquiry for Continuous School Improvement consists of eight chapters, all of which originated as *dissertations in practice*. The chapters authors—who are all former students of Dr. Orr—range from experienced secondary and elementary principals to novice principals leading change initiatives in city and suburban schools. One seeks to transform a whole school, while others focus their case on a single subject matter. Two authors address the needs of distinct student populations, while another is dedicated to cultivating inclusive, schoolwide support for students with special needs. Two lead initiatives that stretch beyond a single school, impacting larger educational communities. The *why* of their efforts is well understood. It is *what* they do and *how* they do it that is the focus. Despite the variation in their approaches and methods, all are grounded in a common commitment to continuous improvement. Each includes an improvement cycle highlighting what and when they took action. All the chapters conclude with a series of challenging questions, impact statements, and carefully drawn self-reflections.

I had the privilege of being a reader for Dr. Orr's dissertations in practice. The process is purposeful, deeply reflective, and the rubric shared with readers in the weeks leading up to the final defense provides guidance to both assess the worthiness of the presentation and shape the interactions between candidate and committee members. Collectively, these stories of leadership and change illustrate the effect and appreciation of the common improvement framework. The contributors each evidence a deep engagement with various leadership styles, provide a valuable literature review relevant to their problem analysis, and share carefully crafted narratives of their efforts to lead others in implementing meaningful change within their schools and districts. Orr has created something greater than the sum of its parts—a compelling argument to educational leadership that centers equity, embraces complexity, and is steadfastly committed to all students, especially those most often marginalized by our educational systems. This volume is a testament to Terry Orr's profound influence on school leadership preparation and practice, and shows proof of the promise that school leaders can lead in impactful ways.

—David Imig
Professor Emeritus of Practice
University of Maryland, College of Education

Introduction

Leading Equity-Focused Inquiry for Continuous School Improvement

Margaret Terry Orr

Leading Equity-Focused Inquiry for Continuous School Improvement describes how eight leaders used equity-focused improvement science principles to increase their efficacy and how their teachers and other staff improved their effectiveness so their students, particularly those facing the most challenges, would gain improved conditions and supports for learning. This book presents eight case studies and a multicase synthesis of how these leaders addressed a myriad of complex educational challenges and critical student needs. It shows how they did so through careful exploration of specific problems and their causes and thoughtfully testing solutions, while working collaboratively with teachers and other staff, whose work most often required change.

THE NEED FOR A CONTINUOUS IMPROVEMENT PROCESS

School and district leaders work in complex environments, encountering scores of problems and decisions daily. The breadth and depth of their responsibilities have been well documented, covering not only administration and operations, but student and staff matters, community engagement, curriculum, instruction, and assessment (Grissom et al., 2021). Policy changes in recent years have shifted educational leaders' roles from management to leadership, and their work from accountability to continuous improvement in student learning and achievement (Bryk, 2020).

Many school and district matters are routine and can be handled with readily available technical solutions. But there remain perplexing problems that warrant closer analysis and investigation to be solved. Added to the need to solve such problems is the press for continuous improvement, to iteratively support change efforts and their fit and effectiveness, since initial solutions are not always successful or even adequate. Thus, continuous improvement requires incremental analysis over time of areas that need improvement, and cycles of adjustments to gain better outcomes over time (Park et al., 2013).

Leading continuous improvement efforts is fraught with challenges and requires skills and capacities for which school and district leaders are typically underprepared (Mehta et al., 2022; Yurkofsky, 2022). The impetus for improvement is often driven by accountability pressures to meet or exceed state performance benchmarks, community expectations, or local competition. Initially, continuous improvement was narrowly defined by formal methodologies, such as the Six Sigma set of techniques and tools for process improvement, created in 1986 by Bill Smith (Tennant, 2001). The continuous improvement model has more recently been successfully used in health care and manufacturing for simultaneously improving efficiency and effectiveness (Park et al., 2013). Continuous improvement has now become more common in the field of education to promote innovation; better, more reliable practices; and gains in student learning and achievement (Tichnor-Wagner et al., 2017; Yurkofsky, 2022). While improving efficiency and efficacy are among the goals of continuous improvement, it also can and should be used to reduce inequities in students' educational experiences and outcomes (Hinnant-Crawford et al., 2023).

With current pressures of accountability and performance improvement, effective leaders must now employ a broader range of strategies to promote continuous improvement in schools. They must depend on collaboration with other educational professionals, relying on their own engagement skills and capacity to foster a culture of learning and expectations of continuous improvement (Bryk, 2020). This requires establishing a vision and direction for improvement work and data-informed planning. But such direction-setting is difficult because schools and districts are awash with data from different sources and reporting periods often unaligned to the time periods and problems when planning is most critical. In addition, the complexity of planning becomes multiplied by competition among problems and priorities, as well as varied staff capacity, motivation, and willingness to pursue improvement or allow continuous improvement to become normative for a school or district culture. Thus, developing a culture of continuous improvement requires leaders to combine attention to specific areas needing improvement with the creation of systems and structures for the inquiry process, engagement of staff in the improvement work, supportive organizational change practices, and evaluation of the impact for further improvement efforts.

CONTINUOUS IMPROVEMENT AND IMPROVEMENT SCIENCE PRACTICES IN EDUCATION SETTINGS

Employing continuous improvement is a means of transformation for both a targeted problem of practice and for a school or district as a whole. Success depends upon how an improvement process is led and what organizational practices are used to support it. Improvement science offers both a framework and process to support continuous improvement (Bryk et al., 2015; Lewis, 2015).

The roots of improvement science are often attributed to Deming's system of profound knowledge. Its four parts are informed by (a) an appreciation for viewing organizations as a system with the interrelated parts, (b) attention to and understanding of variation, (c) a theory of knowledge and how knowledge is gained, and (d) the role of psychology in leading and managing others (Hinnant-Crawford, 2020). Improvement science also has its roots in action research and the work of Kurt Lewin, who promoted the use of cycles of inquiry to collect data and support action to solve a social problem. Lewin promoted action research as a collaborative approach to studying and resolving important social issues with those who experience them directly (Coghlan & Brannick, 2010).

Bryk and his colleagues (2015) outline six principles for improvement science to guide school improvement:

- school improvement through sustained inquiry around problems of practice;
- attention to variation in performance (in pursuit of equity and excellence in student learning);
- application of a systems perspective to account for school, district, and other external influences;
- use of applied research methods and multiple sources of data;
- application of rigorous inquiry practices and reflection on possible solutions and innovation; and
- embracing of a network approach to collaborative inquiry and problem-solving (Bryk et al., 2015).

Use of improvement science principles represents a paradigm "that recognizes the complexity of the tasks that educators undertake and the systems through which they carry them out . . . [whereby] highly variable consequences are the inevitable end result" (Bryk et al., 2015, p. 50). Improvement science practice differs from traditional approaches to improvement work in several important ways. It simultaneously requires a shift in leadership orientation and organizational practices, along with careful inquiry about problems, before proposing solutions, and a concerted effort to develop new approaches or solutions with concurrent investigations of fit and effectiveness (Bryk et al., 2015). These differences are explained further below.

First, improvement science as inquiry requires a sustained focus on the problem of practice from several vantage points. It begins with the assumption that critical or heretofore unsolved problems are not well understood by leaders and their staff and thus require deeper investigation, broader exploration, the challenging of assumptions, and extensive initial study of the problem's attributes from different vantage points. This step centers problem exploration on the "users"—the people who directly experience the problem. In education, the users are typically the students, for example, if the problem is about low math or reading performance or absenteeism.

Second, such attention to the problem requires the collection of information on the users' experiences, optimally from multiple sources of data, including quantitative evidence from existing reporting systems and qualitative evidence gathered from interviews and observations, to "see" the problem from the users' perspectives and encounters. Analysis of these data draws attention to *variations* in users' experiences and outcomes, be they narrow or broad. Thus, rather than consideration only of average score differences among groups, insights about a problem of practice can be gained from examining how scores or measures range in order to question how current practices and systems may contribute to different levels of performance or outcomes.

Evaluating variation is critical because our aim as educators is to establish a standard set of practices, *standardized work processes*, that can predictably yield positive outcomes for most students under most conditions. The narrower the variation in student performance or other measures, the more consistent our practices and their effectiveness are likely to be. Conversely, the wider the variation in student performance or other measures, the less consistent or effective our practices are likely to be. Thus, studying variation can help us evaluate the consistency and effectiveness of our practices and explore how differences in our practices contribute to highs and lows in varied outcomes.

Third is the need to understand a problem through the lens of its context and the system that produces it. Existing approaches, practices, staffing, and resources for addressing the problem differ in different contexts. Moreover, as Langley et al. (2009) is quoted in the improvement field, "every system is perfectly designed to deliver the results it produces" (p. 79). Thus, it is important to step back and see the system as it pertains to a problem of practice, in order to understand how the context attributes and existing approaches work together to yield the current outcomes. Importantly, leadership and staff support are key aspects of the system to examine.

A useful resource for system analysis is the organization of all the contributing factors thematically and pictorially as a fishbone, where a problem is represented by the fish head and each common group of contributing

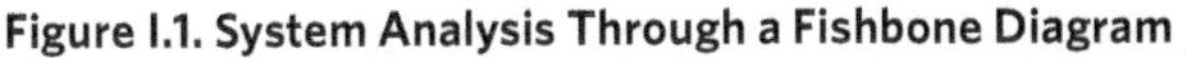

Figure I.1. System Analysis Through a Fishbone Diagram

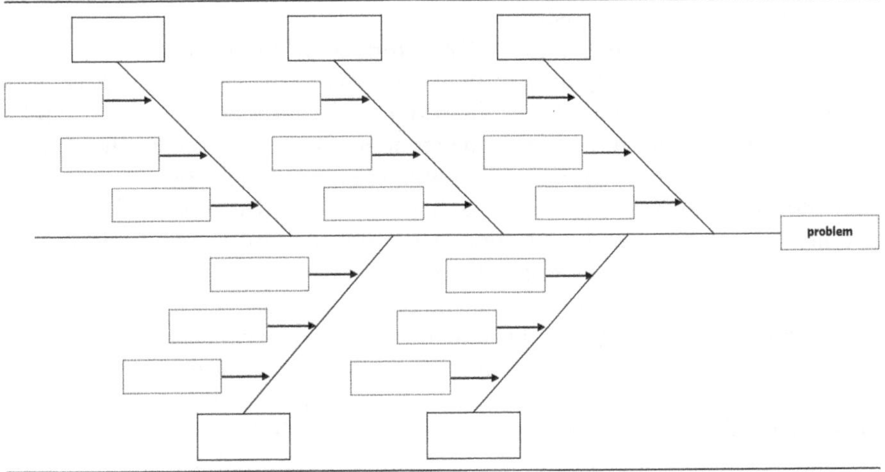

factors are the bones. This visual representation enables leaders and their staff to step back and evaluate how and in what ways these factor groups account for the problem of practice (see Figure I.1).

Such a system analysis can lead to further problem and system exploration through interviews with staff and users about how they experience these contributing factors and how they perceive the causes' or factors' connection to the problem of practice. These interviews can help to surface and challenge strongly held assumptions about what contributes to a problem of practice, how, in what ways, and why, by probing the veracity of these assumptions based on evidence and hypothesizing alternative explanations. This system analysis enables identification of key leverage areas for improvement and theorizing about how a change in one area might lead to measurable improvement in the problem of practice.

In the improvement field, we try to identify which causes or factors, if changed, would offer the greatest potential for improvement. Such identification is defined as the "Pareto principle," as typically 20% of the possible causes contribute to 80% of the variability in a problem (Bryk et al., 2015, p. 176). Solving or otherwise improving the problem situation would therefore entail discontinuing a practice that is not working, adding a missing practice to enhance current efforts, adapting or replacing a practice based on newly revealed assumptions or insights, or some combination, thereof. Typically, one or two high-leverage areas for change are identified, respective changes or alternatives for these areas are identified, and their relationship to a proposed aim as a new theory of action is proposed. These high-leverage areas are defined as the primary *drivers* for change, in that if they are enacted or operationalized, then the proposed aim should improve. These elements—the aim and primary drivers—become an explicit theory of action, which can be stated as:

If we enact (primary drivers), then (aim) should improve.

Before discussing the next steps in improvement science practices, it is useful to step back and apply the first three practices to one school example. In this example, too many 7th-grade students in an urban 3–8 school were receiving low quarterly grades for incomplete or missing assignments across their content courses. The principal met with the teachers to discuss the problem. They came ready to brainstorm solutions—primarily penalties—to increase homework completion. The principal paused the discussion and instead asked several questions about the problem, probing why they thought students were not doing their homework. Their answers centered on blaming the students for being lazy, unmotivated, or lacking parental support. The principal probed deeper—was this all students or only some? The principal then asked the teachers to meet again after collecting more data—to compile their homework completion data for trend analysis by the day or week and student proficiency, and to conduct empathy interviews with a few students to learn why they were not completing their homework.

In this initial step, the principal modeled several key steps: slowing down the process and not jumping to solutions, taking time to begin to frame the problem with greater specificity, surfacing the teachers' assumptions about why students were not completing homework assignments sufficiently, and asking for data to examine variation in the problem and gain the user perspective (how students experience the problem).

When the group met again the following week, they reviewed the data they had gathered. From the quantitative evidence, they could not see any discernible pattern among the students or the days of the week. From the empathy interviews, however, a new picture of the problem emerged: Some students were overwhelmed by the amount of homework and their family responsibilities of caring for younger siblings, and several students complained that the homework was boring, seemed unnecessary, and was rarely checked by their teachers when they did complete it.

Using this information, the principal and teachers decided to collect more information that would allow them to see the system they had created in assigning homework. For the next meeting, they gathered up all the homework assignments for a week and compiled them for analysis. In this examination they learned about the large and uneven quantity of homework they were assigning weekly and noticed that most of the homework was similar—requiring students to complete duplicated worksheets. They also reviewed their practice of spending class time reviewing and grading completed homework and found it had often been inconsistent or missing. Through this analysis, they and the principal were able to construct a fishbone analysis of their problem, discovering that it centered on their practices: poor quality or unnecessary homework assignments; insufficient coherence in pacing homework assignments across subjects weekly; inadequate follow-up on discussing or grading completed homework; and insufficient support for students with competing family and personal demands.

In their analysis, they selected two high-leverage areas to address as easily actionable, setting as their aim to improve students' homework completion rates. These two areas were to modify and even out the amount of homework scheduled weekly across content areas and to become more consistent in grading completed homework. They selected the other two areas for further work—creating more meaningful assignments and supporting students with competing demands or insufficient support during nonschool hours.

The fourth improvement science step is the extension of how *to realize the aim and what to do.* The "how" represents the means by which the primary drivers are activated. The typical means of activating *primary drivers* or changes involve professional learning, changes in systems and structures, reorganization of collaborative practices, and the addition of new programs or practices (Mintrop, 2016). These activators are defined as the *secondary drivers* and represent the primary interventions for improvement.

In turn, the secondary drivers are operationalized in specific ways that represent what are called the *change ideas* for the improvement effort. These change ideas encompass the detailed steps or actions, as there are often many possible alternatives, such as when, where, in what form, and how much professional learning will be required or which form of collaborative practice will be used and how these will be supported. The individual change ideas represent the decisions and actions that are selected to operationalize the secondary drivers. The actions outlined as change ideas typically reflect considerations of the local context, available resources, and policy options. They are modifiable as the proposed interventions are implemented and adjustments are made to better support their feasibility and use.

It is useful in improvement work to make these elements and their hypothesized relationship explicit, using a driver diagram (see Figure I.2). The elements of the driver diagram represent a theory of improvement that is

Figure I.2. Driver Diagram Representing the Theory of Action

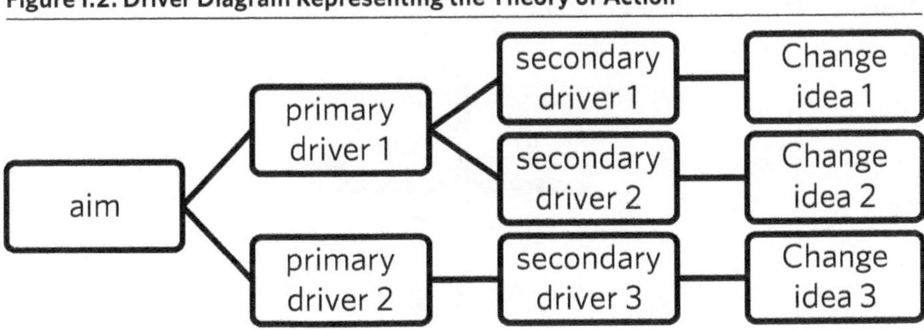

testable, once initial changes are tried out and adapted for use. This model should represent a substantive departure from existing practice reflecting new assumptions about the problem and means of improvement.

Fifth is testing the theory of action through a series of inquiry cycles, focusing first on operationalizing the specific change ideas (were these feasible, operationalized, and implemented as needed or modified for use?). Next is to evaluate whether these enacted change ideas enabled the secondary drivers (for example, did teachers learn new practices through the form and amount of professional learning used, or did the structures and supports enable teacher teams to work collaboratively?). If so, then, in turn, the next step is to evaluate whether the secondary drivers activate the primary drivers (for example, did teachers learn enough in their professional learning to gain new skills and practices?). The final step is to evaluate whether the primary drivers are sufficient high-leverage improvements to achieve the aim. This is the final step in testing the theory of action for improvement (for example, did changes in teacher practice improve student learning?).

The most commonly used inquiry cycle is Plan-Do-Study-Act, which lays out each step in the idea-testing process, both what is tested or tried and how it is evaluated (see Figure I.3).

In the *plan* phase, the proposed change or intervention is mapped out for implementation, addressing necessary logistics, materials, and resources. Simultaneously, those who are enacting the change effort should also be preparing to collect relevant information to document what is being implemented and how to track early impact on the target of change. This can be done by creating tracking forms, fielding pre- and post-assessments, and compiling baseline measures. In the *do* phase, the planned intervention or change is operationalized, with simultaneous data collection on implementation, use, and early impact, as had been planned. After a designated initial period of use comes the *study* phase, in which the documentation on implementation is evaluated to determine the intervention's feasibility and ease of use, and to review feedback on staff and student reactions and suggested improvements in order to evaluate the initial impact. This phase is followed

Figure I.3. Plan-Do-Study-Act Model

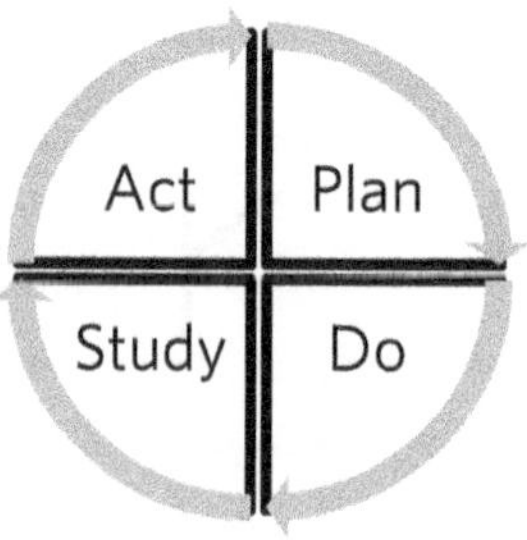

by the *act* phase, in which decisions are made to adopt the tested change or intervention for continued use, adapt it based on early feedback and use experiences, or abandon it as unworkable or inappropriate.

The inquiry process does not end in just one cycle, however. Typical efforts to improve education policies and practices require multiple cycles of testing as change ideas are adjusted to fit the local context, and later as the secondary and primary driver strategies are adjusted, improved, or abandoned, in whole or in part, based on the evidence gathered and the success of the theory of action. Frequently, there are several short initial iterations or improvement cycles as the planned intervention is modified to improve feasibility and use. Later inquiry cycles shift from attending to feasibility to determining the impact of the intervention. Therefore, these cycles are longer in duration depending upon the aim being pursued. The aim is to develop a set of standardized work processes that reliably yield intended improvements for students and staff.

Such processes—testing out change ideas and examining whether these yielded the intended secondary drivers and, in turn, activated the primary drivers and impacted the aim—while seemingly simple steps, are actually quite complex because they require a shift in how a school or district works on problems and tries out solutions. This form of continuous improvement requires leading and organizing in new collaborative ways of working and fostering a culture of problem-solving data use, trust in risk-taking, and learning as a core process for improvement.

Returning to the initial example, let's examine what the teachers and principal did next to develop and test their ideas. Starting with the primary driver of simplifying and creating coherence in weekly homework assignments, the teachers agreed to activate this by establishing shared homework assignment guidelines. The change idea they started with first was to alternate which days each subject-area teacher could assign homework and use their team meeting time to check in on the workload demands of each assignment. For the second primary driver of regularly grading homework, they committed themselves to only assign homework that they would be able to grade in a timely manner. The change idea to support this was to establish this as a shared practice and commit to regularly revisit their progress. By limiting how much homework they assigned weekly, they began to work on making the assignments more meaningful and educative. They tried out these new policies and practices following an initial planning meeting, checking in with one another in subsequent meetings to review what worked or did not and to make modifications. Over time, as they tried out these new practices, they also monitored improvements in homework completion overall and among students for whom they had learned it was most challenging to manage. They not only learned that addressing a problem from the user's perspective would lead to more workable and effective solutions, they also learned to collaborate with one another and the principal in problem-solving, to use data to inform their practice, and to feel safe in trying out changes in practice.

INCORPORATING AN EQUITY PERSPECTIVE

Throughout the continuous improvement process, particularly in using improvement science practices, there are opportunities to incorporate an equity perspective. While continuous improvement research, particularly through improvement science practices, can be effective in pursuit of equity in students' educational experiences and outcomes, it is not a given that it will. In fact, as Hinnant-Crawford et al. (2023) argue, without a conscious use of an equity perspective, there is a danger that it can improve the efficiency of school or district systems and practices without reducing inequities. Thus, it is important throughout that each phase of improvement science inquiry and practice considers how historically underserved students have experienced a problem of practice, the variations in their experiences, and how existing systems and structures may uniquely contribute to their experiences of the problem. The problem exploration phase of improvement work is a critical opportunity to surface and challenge existing assumptions that may contribute to perpetuating inequities. Similarly, when designing and testing solutions, significant attention must be given to how these improve opportunities and conditions for historically underserved students and in what ways. In some cases, according to Hinnant-Crawford et al. (2023), dramatic change may be necessary because inequity is so deeply built into current practices, stating that "some systems are beyond modification and require prophetic imagination and architecture" (p. 118). Thus, for leaders to engage in equity-focused improvement science, they must, as Hinnant-Crawford et al. (2023) advise, center justice in their work and ensure that others with whom they work adopt a critical equity perspective in their shared work.

ABOUT THE BOOK

This book presents eight case studies and a final synthesis chapter that discusses how educational leaders created and facilitated equity-focused improvement inquiry in their schools and districts. Each chapter describes one author's journey, as a school or district leader, through problem identification and exploration to solution generation and testing. The leaders' efforts consist of more than the technical steps of following improvement science principles for continuous improvement; they entail fostering learning and change in their local contexts to build teacher and leader capacity for such inquiry, while piloting new innovations. Each case is designed to both illustrate and model how such work can be undertaken, the impact on targeted problems of practice, and the organizational learning the authors fostered to enable the improvement work.

It is worth noting that all eight educational leaders presented in the following cases undertook their inquiry work by coupling ongoing improvement efforts with their doctoral preparation and dissertation in practice research (Orr & Stosich, 2022). Thus, they were trying improvement science for the first time, purposefully adapting their leadership practices and change strategies as a result. They benefited from faculty support and guidance through their process: challenging their leadership considerations, slowing down their problem investigations (rather than jumping to solutions, as is typical), and helping them establish a methodology for evaluating their improvement work. The leaders also benefited from access to professional journals and publications, where they explored available research on how others unpacked their problem and on workable solutions.

Five cases focus on leaders' work to improve student learning through better teacher practice. In all five cases, the principals established structures and processes to support teacher inquiry and collaboration, including professional learning communities, lesson study, paired collaboration, co-teaching, and coaching. Two cases describe two approaches, one school-based and one district-based, to foster school improvement by engaging teachers and principals in continuous improvement cycles to address local problems of practice. One case describes the experience of one principal who used continuous improvement to create an in-school program and schoolwide support for students with severe disabilities.

Chapter 1, "Improving ELA Instruction for Middle School Black Boys Through Lesson Study and Culturally Relevant Pedagogy" by Rosalyn Barnes, describes how she engaged ELA middle school teachers in adopting culturally relevant teaching practices into their classes using a schoolwide book study and the Japanese lesson study process to improve their instruction and content and better engage their Black boys.

Chapter 2, "Transforming Our Middle School Math Instruction Through an Integrated Approach and Co-teaching" by Josef Haas, describes how, as the assistant principal, he coached his middle school math teachers to use a common integrated math approach, using co-teaching and daily common planning and feedback.

Chapter 3, "Improving Students' Sense of Belonging Through Teacher Collaborative Improvement" by Trisha Fitzgerald, describes how she supported a group of elementary school teachers in adopting and implementing a common morning meeting ritual, through group meetings and reflections, to improve student engagement during the pandemic in grades kindergarten through 5th grade.

Chapter 4, "A Multipronged Approach to Improve Reading Instruction for Students With Disabilities" by Shaundrika Langley-Grey, describes her improvement efforts to enhance the instructional skills of special education teachers. This includes teaching them how to effectively instruct reading to students with special needs while integrating trauma-informed approaches. The chapter emphasizes the iterative process she used in transforming teaching practices, fostering emotional awareness, and increasing reading proficiency among students.

Chapter 5, "Cultivating a Schoolwide Approach to Integrate K–5 Students With Significant Disabilities" by Tashia Brown, describes how as principal she designed and implemented a program for students with significant impairments to be educated in their local elementary school, through targeted professional learning and job-embedded coaching, fostering teacher collaboration and agency, and promoting a more inclusive school culture.

Chapter 6, "Supporting English Language Instruction for All Through a Nested Learning Experience" by Christopher Keough, describes how a director of instruction engaged elementary school teachers in learning to adopt English language instructional practices to support non-English-speaking students, through a collaborative inquiry process.

Chapter 7, "Engaging Middle School Teachers in Improvement Cycles to Increase Achievement" by Gail Joyner, describes how one principal established structures and processes for subject-based teacher teams to learn to use 3-week improvement cycles to strengthen instructional practices collaboratively.

Chapter 8, "Leading Principals Through Short-Cycle Improvement Work" by Kris DeFilippis, details a process created to support multiple principals in learning improvement science while tackling persistent problems of practices. This case study explores the importance of attention to culture and space in the change process.

Chapter 9, "Leading Continuous Improvement: Cases and Findings" by Margaret Terry Orr, provides a synthesis of the leadership actions and organizational practices used by the leaders in these cases and how they have improved teacher practice and reshaped the school and district culture around data use, collaborative problem-solving, and commitment to continuous learning and improvement. The chapter also provides reflections on the theory behind these practices and why these are best suited to support continuous improvement, particularly for these challenging problems. Finally, the chapter reflects upon the equity considerations used in how the leaders focused their problems of practice and engaged others in learning to question existing assumptions and try out new practices that more effectively engage and support students.

REFERENCES

Bryk, A. S. (2020). *Improvement in action: Advancing quality in America's schools.* Harvard Education Publishing Group.

Bryk, A. S., Gomez, L., Grunow, A., & LeMahieu, P. (2015). *Learning to improve: How America's schools can get better at getting better.* Harvard Education Press.

Coghlan, D., & Brannick, T. (2010). *Doing action research in your own organization.* Sage.

Deming, W. E. (1993). *The new economics for industry, government, education.* The MIT Press.

Grissom, J. A., Egalite, A. J., & Lindsay, C. A. (2021). *How principals affect students and schools: A systematic synthesis of two decades of research.* Wallace Foundation.

Hinnant-Crawford, B. N. (2020). *Improvement science in education: A primer.* Meyers Education Press.

Hinnant-Crawford, B., Lett, E. L., & Cromatie, S. (2023). ImproveCrit: Using critical race theory to guide continuous improvement. In E. Anderson & S. D. Hayes (Eds.), *Continuous improvement: A leadership process for school improvement* (pp. 105–124). Information Age Publishing.

Langley, G. J., Moen, R. D., Nolan, K. M., Nolan, T. W., Norman, C. L., & Provost, L. P. (2009). *The improvement guide.* Jossey-Bass.

Lewis, C. (2015). What is improvement science? Do we need it in education? *Educational Researcher*, *44*(1), 54–61.

Mehta, J., Yurkofsky, M., & Frumin, K. (2022). Linking continuous improvement and adaptive leadership. *Educational Leadership*, *79*(6), 36–41.

Mintrop, R. (2016). *Design-based school improvement.* Harvard Education Press.

Orr, M. T., & Stosich, E. L. (2022). Designing the EdD for transformative change. In E. Anderson & S. Hayes (Eds.), *Continuous improvement: A leadership process for school improvement* (pp. 429–450). Information Age Publishing.

Park, S., Hironaka, S., Carver, P., & Nordstrum, L. (2013). *Continuous improvement in education.* Carnegie Foundation for the Advancement of Teaching.

Tennant, G. (2001). *SIX SIGMA: SPC and TQM in manufacturing and services.* Gower Publishing, Ltd.

Tichnor-Wagner, A., Wachen, J., Cannata, M., & Cohen-Vogel, L. (2017). Continuous improvement in the public school context: Understanding how educators respond to plan-do-study-act cycles. *Journal for Educational Change, 18*, 465–494. https://doi.org/ 10.1007/s10833-017-9301-4

Yurkofsky, M. (2022). From compliance to improvement: How school leaders make sense of institutional and technical demands when implementing a continuous improvement process. *Educational Administration Quarterly*, *58*(2), 300–346.

CHAPTER 1

Improving ELA Instruction for Middle School Black Boys Through Lesson Study and Culturally Relevant Pedagogy

Rosalyn S. Barnes

This case study describes how a Black female principal of an urban Pre-K–8 school worked with her leadership team and middle school ELA teachers to improve ELA instruction using culturally relevant pedagogy, through a 10-week schoolwide book study experience and a 10-week Japanese lesson study process. Middle school ELA teachers worked with one another to design shared expectations for culturally responsive teaching and tried out new lessons, observing and measuring improved student engagement and learning, especially among Black boys. Through Plan-Do-Study-Act cycles of inquiry, the principal co-facilitated and evaluated the implementation and impact of these experiences on teachers and improved student learning.

CONTEXT

Urban Academy, a pseudonym, is in a large Northeast city and serves predominantly Black students in grades Pre-K through 8. Although it is one school, it consists of three distinct communities labeled primary, Pre-K through 3; grammar, grades 3 through 5; and middle, grades 6 through 8. I served as the principal with two assistant principals for over a decade.

During my 10-year tenure, I worked to improve student achievement by focusing on (a) school culture and climate; (b) literacy across the curriculum; and (c) the development of professional learning communities focused on data analysis to improve instruction and student achievement. As a Black woman leading a predominately White, female staff, I developed systems and structures to guide each area of improvement. My approach eventually became more collaborative, whereby more stakeholders became more involved in the decision-making process. The school made great strides in developing a positive school culture and climate. Systemic changes decreased the total amount of out-of-school suspensions for the year. The number of students achieving honor and credit roll status increased. However, the school leadership team had not yet addressed our achievement disparities through the lens of equity.

DISCOVERING THE PROBLEM

When we explored our achievement gains for equity differences, the school leadership team, composed of administrators, teachers, parents, and district leaders, uncovered a pervasive problem at our school. Middle school Black boys were not having the same learning experiences as any other identified subgroup in our school and had lower performance and achievement than their peers. We noticed that they were policed, disciplined, and suspended from school at a higher rate than any other group, and were assessed and labeled as special education for mostly behavioral problems at a higher rate.

Problems seem to persist for Black boys in our school most often at the middle school level. This is a very pivotal period for all students, regardless of gender, race, or ethnicity. Developmentally, students begin entering puberty when their bodies, emotions, and social awareness change (Anderman & Mueller, 2010). They are challenged to develop self-management skills, achieve greater independence, and complete more complex academic tasks at home and in school. Students begin to change classes by 6th grade, and they have four major subject classes (i.e., English language arts, science, math, and social studies) and three special classes (e.g., physical education, Spanish, art, and music). There was clear performance evidence and consensus that these changes disproportionately and negatively impacted Black boys.

ANALYZING THE PROBLEM

The school leadership team included the school's administrators, teachers across the content areas who were nominated and voted in by their peers, and two parent volunteers. During our monthly meetings, the leadership team and I conducted data dives with an equity focus, exploring why our middle school Black boys were constantly lagging behind their peers in achievement and performance in literacy.

In a September 2019 staff meeting, before the onset of the COVID-19 pandemic, we used the fishbone diagram, a tool of improvement science (Bryk et al., 2015), to examine this problem further. I wanted them to be part of the process of determining if this was a problem worth addressing. We also used a root cause analysis protocol like the "five whys," to consistently ask the question "why?" in our small group, in order to engage our thinking around the possible cause of the disparity. We also collected additional data to learn more about the problem and the system that produced it.

I conducted empathy interviews, which offered personal accounts from some middle school literacy teachers and middle school Black boys about how they experienced the problem. I formulated similar questions for the teachers and students. After getting consent for the students from the parents, I conducted the interviews virtually.

Interviews With Teachers

When I asked the teachers about planning lessons and expectations for students, several themes emerged. Two of the three interviewed teachers believed they had high expectations for their students' literacy abilities but could not provide examples of successful lessons that were rich in content or high-level literacy practices. When asked specifically about culturally responsive practices, the teachers shared strategies that were limited to the teacher's selection of books based on holidays like Black History or Hispanic Heritage Month. When asked about the school's operational practices as they related to discipline and referrals to special education programs of mostly Black boys, all teachers expressed reluctance to reply. It was evident that they were concerned about my perception of their responses as their (Black) principal. One teacher smirked, "Come on, you want me to say it." Although I had expressed, in writing, that their participation in the interviews was totally voluntary and their responses would not affect their evaluation as teachers, they were still reluctant to speak their own truth and that of the school. All their responses, however, aligned with the school-level data.

Overall, the teachers perceived that their low-level expectations for students and lessons were appropriate. They confidently spoke about their students and what they deemed successful literacy lessons. However, these lessons focused on developing test prep skills, reading and answering questions, and following procedures. Questions about school-level operational procedures caused visible discomfort, but they nevertheless truthfully provided answers to the questions. All three teachers agreed that middle school Black boys made up most students disciplined, out-of-school suspensions, and special education referrals.

Interviews With Students

I interviewed three Black middle school boys, two general education students and one student with disabilities. I wanted to understand the boys' experiences in literacy class and their relationships with their teachers and peers. When asked about their achievement and performance in literacy classes, two of the three boys agreed that they had performed better in the primary grades. When probed to describe a successful lesson, the boys shared similar experiences: When they followed directions, the teacher acknowledged their success. For example, when one student was asked to write a response to a prompt, at each paragraph he checked in with the teacher, and she affirmed his success before he could move on to the next paragraph. Another student conveyed that he was not always successful but had started paying more attention and following directions. Success for these Black boys had nothing to do with mastery of content, high-level critical skills, or innovation; success was reduced to being compliant or following orders.

When asked about whether the classroom lessons included their culture or interests, one student recalled a lesson with Myers' (1999) book *Monster* when he was in 7th grade. He explained how he connected to the events of the story: He had had to personally call 911 because someone was shot. He and his friends stayed with the injured person until help arrived. What appeared very normal and relevant to this young man was heartbreaking and traumatizing for me, knowing that the teacher had chosen this book to be culturally relevant. Yet our 12-year-old students experienced this type of trauma and were okay talking about it as part of their life. These empathy interviews were powerful in helping me to gain insight into what was happening in the classroom by listening to the students, rather than trusting what was written in the lesson plans.

When asked about access to high-level classes like algebra, which would ensure their success in high school, or school clubs like STEM that would prepare them for future jobs, none of the students reported their enrollment. Yet all perceived that they could have chosen to take part in these classes or activities based on their interests. The reality was that they were not aware that the algebra class was reserved for students who passed the state assessment and performed well in their math courses. The STEM club, in addition to requiring high scores in math and science, required students to have teacher recommendations. The makeup of the algebra class and STEM club was mostly White and Asian students.

When asked which students they perceived as most frequently disciplined or assigned out-of-school suspensions, they all agreed that it was Black boys. When probed further, one boy remarked that some of his Black male peers usually played too much and got in trouble for playing. He admitted that "when I got to eighth grade, I decided to stop playing because I wanted to graduate and participate in all of my activities." Once again, the natural youthful pleasures of childhood were perceived as grounds for harsh discipline and removal from the learning experiences.

Overall, the interviewed students struggled with articulating their thoughts about their experiences in their literacy classes. Their responses suggested that success in their literacy classes was characterized by their ability to follow the teacher's procedures. Based on their responses, I concluded that culturally relevant texts or activities were extremely limited. If included at all, they appeared to showcase the negativity and trauma plaguing urban communities.

Research Literature Review

I reviewed available research for additional insights into this problem. Unfortunately, this situation was not unique to Urban Academy. In the United States, Black children have historically been denied the same educational opportunities and resources available to their White counterparts (Lawrence, 2005). Black boys, in particular, encounter racism from a mostly White female workforce (Hussar et al., 2020). Hammond (2015) suggests that Black boys have not received adequate literacy and content instruction because they are disproportionately disciplined and removed from class. Yet student achievement and performance in literacy are found to be strong predictors for achievement and success in high school, college, and career (Cunningham & Stanovich, 2003; Sparks et al., 2014).

Systems Analysis

The information gained from these interviews was very telling. The leadership team and I had preconceived ideas about the teachers' execution of instruction, but learning the students' perspectives fueled our urgency to explore and review available data on student demographics, academics, and discipline. We further investigated the root causes of this pervasive problem for middle school Black boys, conducting a comprehensive analysis and revising our fishbone diagram to group the factors that contribute to the problem.

The head of the fishbone diagram represented our problem: the underperformance and underachievement of middle school Black boys. As a team we brainstormed possible factors that could be contributing to the problem, drawing on our evidence, and labeled each factor as a bone. Among these were that our curriculum, materials, and resources did not explicitly address the culture and interests of Black boys, causing them to disengage intellectually. Learning activities that did not support linguistic diversity, multiple intelligences, or different learning styles contributed to the problem. School policies and operations that targeted Black boys and systematically removed them from the normal learning environment also contributed. We speculated that teachers might have implicit bias toward Black boys, were not equipped or unwilling to differentiate instruction, or offered low-quality instruction. Finally, families and community environments that loved and nurtured Black boys but did not demonstrate high expectations for learning and high academic achievement might have contributed, too.

After identifying the fishbone categories, my leadership team and I facilitated schoolwide small-group meetings to complete the diagram, generating

Figure 1.1. Fishbone Diagram of Factors That Contribute to Underperformance of Middle School Black Boys

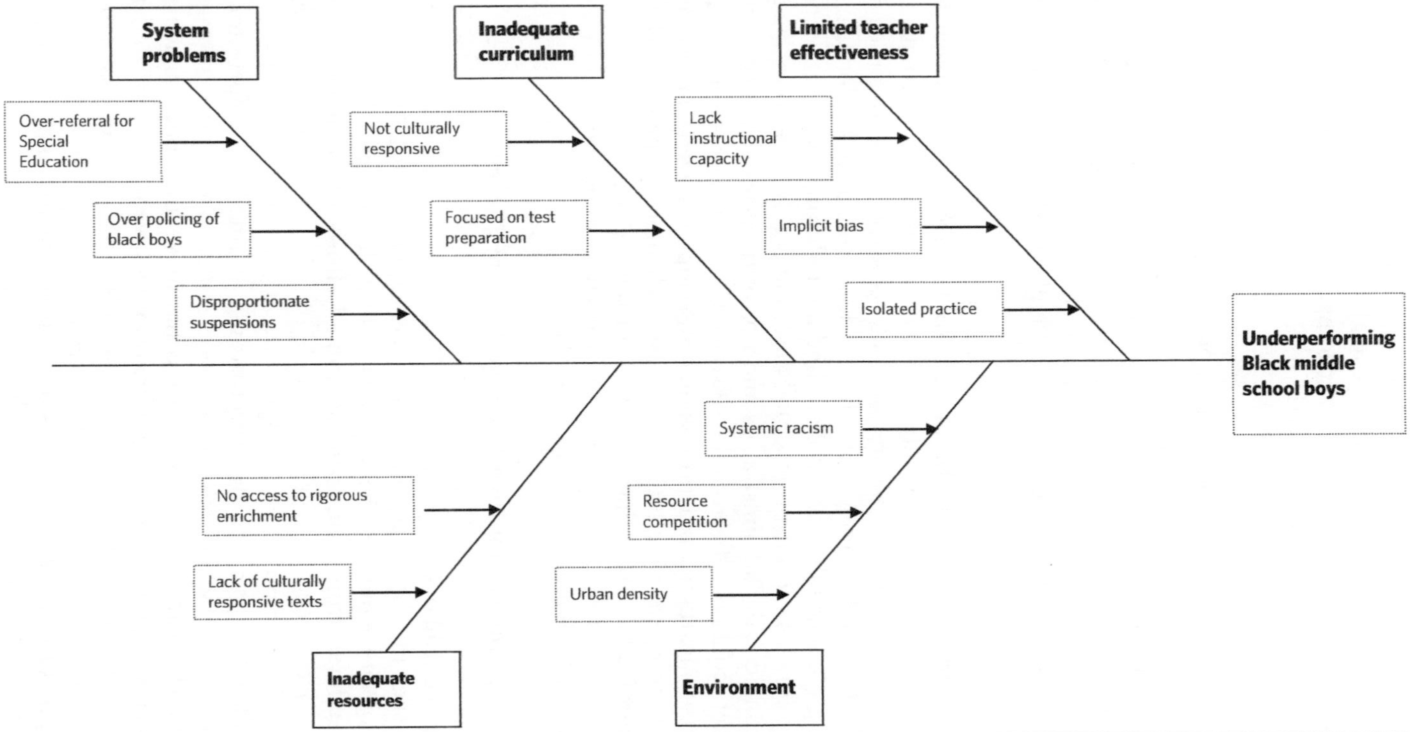

factors that might contribute to the problem by category. Then the team compiled the information from the small-group fishbones to develop a single robust fishbone diagram that encompassed perspectives from the entire school community (see Figure 1.1).

DESIGNING THE SOLUTION

My leadership team and I decided to use improvement science strategies to respond to the urgent and intransigent problem of practice related to Black boys' achievement. It appeared to be an effective way for us to examine and evaluate our problem of practice, select high-leverage areas for intervention, identify change solutions to try, test change ideas, and gain immediate data about our progress to make adjustments or scale up.

We knew we had to begin with some form of professional learning. My staff was used to job-embedded learning, using contractual time from 8:00 a.m. to 8:30 a.m. before the students arrived. We also used monthly after-school staff meetings for schoolwide professional development. By adjusting the schedule, I was able to find an additional preparation period to utilize for this specific professional development. If there were any scheduling conflicts, the administrators and I prioritized providing coverage so all teachers could benefit from the sessions. Unfortunately, in-person teaching, in-person learning, and professional development were interrupted when we had to operate remotely on a revised schedule during COVID-19 in the spring of 2020. Adopting improvement science was beneficial because we could do most of the work online in virtual team meetings, since the structures and protocols were already in place.

Selecting Solutions for High-Leverage Areas of Change

Using the fishbone diagram, the leadership team and I decided to focus on the issues in our direct sphere of influence, rather than those beyond our control. For example, the school was in a densely populated urban area that suffered from long-term intentional efforts of the federal, state, and local governments to segregate people of color. Although the members of the community produced a rich culture of diversity and lived experiences, they also were plagued by overcrowding and had to compete for limited resources. The school system was not equipped to deal with these challenges. The team and I believed we could make an impact on achievement by addressing our pedagogy and the resources we provide for students.

Our aim was for Black boys in middle school to feel seen and valued, while improving their literacy achievement and performance. We proposed doing that by giving them access to (a) an antiracist, culturally relevant curriculum and (b) high-quality teaching using high-level, content-rich, literacy

Figure 1.2. Driver Diagram to Improve ELA Teaching and Student Learning

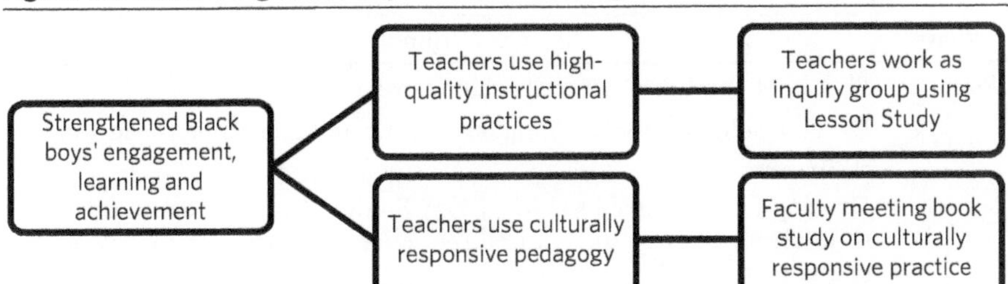

instructional practices that engaged all students. These became our primary drivers for improvement (see Figure 1.2).

We purposefully started with the teacher-centered primary driver of developing high-quality teaching using content-rich instructional practices and culturally responsive materials. The team decided that to activate this primary driver and reach our goal, we would need to engage the teachers in professional learning on culturally relevant pedagogy and improve their lesson planning and instructional practices.

Using available research, we collectively decided to try two change ideas (which we pursued and tested through separate concurrent Plan-Do-Study-Act cycles): (a) a schoolwide book study using *Culturally Responsive Teaching and the Brain* by Zaretta Hammond (2015) to address implicit bias and learn culturally relevant pedagogy, and (b) adoption of the Japanese *lesson study* approach (Doig & Groves, 2011) for the middle school literacy teachers to improve instruction. The schoolwide book study was to be an opportunity to provide knowledge and support to the instructional and support staff by reading together and engaging in learning activities, including discussions, role-play, and introspection to confront biases and gain strategies to implement immediately.

The Japanese lesson study approach, unlike other more formal means of professional development, is school-based, voluntary, and organized by teachers to research their own practices through iterative trial-and-error learning, reflection, and peer support. The lesson study consists of four main phases: (1) goal-setting and planning, (2) teaching the lesson, (3) post-lesson debrief, and (4) consolidation of learning. We planned to use this to support 6th–8th-grade ELA teachers in creating more culturally responsive, student-centered lessons and testing the impact on their Black male students.

We planned to test these two change ideas through consecutive Plan-Do-Study-Act (PDSA) cycles over 20 weeks. I used this work to examine how a multipronged intervention, which emphasized culturally responsive practice, could increase engagement and the literacy performance and achievement of Black boys in middle school (see Table 1.1).

Table 1.1. Overall PDSA Cycle

Phase	Action
Plan	Plan book study on culturally responsive teaching
	Develop schedule for planning, executing, and debriefing the lesson study
	Develop lesson aligned to New Jersey Student Learning Standards (NJSLS) for literacy and cultural relevance to be used for the lesson study
	Develop pre/post-surveys and semistructured interviews
Do	Facilitate schoolwide book study
	Facilitate two rounds of lesson study
	Administer pre/post-surveys and interviews
Study	Analyze survey data with pre-post comparisons
	Code and analyze interviews
	Analyze lesson study assessment data
Act	Revise the tools
	Develop a second round of interventions
	Adjust the intervention as the school moves to fully in-person instruction

Planning Implementation

The school leadership team and I began the first week back to school in the fall of 2020 to plan out the two consecutive cycles. We decided to begin with an 8-week schoolwide book study PDSA cycle with 67 instructional and support staff (child study team, school counselor, crisis intervention teacher, paraprofessionals, and instructional coaches). At the request of the staff, the book study was extended to 10 weeks.

Then we scheduled the lesson study PDSA cycle with the middle school ELA teachers for the following 8 weeks. To close out, I utilized a final week to reflect, identify accomplishments, and explore the implications with the staff. Thus, this improvement work occurred over 20 weeks.

IMPLEMENTING THE CHANGE

The Book Study

Beginning in October 2020, all teachers and support staff were required to engage in the virtual schoolwide book study about culturally responsive pedagogy. We divided the staff into small groups of eight teachers and support staff members, each led by an assigned facilitator. The school leadership team, group facilitators, and I met weekly to discuss the expectations of the book study, provide check-ins and feedback, and maintain continuity. All sessions were held virtually due to COVID.

In each group, the facilitator planned discussions, activities, and tasks for the weekly readings. At the discretion of the facilitators and group members, the activities might have varied among groups. Initially, the groups were scheduled to discuss two chapters per week, but the facilitators reported that groups requested more time to discuss each chapter, so we decreased the readings to one chapter per week.

During our facilitator meetings we discussed how valuable it would be for others to hear about experiences from other small groups. Therefore, we added three virtual whole-group sessions to check in, promote cross-group discussion, and enable whole-group modeling for using culturally relevant text and content. When asked, I modeled culturally responsive teaching using four texts to plan lessons that were relevant to the students in Pre-K to grade 8. Utilizing picture books as mentor texts, I read the texts and pointed out content to explore, connect, and engage students. I provided concrete learning activities across the grade levels for each text, and opportunities to discuss how to adapt the mentor text to particular grade levels. This practice proved beneficial to the teachers because they appreciated having an administrator demonstrate how to plan and execute a lesson.

Over the course of 10 weeks, the leadership team and I observed that attendance in this schoolwide professional development was at an all-time high. Usually, only 50–60% attended morning professional development sessions due to lateness, other scheduled meetings, or simply lack of interest. Now we noticed a new commitment to the work during this professional development. The facilitators also reported high levels of engagement, which they defined as actively participating in discussions, completing activities, and demonstrating their learning to peers. At times there were conflicting meetings that support staff members were required to attend, but those participants requested the notes and still completed their group's assignments. The members were so engaged that they requested that the book study be extended from 8 weeks to 10 weeks. We saw the staff take ownership of their professional learning time and growth, working with their facilitators to make decisions about which topics to explore or extend, scheduling, and how best to maximize their time.

During those sessions, the participants learned about culture and how it programs the brain. Teachers explored the broader nature of culture and learned to not limit their focus to food and celebrations when planning lessons for diverse populations. They learned about emotional intelligence, implicit bias, and how microaggressions affect the learning environment, making it unsafe for some students to engage. They discussed practical ways to build relationships with students and build their capacity, independence, and confidence as learners. Whether they were in a small group or the whole group, participants freely shared their learning experiences, personal convictions, challenges, and next steps.

One activity that started as a small group but evolved into a whole group was staff sharing their own cultural stories. It was a suggested activity in the text, and the staff really embraced it as an opportunity to build relationships and create a culturally relevant environment. A "cultural story" is defined as a presentation of one's family history, values, and cultural beliefs. In the small-group sessions, each group discussed and decided how they would incorporate the three levels of culture discussed in Hammond's (2015) book in their cultural story to help others understand who they are and their values, beliefs, and worldviews. Over several weeks, participants volunteered to present to their small group, with feedback and reflections from their peers.

After a few small-group presentations, the facilitators shared how they were "in awe" of the presentations and the reception by peers. They reported how staff members encouraged their peers and that some were in tears as they witnessed the lived experiences of their colleagues. The facilitators suggested that some participants present to the whole staff in the middle of our weekly sessions. We all agreed. During our whole-group sessions, teachers and staff shared their family history in the United States, holiday customs, and family values of respect for leadership, community, and education. During the presentations, you could see the physical shaking and tears of presenters as they shared their personal histories, lived experiences, and even trauma.

For example, one teacher presented her cultural story in the form of a multimedia animation about home life. She shared how her family grew up in poverty, and how she remembered family gatherings with her favorite meals, visiting relatives, storytelling, and dancing. She shared how her teacher and some students made disparaging comments about her hair and how her 2nd-grade teacher refused to pronounce her name correctly, making her feel like something was wrong. She expressed how those experiences shaped her and made her very self-conscious of how she interacts and builds relationships with all her students.

Although most of the participants shared their cultural stories in small groups, four of the 67 completed the task but declined to share with the group. One teacher called me personally and said, "I just can't share my story with my colleagues. It is not a pretty picture." I encouraged the teacher to continue her own personal journey of first showing up for herself and then for others.

Overall, the data collected from observations, notes, and reflection surveys revealed the teachers' plans to use knowledge of cultural awareness, build learning partnerships, and develop intellectual capacity for students.

The teachers planned to use the book's teacher-provided prompts to address their deficit thinking about students and the culture stories to get to know the students. They planned to help students by utilizing the four macro-level instructional strategies: Ignite (cueing the brain to pay attention), Chunk (making information digestible), Chew (actively processing new information), and Review (having a chance to apply new learning).

I noticed the implementation of these strategies and teaching practices almost immediately. During my regular classroom observations, I witnessed teachers across the grade levels and content areas including culturally relevant texts and activities to engage the students. Some teachers facilitated opportunities for the students to share their cultural stories. Many teachers were observed helping to build students' intellectual capacity by using the four strategies of processing information. In addition, the teachers requested to continue utilizing book study as a form of professional development. They valued the opportunity to learn alongside their peers to gain research-based ideas, strategies, and techniques to apply in their classrooms.

The Japanese Lesson Study

Next, we began a 10-week cycle of trying out the Japanese lesson study of new lessons with seven middle school literacy teachers who had also participated in the book study. Three teachers identified as Black and four as White. All had at least 17 years of experience teaching middle school literacy at Urban Academy. During the empathy interviews, three had reported that their focus was on procedures and compliance in literacy, rather than student-centered literacy instruction. In addition, most of them reported having had no prior training on how to use culture in lesson planning and execution.

Our Japanese lesson study of new lessons consisted of three weekly parts. During Week 1, the team of educators planned a 6th-, 7th-, and 8th-grade lesson together with objectives, activities, and assessments. We were guided by the New Jersey Student Learning Standards (https://www.nj.gov/education/standards/) for middle school literacy and a culturally responsive observation tool adapted from Freebody and Luke's (1990) four resources model for literacy. In the adaptation, our four sections included: (1) high-quality questioning and discussion techniques, (2) culturally relevant texts/content, (3) connection to specific experiences for students, and (4) literary analysis. This tool was effective in identifying the elements we expected to assess to ensure that the lesson was high-quality and culturally relevant. We intentionally sought mentor texts and activities to engage Black boys as they related to images, student interests, community activities, and social issues.

During Week 2, the lesson was delivered and observed by other teachers from the same grade levels who collected data using the culturally responsive observation tool. The observing teachers tallied the literacy instructional moves made by the teacher and took low-inference notes that consisted solely of the observable. Finally, in Week 3, the entire team debriefed the observations and the findings of the observed lesson. During these scheduled learning times, we began with teacher-developed norms to analyze data, discuss curricula, and review student work.

Adopting the lesson study process was more complex than we imagined. We spent countless hours beyond our scheduled contractual time just planning the model lesson. It took a long time for the team to unpack the New Jersey Student Learning Standards to ensure that we were planning appropriate outcomes aligned to the standard. Coupled with the culturally responsive observation tool, we vetted each question, strategy, and student activity.

During discussions, the teachers acknowledged that prior to this work they did not properly unpack the standards before attempting to teach lessons aligned to them. Further, "teacher proof" programs that listed the objectives, standards, and suggested activities made the teachers believe they were teaching to the standard. One teacher remarked how she noticed that the caliber of lessons and activities differed from prior ones. She attributed the disparity to the lack of opportunities to unpack the standards collaboratively and build a consensus.

The teachers appreciated having the observation tool to guide their planning. When they understood clearly what was expected, it made lesson planning easier. Some suggested that the tool be published and utilized schoolwide to ensure that all lessons were culturally relevant in order to engage all students, with a particular focus on Black boys.

During the observations, as the observed teacher facilitated the lesson, the team of observers tallied the teacher's moves as they related to high-level questioning and discussion techniques, culturally relevant text/content, connection to specific experiences of students, and literary analysis. The team took low-inference notes to substantiate our tallies. After the observation, we debriefed to calculate our tallies, offer evidence for them, and discuss ways to improve student outcomes. If necessary, we collectively adjusted the lesson and sent the teacher back in to re-teach. The students were receptive to the reteaching because we shared with them how this activity was helping us be better teachers, coaches, and administrators for them. We were able to complete the 6th-grade lesson with two classes, the 7th-grade lesson with two classes, and the 8th-grade lesson with two classes. As we completed each lesson, we saw our progress. Through constant discussions with the tool and the evidence, our expectations became calibrated.

During the debriefs, teachers remarked how powerful it was to see their colleagues execute lessons. They discussed how the best plans might be altered in real time because of the needs or interests of the students. The observed teacher stated, "I forgot to build the background on the author and ask that question." Another offered the possibility of pre-planning the higher-order thinking questions so students could engage in critical discussions. Teachers explained that watching others in action helped them improve their pedagogy.

The teachers were amazed by how the Black boys emerged as leaders during the high-quality discussion techniques they tried, like Socratic seminars. They observed that some Black boys were leading the discussions, countering responses, and providing feedback to their peers with textual evidence. Simple engagement techniques like "cold calling" allowed for students with disabilities to get their responses ready and engage in the discussion. During one observation, a student who stuttered was given appropriate wait time and then was able to offer his thinking to the discussion. When another student added to his response, the student who stuttered thanked his peer for waiting. The observers were in tears. In another example, we noticed how well students were able to connect to their readings from Langston Hughes. They related to the community characters, themes, and dialect of the text. One student remarked that the main character reminded him of a neighbor on his block.

The teachers and I also dug into emergent problems. For example, in a 7th-grade class, the Black boys were more comfortable with leading and speaking than recording their responses. Some Black boys did not write their responses on the exit tickets. As the team considered their hesitancy, we attributed this to their fear of being marked wrong. After a discussion with the teacher, we decided the teacher should go back, provide time, and encourage the students to record their responses on the exit ticket. We found that after the discussion and giving the students another opportunity to complete the ticket, 100% of the Black boys did so. The team agreed to address the anxiety Black boys felt about their written work by providing extra time and opportunities to revise and resubmit as needed. After all, the goal was to achieve mastery of the concept or skill.

RESULTS

The results of the book study and literacy lesson study showed that these had a layered impact on teaching practices as well as on students' engagement, performance, and achievement. The lesson study gave teachers sacred time to collaborate, plan, and give critical feedback to one another. As a result, the teachers were able to apply their learning from the book study and see firsthand how the strategies and techniques impacted Black boys' engagement, performance, and achievement. Together we saw the impact firsthand, as we watched the joy in Black boys as they achieved new levels of success.

Impact on Students

For the middle school Black boys involved in the intervention, we saw an instant shift in their willingness to engage with the content, discussions, and activities of the lesson. It was exciting to the observers to watch the Black boys, during lessons, take on leadership roles while engaging in high-level literacy practices, including leading and countering arguments, completing character analyses, and evaluating authors' purpose. One young boy was so excited to share his cultural connection that he seemed hurt when the teacher facilitated a cold call because she wanted a response from every student. In a Socratic seminar, we witnessed the boys using sentence starters on note cards to add, affirm, or challenge the responses of their peers. Visible smiles were evident as all boys engaged freely or with support in the high-level literacy activity.

The pre- and post-interim literacy assessment administered to 59 middle school Black boys in the fall and the winter also showed significant positive change. The assessment tested high-frequency words, phonics, word recognition, vocabulary, spelling, and comprehension. In all but high-frequency words, there was a significant positive statistical difference in their scores.

An unintended benefit was that the increased engagement of Black boys decreased the number of times they were sent out of class for discipline issues, which we attributed to the shift in the teachers' perceptions and treatment of them. After engaging in the schoolwide book study and lesson study, teachers were less likely to send Black boys out of the learning environment for discipline. Teachers now used the knowledge strategies and techniques, such as chunking and questioning, to ensure that Black boys were not missing out on valuable, high-level instruction.

Impact on Teachers

At the close of this improvement effort, the data suggested that the multipronged professional development strategies, based on our evaluation of the Plan-Do-Study-Act cycles, had a positive effect on teacher practice. Feedback from the teacher surveys, interviews, and reflections revealed that participating staff were able to honestly explore their implicit bias toward Black boys and saw how those biases impacted the way the Black boys performed in comparison to their peers.

By the end of our effort, all participating teachers believed they could implement some of the strategies to ensure culturally relevant practices. During learning walks and formal observations, administrators noted the inclusion of culturally relevant practices in primary, grammar, and middle school classes. Teachers selected culturally relevant texts, facilitated high-level literacy tasks for all students, and allowed students to co-create lessons by sharing their culture and interests.

Our administrative team and district content supervisors saw firsthand immediate changes to the culture of the school and professional learning. During their regular grade-level and content professional learning communities, teachers discussed and planned opportunities to conduct Japanese lesson studies to improve their teaching practices and students' learning. Requests were made to the administrative team for support in scaling up to benefit other teachers and grade levels. Simultaneously, teachers took ownership of their professional learning and requested launching a subsequent book study. They decided they needed more support with methodology and a possible framework to guide them. They researched and suggested the text *Cultivating Genius* (Muhammad, 2020). We purchased it for every staff member, and they launched the study.

The school leadership team brought the suggestion of utilizing the culturally relevant observation tool (Freebody & Luke, 1990) adapted for the Japanese lesson study to use as a guide for planning, observing, and providing feedback on all lessons. Without prompting, some middle school teachers created a category in the lesson plan template for cultural relevance.

Throughout our improvement work, teachers began to call out their own implicit bias and that of their peers. Many could pinpoint their root causes or a reason for the biases, and they were encouraged and supported while they sat in the discomfort without making excuses. As a school, we were committed to addressing the biases to make some actionable changes to positively impact Black boys and all children.

Impact on the School

This improvement process created a major organizational shift in the school because of how I included others in making decisions about curriculum, professional development, time schedule, and budget. I empowered the school leadership team by stepping back myself and allowing them to honor the voices of the teachers and make the changes they needed. The facilitators and staff were able to make decisions about their time, procedures, and resources. When they saw that their voices and commitment were respected, they began to take increasing ownership of the goal of the improvement work and commitment to improving the performance and achievement of middle school Black boys.

When staff saw the transformation of my leadership style, they themselves began to transform for the purpose of the goal, but also for the improvement of the school community as a whole. That shift was powerful for me because it was the first time I felt that the whole school community owned a shared vision and mission for the school. The goal was no longer just what we crafted together in meetings. It was alive in how every member was working toward it daily; there was evidence of that work in our actions, planning, professional development, lesson implementation, and the improved student engagement and performance.

Through this improvement science effort, the culture of our school shifted tremendously. There was growth in performance and achievement in literacy for our Black boys because of implementation of the change ideas. But most importantly, we had heard from the powerful voices of children about how they had experienced the problem of unequal treatment and later the excitement they felt when they achieved success. We marveled at the exponential changes in teachers' commitment to personal and professional growth. By the end of the effort, virtually the whole staff was willing to acknowledge their implicit bias and how it impacted their teaching and, ultimately, student learning. The transformation of their beliefs, philosophies, and pedagogies was evident in our observations of teaching and their student interactions. At the end of the effort, there were requests to continue the work and scale up for all grade levels and different content.

LEADER REFLECTIONS

Confronting Assumptions

As a Black woman leading a mostly White female staff, I had to be courageous in looking at this problem of practice from an equity lens. I had my own assumptions about the fragility of White women in relation to Black men. I had some experiences with White women claiming to be afraid of Black men without any provocation. I have also witnessed White women express their explicit bias against Black boys in school and community settings, often seeing them as men and criminalizing their youthful acts. Hence, I intentionally described them as "boys" throughout my principalship and this effort.

Tackling this problem of practice required me to address my own assumptions and offer a safe space for my teachers to do the same. We collectively had to sit with our beliefs, assumptions, and biases and then challenge one another to change. My challenges could have been misconstrued as harassment or intimidation because of my position of authority. Nevertheless, I pursued this problem because I believed it would benefit the Black boys, and ultimately all students and staff.

Transforming Leadership

For me, that courage led to the emergence of my transformational leadership style and its impact on me and others. I had been used to a hierarchical, top-down approach to decision-making. I alone had decided if there was a problem. And I alone had to find solutions and then share them with the staff, and assumed that to be successful, the staff just needed to follow my procedures.

Improvement science pushed me to adopt shared decision-making. Through this, teachers took ownership of their learning and made the success of the students our collective responsibility. In turn, I slowly released my hand and welcomed shared decision-making. I learned from listening to those who experienced the literacy problem and allowed them to engage in every stage of the work to solve it. As a result of this new approach, the teachers came to own the process, made changes in the way they worked, and grew as a collaborative team. I observed them supporting one another and witnessed teachers push the thinking of their peers even when it got uncomfortable.

We became a cohesive unit of trust and accountability throughout this work for the benefit of our students and the growth and development of the teachers. There was clearly more work I had to do throughout my tenure to get the school out of Focus Status,[1] build a safe learning environment, and change the low expectations for learning. The staff now trusted me to do that work with integrity and with the best interests of the faculty and student body at heart.

QUESTIONS

1. The principal sought input on the problem from a few teachers, through empathy interviews and discussions with her leadership team. How else could the principal engage the whole staff in exploring the problem and its causes before developing solutions?
2. The principal sought student voice about the problem through empathy interviews. How else could the principal and other staff incorporate student voice throughout the problem exploration and solution-testing processes?
3. The principal explicitly chose to incorporate distributed leadership practices as part of her improvement work. How did that contribute to the success of the improvement work and its impact on teaching and student learning?
4. Why was this approach to improving Black male literacy performance successful, since it did not explicitly target Black boys as a subgroup?

1. In New Jersey, Focus Status designates a school that has low subgroup performance or large within-school performance gaps. https://www.nj.gov/education/doedata/prfschools/TechnicalGuidance.pdf

REFERENCES

Anderman, E., & Mueller, C. (2010). Middle school transitions and adolescent development. In J. Meece & J. Eccles (Eds.), *Handbook of research on schools, schooling, and human development* (pp. 198–215). Routledge.

Bryk, A. S., Gomez, L., Grunow, A., & LeMahieu, P. (2015). *Learning to improve: How America's schools can get better at getting better*. Harvard Education Press.

Cunningham, A., & Stanovich, K. (2003). Reading can make you smarter! *Principal, 83*(2), 34–39.

Doig, B., & Groves, S. (2011). Japanese Lesson Study: Teacher professional development through communities of inquiry. *Mathematics Teacher Education and Development, 13*(1), 77–93.

Freebody, P., & Luke, A. (1990). Literacies programs: Debates and demands in cultural context. *Prospect: An Australian Journal of TESOL, 5*(3), 7–16.

Hammond, Z. (2015). *Culturally responsive teaching and the brain: Promoting authentic engagement and rigor among culturally and linguistically diverse students*. Corwin.

Hussar, B., Zhang, J., Hein, S., Wang, K., Roberts, A., Cui, J., Smith, M., Mann, F., Barmer, A., Dilig, R., Nachazel, T., Barnette, M., & Purcell, B. (2020). *The Condition of Education 2020*. National Center for Educational Statistics.

Lawrence, C. (2005). *Forbidden conversations: On race, privacy, and community (a continuing conversation with John Ely on racism and democracy)*. Yale Law School.

Muhammad, G. (2020). *Cultivating genius: An equity framework for culturally and historically responsive literacy*. Scholastic.

Myers, W. D. (1999). *Monster*. Harper Collins.

Sparks, R., Patton, J., & Murdoch, A. (2014). Early reading success and its relationship to reading achievement and reading volume: Replication of '10 years later.' *Read Writ*, 27, 189–211. https://doi.org/10.1007/s11145-013-9439-2

CHAPTER 2

Transforming Our Middle School Math Instruction Through an Integrated Approach and Co-Teaching

Josef Haas

This chapter describes how a new vice principal used improvement science to improve his urban charter school's math instruction. The vice principal and 8th-grade math team members designed and tested an instructional framework to address students' gaps and add authentic problems in the 2018–2019 school year. They expanded their use to the 7th grade in 2020–2021. The vice principal improved the teachers' practice and planning for instructional differentiation by co-teaching one math section and meeting daily for co-planning. He and the math teachers refined the instructional model and monitored teacher and student progress even when the school turned to fully remote learning starting on March 15, 2020, and continuing for the entirety of the 2020–2021 school year. The results showed strong and sustained math performance improvement for both grades, improved teacher instructional efficacy, and sustainable collaborative meeting processes.

"I hate math" is an all-too-common complaint that I have heard uttered by students and adults at my own school. Most of us were taught by a teacher lecturing and telling us how to memorize rules applied to abstract problems. Many would remember directions like "find the least common denominator" and "simplify the fraction" that we followed by gritting our teeth and fighting through the boredom of the classroom, counting down the minutes until the class was over. Under the old-school lecture-and-memorize model, only the compliant would prevail, leaving those unconvinced of the benefits of math asking, "When are we going to use this in real life?" Is there a better way? How can a math teacher get students to understand why math works and how it actually applies to their life? Not surprisingly, the school's students were performing poorly in math across grades.

This chapter presents a story about how I, a middle school vice principal, was able to significantly improve students' mathematics achievement by supporting the teachers of one co-teaching team through daily planning and teaching together, using a new model of teaching math that promoted understanding. I used improvement science practices (Bryk et al., 2015) to investigate the problem and design and test these new strategies for their impact on student math learning.

CONTEXT

Manor College Preparatory Academy (MCPA) (pseudonym) is a charter middle school comprising grades 6 through 8. Located in the Bronx, New York, the school served 326 students in those grades, of whom 98% were black or Hispanic, and 89% were designated as low-income. There were 27 teachers, many of whom, while experienced, were teaching outside their subject area. The school's math teaching teams consisted of two teachers in the 6th grade, two teachers in the 7th grade, and two teachers in the 8th grade.

Since MCPA began operation in 2015, it has underperformed on every measure of a school. In 2018, after its third year of operation and poor performance, and following a state review, MCPA's board was forced to replace the entire administrative team and most of the teaching staff. That year, I became the vice principal of STEM (Science, Technology, Engineering, and Mathematics) at MCPA and joined a new team of administrators and staff who were hired to turn MCPA around or risk its closure by 2021.

MCPA was organized into four student cohorts per grade using a fully integrated co-teaching (ICT) model. Our ICT model meant that each content class consisted of two to three teachers (including one designated as the special education teacher) who served all students together schoolwide: students with disabilities (SWD) and English language learners (ELL), as well as general education students. The teachers on each team taught each class together and planned the lessons together. MCPA adopted this approach because we, the leadership team, believed that it was the most effective and most equitable way to meet the needs of all our students.

As the vice principal of STEM at MCPA, I oversaw and supported the math and science teams, and half of the noncontent classes (PE and computer science), through biweekly observation and feedback cycles and curricular/lesson planning support. It was also my responsibility to work with the rest of the administrative team to accomplish other administrative duties such as scheduling, planning events, reporting, and problem-solving.

DISCOVERING THE PROBLEM

Although the problems of MCPA ranged widely, my reform efforts were focused on improving math performance, which, as measured by standardized state assessments, was lower than in any other content area in the school. Importantly, if MCPA's math performance did not improve drastically, the school's charter would not be renewed, and the school would be shut down. Therefore, my goal was to increase MCPA's performance to at least meet the New York State average performance in a way that was sustainable with systems and routines that would continue to move the school forward.

ANALYZING THE PROBLEM

My focus on math improvement began in 2018 with an analysis of the school's broader student math performance problems. The math teachers and I looked at recent New York State Exam data, the New York State Education Department (NYSED) reports, and the curricula and resources that were provided to the teachers. We also conducted teacher and student interviews in attempts to best understand how MCPA operations affected student learning. Using these data, I conducted a root cause analysis on how the overall problems of the school and the problems specific to math instruction impacted student math outcomes. I found that the major problems contributing to poor student achievement in math at MCPA stemmed from MCPA's ineffective systems (or lack thereof) for teacher supervision and support, student behavior management, incoming student readiness, data access and use, instructional planning, and math curriculum. These system factors are shown in the fishbone diagram (Figure 2.1) and are discussed below.

Incoming Student Readiness

Our data analysis showed that most students entered 6th grade with weak math skills. According to the diagnostic I-Ready exam given in September 2018, only 15% of 6th-graders were on grade level, while 42% were two or more grade levels behind. Although 28% of MCPA students were SWDs (which was higher than the city average), the systems in place to provide support for SWDs were ineffective. In particular, the previous administration provided no support or expectations to teachers on how to differentiate instruction within the classroom given these students' weak math skills.

Limited Data Access and Use

When the current administrative team arrived at MCPA, no schoolwide data were available and there were no prior interim assessments or schoolwide

Figure 2.1. Fishbone Diagram of the Factors Contributing to Low Student Math Performance

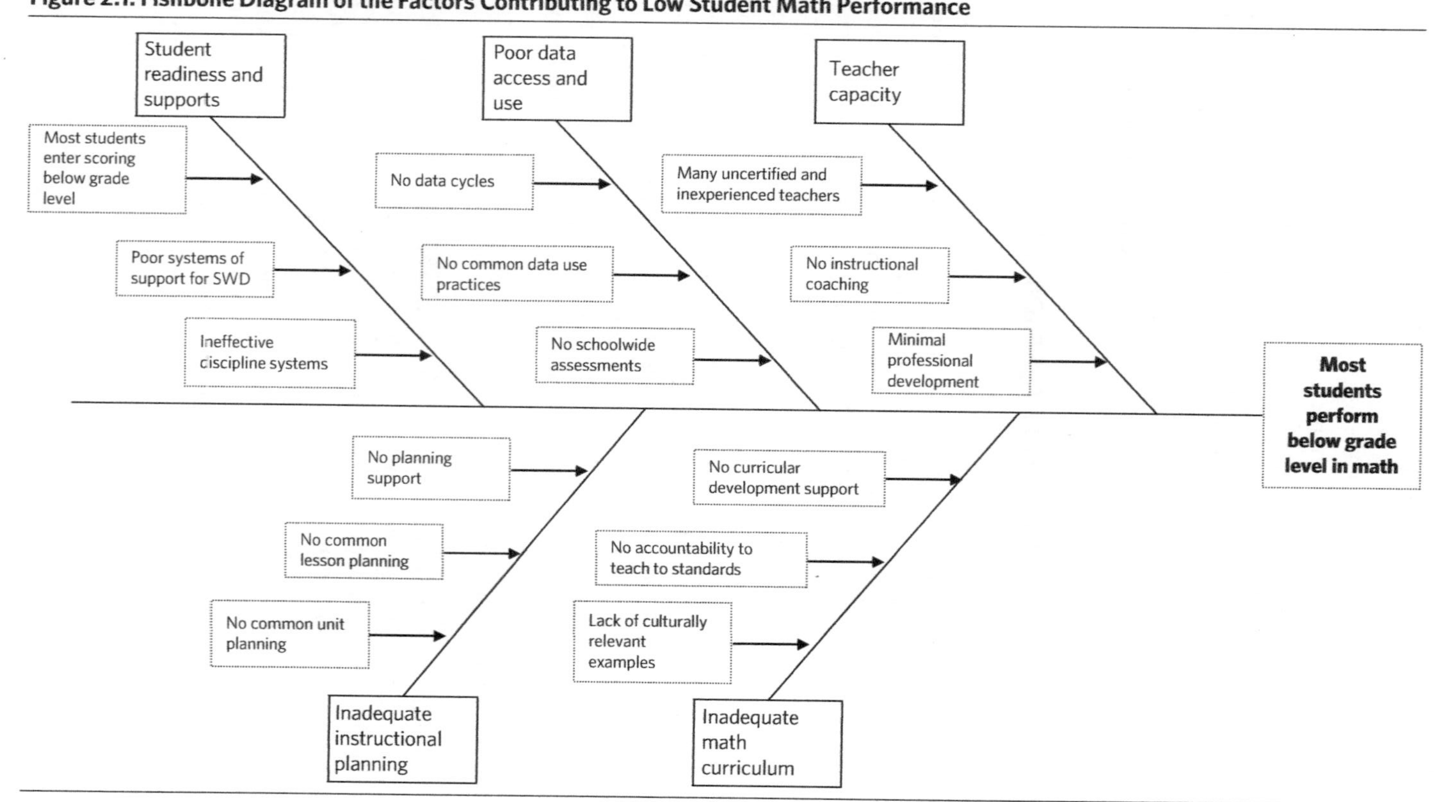

forms of data collection. Therefore, the New York State exams were the only measures of progress. Although teachers created their own exams for their class, there were no data cycles or time set aside for teachers to collaborate and discuss their data. Moreover, as noted in meetings and observations, the teachers appeared to be ill-practiced in using data for instructional planning.

Inadequate Math Curriculum

I learned in my initial review that there was no common math curriculum or related instructional resources. Nor was support provided for developing the curriculum or maintaining accountability that instruction to be aligned to the standards. Staff members stated that the former principal had told teachers to "just teach what you are passionate about," which led to inconsistent and uncoordinated content. The lack of common expectations made vertical alignment almost nonexistent. To support their instruction, teachers would typically draw from the state math curriculum with little adaptation or alteration.

Inadequate Instructional Planning

MCPA had major issues regarding instructional planning. No support had been provided by the administration for planning: no common lesson plan or unit plan expectations, no feedback on any planning materials, and no common expectations on how to conduct an effective lesson. Teachers were not given any coaching or instructional supervision. The existing environment at MCPA was not conducive to collaboration among staff members, as planning space for teachers was limited to one room with separately assigned cubicles, making it difficult for teachers to work together.

Lack of Teacher Supervision and Support

From the New York State midterm site visit report (for the charter renewal) and conversations with staff members, I found several teacher staffing, supervision, and support practices that contributed to student underachievement in math. First, many teachers in the math department were inexperienced and uncertified. Second, some teachers were consistently absent or late, and there was no system of administrative discipline to minimize staff absenteeism. Third, although teacher teams taught together and could learn by working together, there were few opportunities for joint professional development. The only professional development opportunities organized by the previous administration were occasional math content meetings, which were reportedly particularly poorly organized.

Poor Student Behavior Management

When starting at MCPA, the principal and I quickly learned that there was a lack of consistency in behavior management and no common discipline systems in place. Staff reported to us that without a schoolwide system of student discipline, they were expected to mete out their own discipline, even if it meant holding their own after-school or lunch detentions. To learn more, the principal and I informally interviewed about 10 students who were available and willing to talk. The students reported that they acted very differently from one class to the next and were confused by the different sets of rules and procedures in each classroom. Accordingly, students ran the school; they did whatever they wanted except in certain classrooms. Our initial assessment of the level of property damage verified the lack of behavior management. We had to replace most whiteboards and much of the lab equipment and other instructional materials because they had been destroyed.

Initial Improvements

Considering the state of disarray at MCPA when we started in fall 2018, the principal and I, along with other staff, took several steps to add critically needed systems and create a stable school environment. We implemented responsive classroom training across the school; updated our disciplinary code of conduct in our faculty handbook; and overhauled our behavior management system to establish consistency, developmental appropriateness, and responsiveness. We also implemented use of a common lesson plan and unit plan templates to ensure a common lesson structure within the classroom, including standards alignment, differentiation strategies, and co-teaching strategies. We implemented ICT within every classroom, complete with professional development on co-teaching. We provided biweekly instructional coaching cycles and feedback on planning materials in every classroom.

Several other improvement efforts were made during the 2018–2019 school year that directly related to improving math achievement. We hired four new certified and experienced math teachers. We implemented i-Ready Diagnostic assessments (https://www.curriculumassociates.com/programs/i-ready-assessment/diagnostic) to track progress in math and ELA, and quarterly standards-based interim assessments with data analysis cycles.

DESIGNING A SOLUTION

Although these above changes and initiatives were essential, alone they would not yield a significant increase in mathematics achievement. Thus, additional solutions were required. To provide support to my math teams, as the vice principal, I needed to find the most effective practices for strengthening teaching, planning, and using data to facilitate the best possible math instruction and support, particularly for students with limited foundational math skills.

Given that a remarkably high percentage of our students lacked prerequisite knowledge, the math teams and I concluded that our math coursework needed to be modified and differentiated to develop missing skills while also building new ones. Doing so would be complicated by the fact that we were using the ICT model, so each classroom would expect to have a unique set of students and learning challenges. Consequently, teachers at MCPA needed the skills not just to facilitate highly effective instruction but also to continue to adapt to meet the their diverse students' challenging learning needs.

Based on these circumstances, I concluded that the math teachers needed highly effective systems of co-planning and analyzing their students' data, and the means to continuously adapt their instruction to improve student learning. Further, we required new ways of providing professional learning to help teachers to develop their expertise. I turned to two major levers to improve math achievement for all students: focusing on ways to improve instructional practices and creating systems in which teachers continuously supported one another instructionally. To accomplish these goals, it was necessary not only to identify exemplary math instructional practices but to support their use through an effective means of professional development combining co-planning and modeling instruction.

First I worked with the teachers to design our own teaching framework, integrating prerequisite skill development and teaching conceptually; adopting a job-embedded approach to professional development that combined daily co-planning and co-teaching; and enhancing the curriculum with authentically created materials. This approach to improved math instruction and learning proved to be incredibly successful and served as a prototype for future school years.

The Integrate-Conceptualize-Adapt (ICA) Model

Our first step was to develop a shared teaching model that incorporated highly effective instructional strategies. In my previous work as a math teacher, I had experimented with various instructional strategies to support student learning. As the vice principal, I used them to coach the rest of the 8th-grade math team through daily planning meetings throughout the 2018–2019 school year. Through trial and error and regular discussion, the team was able to refine its teaching methods and identify what was most effective about our teaching. This exercise led to establishing a shared math instruction framework and team approach that included three high-leverage tenets that we concluded, if used consistently, would foster significant gains in student achievement. We called this the Integrate-Conceptualize-Adapt (ICA) Model based on three practices:

- *Integrate prerequisite knowledge.* We revisited every prerequisite skill necessary to be successful for the new skill being taught, even if an on-grade level student was expected to know it. The reasoning was that for any given lesson, there would be at least one student who was not familiar with the prerequisite skills and knowledge needed to access the skill. This strategy provided a refresher for other students, building their fluency with that particular skill. Students were presented with manipulatives and visual models whenever possible to represent each concept. They were also given the opportunity to discuss their learning together, to be exposed to different approaches, and to solidify their understanding through collaboration.
- *Teach math conceptually.* We focused on the concepts needed for each skill and presented them in a way that was understandable and relatable.
- *Adapt through daily co-planning.* By analyzing summative data (performance data such as exit tickets, quizzes, and exams) and formative data (observational data such as student behavior, engagement, how students worked through their tasks, and any other classroom observations), teachers were to evaluate their instruction as a whole and how they met individual student needs. Based on their regular analysis, discussions, and evaluation, they could adapt instruction to meet the needs of any group of students.

While these three tenets do not account for every aspect of good teaching, we concluded that they were the main aspects of our teaching and planning that would be most impactful for our students' mathematics achievement. The last component, *adapt*, allowed teachers to continue to improve their instructional practices to not only improve their overall teaching skills but also to refine their practices to meet the unique needs of any classroom.

Co-Teaching and Co-Planning

I worked with the 8th-grade team to develop an approach that integrated these three practices as one intervention. I adopted co-teaching and co-planning as a professional learning modality to support their development. Given that MCPA leaders had decided to institute the Algebra 1 Regents Curriculum for all 8th-grade students (a curriculum typically taught to 9th-grade or honors-track middle school students), the 8th-grade teachers needed additional instructional support. To do this, I co-taught one of the four 8th-grade sections and engaged in daily co-planning with the other two members of the algebra team (I had successfully taught 8th-grade algebra for all at another school the year prior) throughout the year.

Given that my required biweekly teacher observation and feedback cycles were a limited means of supporting professional learning, I decided I could more effectively strengthen teachers' practice through daily co-planning (along with the daily co-teaming). This approach combined modeling effective teaching practices with data-informed lesson planning, discussion, and reflection on these practices. My plan was to meet daily with the math teams to discuss formative and summative data, make adaptations to our instruction, and work as a team in all aspects of planning for all four sections of that grade. I used the tenets of the ICA teaching framework to coach the teachers and model instruction. Although I did not teach in three sections, I assisted in their co-planning.

We experimented with meeting protocols and the most high-leverage topics of discussion for our daily meetings, finding that informal meetings were more enjoyable than using a daily meeting protocol. However, we made sure we prioritized the upcoming lesson and discussed formative and summative data, creating a consistent, but informal, instructional improvement process with limited use of a formal discussion protocol.

Use of an Authentic Curriculum

We developed and used real-world scenarios that were relevant to students' lives, and then moved on to abstractions so that concepts were grounded in reality that students could then apply to the abstract problems. This was an alternative theory of action, given that many curricula are based on the opposite approach, in which students memorize steps to solve problems in the abstract (often without understanding what they are doing) and then apply those skills to solve real-world problems. For 8th-grade algebra, I shared an authentically created curriculum that I had developed over 3 years at another school and found to be successful instructionally and specifically relatable to students in the South Bronx. It included scenarios that our students would understand and could be rewritten to include other students, teachers, local business, and areas within the city and surrounding neighborhood. For example, as one teacher explained, "Making a problem about buying a chopped cheese [a popular Bronx sandwich] as opposed to, like, renting a golf cart, that would be a big difference."

Early Design Evidence of Effectiveness

We tested the efficacy of this model using a Plan-Do-Study-Act (PDSA) cycle in which we implemented the above planned changes in the 8th grade and tracked student progress. By the end of the 2018–2019 school year, math proficiency had increased only in the 8th grade. The 8th-grade students' math

Figure 2.2. Driver Diagram

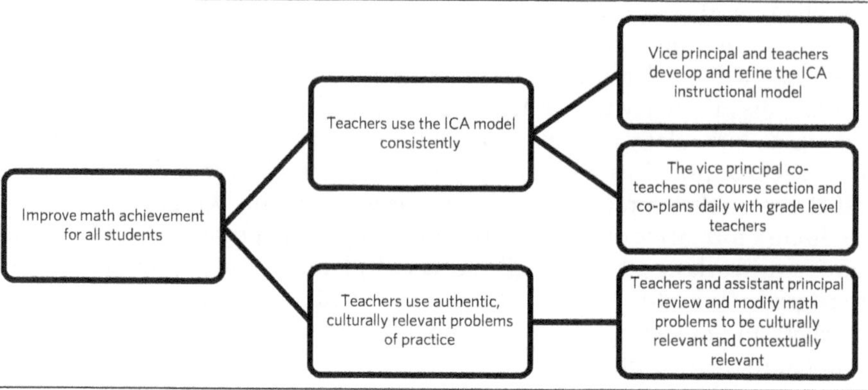

proficiency increased from 19% proficiency the prior year to 73% across all 8th-grade sections (not just the section taught by the vice principal). Based on our experience in developing and refining the model in 2018–2019, I developed the driver diagram to include change ideas and outcome measures to test this model further in other grades. As shown in Figure 2.2, my change idea to operationalize the secondary drivers was for me to co-teach one section of 8th-grade math and continue to meet with the team regularly for co-planning. We then engaged in subsequent PDSA cycles to continue testing these combined changes in the 8th grade (2019–2020) and in the 7th grade the subsequent year (2020–2021; see Table 2.1).

IMPLEMENTING THE CHANGE

Our trial experience with the above-described approach to improving 8th-grade math instruction in 2018–2019 proved to be successful, as evidenced by student assessments, and it served as a prototype for improving our school's math instruction more generally. Thus, the math teams and I agreed that we would continue to use the approach with the 8th-grade team in 2019–2020, and continued to iterate on our initial PDSA cycle, making and testing additional improvements. The following year we expanded its use to the 7th-grade team, with less intensive support for the 8th-grade team, as a subsequent PDSA cycle to test both scaling up the model to another grade and gradual release to the teachers. Thus, I continued to co-teach one algebra section and engage in daily co-planning with the 8th-grade team during the 2019–2020 school year.

To fully implement the ICA framework and co-teaching component with the 8th-grade team in 2019–2020, the math teachers and I organized instructional time differently to strengthen student engagement by adding

Table 2.1. PDSA Cycle

Phase	Action
Plan	Schedule co-teaching and co-planning Adopt the ICA model Add culturally relevant math problems
Do	Engage in co-teaching and co-planning throughout the year Assess students' formative performance Observe teacher practice
Study	Evaluate student progress quarterly and compare within and among grade levels Monitor teacher engagement in co-planning and teaching practices
Act	Adjust the curriculum Adjust instructional practices Agree to expand to other grades

more choice and using problems of varied difficulty for instructional differentiation. We typically started class with a "Do Now" that offered three different problem options from which students could choose one to solve. After debriefing the Do Now questions with the students through call and response, we (a) presented a practice problem that the teacher modeled how to solve, and then (b) assigned a guided practice problem in which we used call and response for students to work together to solve the problem. Next, students worked on practice problems together within strategically assigned groups, while the teachers circulated to assist them as needed. The problems were arranged in order of gradated difficulty, allowing every student in the class to solve the first problem or to proceed to problems that were more challenging for them. Each lesson ended with an exit ticket to collect summative data on the objective for the day. Although we occasionally conducted projects, exams, or other activities, we all followed this typical lesson structure.

As a coach that year, I drew on my prior teaching experience and demonstrated how to teach a lesson in a way that was most understandable to students. I described what visuals to use, what prerequisite skills students might be lacking, and how best to address those prerequisite skills. I also explained in detail how lessons related to and built upon one another. It is difficult for even an experienced teacher to understand a curriculum well enough to teach most effectively in the first year of using that curriculum. For co-planning in 2019–2020, the 8th-grade teacher team and I met informally daily. Considering that we met every day, we knew what topics needed to be covered, divided and assigned our classroom responsibilities, and clarified the lesson for the day. We also discussed newly collected formative and summative data and made changes to our instruction to better meet the needs of our students based on the data. We found that it was beneficial to periodically (every month or so) use a double loop in which we reevaluated our responsibilities and discussed what was working well, what was not working, and what changes needed to be made to our meeting and planning process. Unfortunately, we were unable to determine final student gains because we had to switch to online learning when the COVID pandemic began that spring. Despite this challenge, I was well positioned, being a co-teacher as well as a vice principal, to help them and other teachers transition to online learning.

During the 2020–2021 school year, despite continuing with online schooling, I brought my co-teaching and ICA method of teaching math to the 7th-grade math team as planned, co-teaching one section and planning daily with all the 7th-grade math teachers. Meanwhile, I transitioned the 8th-grade math team to work more independently. The team continued to use the ICA model and daily co-planning, but with only my support through my biweekly observations and feedback.

There were some modifications in 2020–2021 when I switched to working with the 7th-grade math team. As before, I taught one section of 7th-grade math for the 2020–2021 school year and assisted, through daily co-planning, with all aspects of planning and responsibilities for every section of the 7th-grade cohort. The difference was that the 7th-grade math team (me included) adopted a new curriculum that one new 7th-grade teacher had used the previous year. We made adaptations to the lessons within the curriculum to incorporate prerequisite knowledge into our instruction.

We continued to teach conceptually, using the ICA framework, but our instructional practices were slightly different from the instructional practices utilized to teach 8th-grade algebra. In 7th-grade math, we incorporated visual models into our instruction, but we utilized fewer authentically created real-world problems than in 8th-grade algebra the previous year. We also made some modifications to the word problems to make them more relatable to our students, but we found that we could not entirely rewrite the curriculum in a single year while also fulfilling our other responsibilities; therefore, many problems were left unchanged from the original curriculum. But the 7th-grade math curriculum included more foundational concepts that were easier to illustrate with visual models than the concepts taught in the 8th-grade algebra curriculum. As I had with the 8th-grade teachers, the 7th-grade math teachers and I continued with daily planning meetings via Zoom. In these meetings we assigned classroom responsibilities, planned our instruction, discussed formative and summative data, and made improvements to our instruction based on the data we discussed. The math teams and I continued to track our improvement using the PDSA cycle process to document implementation and assess student progress, using i-Ready formative assessments and New York State assessments.

RESULTS

Impact on Students

We measured the effects of the intervention for 8th-grade algebra during the 2019–2020 and 2020–2021 school years and for 7th-grade math during the 2020–2021 school year. While we could measure 2018–2019 school year students' success by using the June 2019 Algebra 1 Regents Exam results, it was not administered in June 2020 and June 2021 because of COVID. So we needed to turn to other assessment sources.

First, we evaluated student performance attainment by year for comparable grades. Since 8th-grade students took the same interim exam in the 2018–2019 and 2019–2020 school years, the results could be compared. We also tested the students using a redacted version of this exam for the 2020–2021 school year and compared their question-by-question performance to the 2018–2019 school year students. Similarly, we compared the scores of the 2020–2021 7th-grade cohort to the 2019–2020 7th-grade cohort using i-Ready interim data.

We measured growth over the 2020–2021 school year by comparing students' September initial i-Ready exam results with the midyear February i-Ready exam results. Finally, to determine the rate of student growth, we compared the 7th-grade cohorts scores for 2020–2021 to their scores as 6th-graders in 2019–2020 using midterm i-Ready assessments. These comparisons and the supports and assessment used are summarized in Table 2.2.

At the end of the 2019–2020 school year, we compared the results of the two March 8th-grade assessments for the 2018–2019 and 2019–2020 school years. Despite the disruption of the COVID lockdown, the results on both exam results were virtually identical: The 8th-grade algebra 2019–2020 cohort showed 41% proficiency, which was comparable to the 39% of the 2018–2019 8th-grade algebra cohort.

In the 2020–2021 school year, which was taught completely remotely, we had to take some topics out of the curriculum and thus could only compare the two groups of students by course-relevant test items, rather than by the full exam. The results were very positive, with strong improvement among the 7th-grade students and sustained improvement among the 8th-grade students. The students answered as many questions as were covered in the March interim assessment (no end-of-year assessment was evaluated comparatively), and performance on them was compared with the scores

Table 2.2. Math Support Interventions by Grade Level and Measurement, by Year and Grade

Focus of Intervention and Measurement	School Year		
	2018–2019	2019–2020*	2020–2021**
8th-grade support and measurement	8th-grade algebra co-teaching, co-planning, ICA • Measured by Algebra Regents exam and March interim exam	8th-grade algebra co-teaching, co-planning, ICA • Measured by March interim exam	8th-grade algebra sustainability ICA • Measured by partial March interim exam
7th-grade support and measurement		• Same year 7th grade used as a comparison	7th-grade math co-teaching, co-planning, ICA • Measured by i-Ready Exam growth • Compared with same year's 6th graders and prior-year 7th grade

*Fully remote instruction starting March 15, 2020.

**Fully remote instruction for the entirety of the school year.

of the students in the 2018–2019 school year. After comparing the results, we found that the 2020–2021 school-year students performed better on the common assessment questions.

To evaluate the 7th-grade cohort's growth during the 2020–2021 school year, we compared its March i-Ready proficiency scores to its 2019–2020 6th-grade i-Ready scores and to the 2019–2020 7th-grade cohort's i-Ready score growth. The 7th-grade 2020–2021 cohort showed improvement by outperforming both comparison groups (34.8% were proficient in 2020–2021, compared with 13% for them as 6th-graders and 15% for the prior 7th-grade cohort). However, the 7th grade's proficiency was not as improved as the 8th-grade cohort's in 2020–2021, which was 56.7% (an improvement over the prior 8th-grade cohort's).

The teachers and I discussed the reasons for the differences in growth for the 7th- and 8th-grade cohorts. We concluded that these differences were due in part to the authentic curriculum that the 8th-grade math team used, which prioritized real-world problems meant to be relatable to our students, in contrast with the 7th grade's purchased math curriculum. While the teachers had modified some of the problems, most were packaged curriculum problems that were not as engaging and relatable to our students. The use of real-world problems, in contrast, appeared to have been more engaging and drew upon knowledge that was already understandable and relatable to our students, which helped students to conceptualize problems more than the 7th-grade math curriculum.

Taken together, however, we concluded, based on the assessment results, that our multipronged approach to improving students' math learning worked. The combination of the ICA instructional approach (which combined teaching conceptually, concurrently developing prerequisite math skills, and using data to adapt instruction), daily co-planning with formative and summative evidence, and incorporation of authentic real-world problems enabled the teachers (and me) to help students learn math better, closing their performance gaps.

Impact on Teachers

At the end of the 2019–2020 school year, I invited several 8th-grade teachers to reflect on the benefits of the multipronged intervention, particularly the co-teaching and instructional coaching, and to describe changes in their instructional practice. All three teachers explained that although they were experienced math teachers, they were new to teaching the algebra curriculum. They indicated that they greatly benefited from the instructional coaching they received on the skills and concepts of the algebra curriculum from the vice principal. As one teacher explained:

> I was a newer teacher to the content, so, obviously, having someone that knew the content really well was beneficial, [and was] able to understand the different concepts, understand what's going on; [and] to have a lot more support with building lesson plans and understanding what it is that I was building.

Several teachers pointed out that they have learned from me different ways of using visual models, student-centered teaching strategies, and use of instructional technology when teaching students remotely.

Improved Teaching Practices

Through the adoption of the ICA model and the regular coaching support, I observed that all the math teachers built prerequisite knowledge development into their courses, and no longer assumed, as one teacher remarked, "that the student knows every single skill they've ever learned in the years past." All teachers explained that they made curricular modifications to incorporate teaching prerequisite knowledge into their instruction and could provide specific examples when asked and adapting their instruction based on daily planning meetings.

All the teachers also took steps to teach conceptually by using visual models and relatable real-world problems to help students understand concepts. The algebra teachers reported that they utilized visual models whenever possible but found certain algebra concepts difficult to represent using visual representations. The teachers of the 7th-grade team placed more emphasis on using visual models to illustrate concepts in their instruction.

Improved Instructional Practice Through Co-Teaching and Co-Planning

By co-teaching with several teachers, I learned more about their strengths and weaknesses and used co-teaching to model for and coach them. All the teachers with whom I co-taught remarked on how beneficial this was for them and potentially for any teacher, and spoke about their lack of discomfort with teaching with an administrator.

Co-planning also impacted teachers' practice by improving their meeting and data use practice and learning to continually support one another. All the teachers commented that they made at least some adaptations to improve their data-use practices in response to our daily co-planning sessions. They learned how to learn with one another. I observed peer-facilitated learning during the daily planning meetings. When reflecting on the year, a new 7th-grade math teacher cited benefiting from curricular support from a teacher with prior 7th-grade math curriculum teaching experience, noting that "we all have different backgrounds, and I think we all have something to offer."

All the teachers interviewed made changes to their instructional practices based on their data-based daily planning meetings. The most significant benefit of instructional coaching that teachers reported was curricular support for the new curriculum and the ICA framework, particularly for the teachers who were exposed to a new curriculum for the first time. Although the math teachers were experienced with effective math instruction, they required support to transition their practices to a new curriculum in both 7th and 8th grades and to incorporate the ICA framework. They agreed that the administrative co-teaching intervention was more effective leadership support than the biweekly observation and feedback cycles.

Impact on the School

The intervention was shown to have additional benefits by providing me, the vice principal, with a tool for diagnosing the effectiveness of school instructional policies and systems. There was also evidence that the administrative co-teaching intervention positively impacted the school organizational culture by improving teacher perceptions of the administrators and by giving teachers a more direct outlet for their concerns to be heard and acted upon by the leadership team, particularly during COVID.

After the 2020–2021 school year, the MCPA board of trustees replaced the principal, which was a highly unpopular decision among the MCPA staff. This change led to new schoolwide problems and consequences that demoralized the staff and their ability to continue the improvement work. The multipronged intervention was sustained in part in the school, even after replacement of the principal. The new principal found the daily team planning and data use to be a critical approach for the school.

LEADER REFLECTIONS

Nature of the Work

My approach to improving math instruction at MCPA was based on the principles of improvement science (Bryk et al., 2015) and student-centered instructional practices. I used these principles to shift the way I would lead improvement work with the teachers and the learning experiences we would create for students. This leadership shift began with my staying problem-centered. Central to developing and refining the ICA model and our co-planning was to return again and again to the math learning challenges that our students were experiencing and how to adjust practice to better meet their learning needs. I also adopted a focus on variation, helping teachers learn to use data to identify differences among their students, and use this information to drive instructional differentiation and focus on developing students' prerequisite knowledge concurrently. I also was sensitive to variation in the teachers' knowledge and skills, adapting my support accordingly. We also worked iteratively in a series of PDSA to try out how we used our co-planning and how to incorporate more real-world problems. As noted above, we would plan our change approaches, try out new approaches, use data to evaluate what worked, and make decisions about changes for the next cycle. As part of the improvement process, we successfully worked toward standard work processes—in the ICA model and our co-planning meetings—that yielded more reliable, positive results over time.

I used a very novel approach to supporting teachers' professional learning: co-teaching. While this strategy is often used by instructional coaches, it is not typical for administrators with full workloads. I chose to co-teach and co-plan with one team at a time for several context- specific reasons: the teachers' lack of teaching this math content; the lack of a shared, instructional effective math curriculum; and the students' math knowledge gaps. By working with the teachers lesson-by-lesson each day, we were able to build the curriculum by using authentic problems. I modeled effective instructional practices, and the teachers became adept at using data to differentiate instruction. Moreover, I was able to sustain my support of their work over time, since I was co-teaching the course with them.

Finally, I also drew on adaptive leadership (Heifetz & Linsky, 2017) in several important ways by co-teaching and co-planning. This entailed giving teachers voice throughout the process, coupled with my working in collaboration, even side-by-side when co-teaching and co-planning. My goal was to ensure that the teachers were co-constructing and, consequently, were valuing the solutions we were developing. In this way, I was able to strengthen their capacity to lead the work within their own teams over time.

Efforts to Meet Challenges

Due to the development and use of this administrative co-teaching math intervention, I improved my abilities as a teacher not only by continuing to practice but also by learning from the people with whom I co-taught. This learning was especially important when we were forced to transition to remote instruction. Remote instruction was new for everybody, and it might have been difficult for me to help create effective systems of instruction designed to help teachers facilitate remote learning without experiencing remote teaching and learning myself. However, I was able to provide effective support to my teaching teams outside of the administrative co-teaching intervention through biweekly observation and feedback cycles because of what I learned from continuing to teach in my own classroom (in person and virtually). I was also able to represent a teacher/user perspective when working with our administrative team to make improvements at MCPA.

Although most of the consequences of administrative co-teaching were beneficial, there was one drawback: the amount of work and time required. Leadership meetings had to be scheduled around my teaching and planning time. While I was teaching, I could not effectively address issues within the school; I had to rely on other administrators to cover for me. Administrative co-teaching required me to work outside of regular hours. There was no way for me to complete all my administrative responsibilities and teaching responsibilities effectively within general working hours. I worked until late at night every day and weekends to stay caught up. However, I was passionate about teaching and did not want to give it up.

For the intervention to be implemented by an administrator, the individual will have to be willing to take on a heavy workload that may not be manageable within a regular work schedule if the administrator has a level of administrative responsibilities similar to mine. The principal also has to be on board with scheduling meetings around the administrator's teaching schedule, and the principal must also be on board with the administrator not being available while the administrator is teaching.

EPILOGUE

Despite our success with this multipronged intervention, I decided to leave my role and the school after the following year (2021–2022), given persistent building and broader educational system problems.

QUESTIONS

1. This improvement science intervention brought together several research-based student learning strategies—using relatable math problems, incorporating instruction in foundational math skills, differentiating instruction to meet learner needs. How might these strategies be replicated in other math courses and other content areas?
2. The administrator co-teaching approach required a vice principal with both content knowledge and instructional experience. How might this approach be modifiable, if at all, when these proficiencies do not exist?
3. The vice principal adopted several adaptive leadership strategies to facilitate rapid instructional improvement. Which of these were most critical, and why did these work in such a challenging environment and under challenging conditions?

REFERENCES

Bryk, A. S., Gomez, L. M., Grunow, A., & LeMahieu, P. G. (2015). *Learning to improve.* Harvard Education Press.

Heifetz, R. A., & Linsky, M. (2017). *Leadership on the line.* Harvard Business Review Press.

Improving Students' Sense of Belonging Through Teacher Collaborative Improvement

Trisha Fitzgerald

This chapter describes how an elementary school principal supported 9 K–5 teachers in strengthening students' sense of belonging in their classroom community during COVID, using a series of Plan-Do-Study-Act (PDSA) cycles to try out Morning Meeting and share results with one another. She adopted a collaborative inquiry group process for teachers to meet weekly to discuss their experiences, problem-solve, and reflect on their practice. Based on the teachers' success and other teachers' interest, the school adopted Morning Meeting more broadly, and the principal structured collaborative inquiry groups for all teachers for other improvement work.

How does a school create a sense of belonging for all students when the ways that teachers engage them vary by each teacher? It all starts with the teacher's classroom practice! This chapter describes how a selected group of teachers from across grade levels and I, the school principal, engaged in the improvement science process to learn how the practice of Morning Meeting could increase a student's sense of belonging within the classroom community. We used Goodenow and Grady's (1993) definition of school belonging as the extent to which children feel individually welcomed, respected, included, and supported by others within the school social environment. Specifically, this chapter presents the processes and protocols put into place to enable teachers to see the benefit of facilitating Morning Meeting with students and the benefit of reflecting and working together with colleagues to improve their own practice.

This collaborative work took place over an 8-week period and used improvement science in two tandem iterative Plan-Do-Study-Act cycles. The intention was to better understand how Morning Meeting could do the following: (1) decrease variation in students' sense of belonging within their classroom community, and (2) increase individual students' feelings of belonging. It was also designed to understand how teachers' shared learning experiences, rooted in active reflection and collaborative critical inquiry groups, could deepen and sustain classroom practices. To provide evidence for the results of the inquiry cycles, I used pre- and post-intervention surveys for students, as well as findings from teachers' reflective journaling and critical inquiry groups, and interviews with teachers. Only teachers who had been trained in the *Responsive Classroom* approach were asked to participate. Responsive Classroom (https://www.responsiveclassroom.org/) is a research-based set of practices designed to help teachers create a joyful and engaging learning environment. Morning Meeting is one of these practices. In all, three kindergarten teachers, one 1st-grade teacher, one 3rd-grade teacher, two 5th-grade teachers and two special education teachers volunteered for this inquiry experience.

CONTEXT

This project occurred in a K–5 elementary school of about 360 primarily White students in a suburban, high-performing district located on the outskirts of a major city. The district includes four neighborhood elementary schools, one middle school, and one high school. While the overall population of the town is not very diverse, this school and the high school both qualified for Title I funds because of the proportion of low-income students.

Based on state standards-based assessments, this was a high-performing district. To maintain this performance, our school's instructional focus was on math and English Language Arts content areas, with small-group instruction based on achievement levels rather than students' social relationships. The school had established a Positive Behavior Interventions and Supports (PBIS) system but focused solely on rules. Whole-school assemblies did not encourage the participation of all students, and though it was a diverse school, the issue of race and racism were most often left undiscussed.

This project took place during the 2020–2021 school year, after schools had physically closed the prior spring due to the COVID-19 pandemic and continued virtually, with limited online student and teacher contact time, using prerecorded teacher videos for instruction. During the 2020–2021 school year, the majority of the students returned to in-person learning but split to follow an abbreviated cohort schedule. Cohort A was in-person Monday and Tuesday and Cohort B was in-person on Thursday and Friday. The two cohorts alternated in-person on Wednesdays. When not in-person, students attended school virtually. Therefore, during this time, classroom teachers were simultaneously navigating about 10 students learning in the physical classroom (seated apart) and about 10 students learning online.

DISCOVERING THE PROBLEM

As the building principal, I typically look at several data points, including office referrals, informal observations of classroom practice, and informal conversations with teachers and students, to monitor the school culture. It was when I began to unpack this information that I noticed the varied experiences students had relative to their sense of belonging within their classroom community. So, how does a problem with a student's sense of belonging manifest, I wondered? I used Goodenow and Grady's (1993) definition of school belonging as a guide to investigate.

For example, I noticed that 99% of the students sent to the office to work someplace other than the classroom or to see the principal were male. About one-fourth of them were repeat visitors. Yet, the majority of the students had not been sent to the office in prior years. In conversations with me, these students most often justified their visit to the office by explaining: (1) "my teacher just doesn't like me"; (2) "I don't fit in well with my classmates"; (3) "I [insert behavior or action] to get away from my teacher"; or (4) "my teacher just doesn't get me." The students' classroom teacher said that they had not broken any rules but were "distracting" to the other students in the class. These responses suggest that the students did not feel a sense of belonging or feel like they fit in, so they acted out as a way to escape the space where their uncomfortable feelings arose. Consequently, the classroom teacher separated the students not only from the uncomfortable feelings but from the learning environment.

Through informal observations and conversations throughout the school building, I noticed that some teachers engaged students on a social-emotional level, to varying degrees, while others did not engage students at all. For example, in some classrooms, teachers engaged students in daily community-building activities, such as greeting one another in different languages; using hand signals such as a fist bump, high five, or handshake; and playing games that required students to work together toward a common goal. During these community-building activities, students and teachers were observed smiling, laughing, and allowing themselves to become vulnerable with one another while creating a deeper connection. The positive impact of this community-building was witnessed throughout the day as students and teachers worked together to learn and grow.

Conversely, other teachers focused solely on the academic component of school, with no time spent on the social-emotional context for learning. In classrooms where time was not spent on these social-emotional learning techniques, students were often observed working in isolation on a task instead of working with a partner or small group. In essence, the teacher was not allowing learning to emerge from discussions among students.

In observing the teachers who took the time to engage students in activities or support them with issues, such as disagreements on the playground, I saw them responding to each child's individual needs. However, when observing teachers who did not engage with a student in these situations, they appeared to be sending the message that they did not care about the child. The latter type of teacher practice was illustrated by student comments such as "my teacher says she can't help with [insert any social issue] because we have too much to do," or "my teacher won't listen to me and told me that what happened at recess wasn't that important." For students, this lack of responsiveness seemed to feed disengagement from school because they did not feel like valued members of the classroom community.

Since not all inappropriate behavior gets the attention of the principal, the question arises as to why some students ended up in the office while other students who acted out or were disengaged did not. Goodenow and Grady (1993) suggest that "unless students identify with the school to at least a minimal extent; feel that they belong as part of the school; and believe themselves to be welcomed, respected, and valued by others there, they may begin the gradual disengagement process of which officially dropping out is only the final step" (p. 61). While students at this elementary school were far from being at risk for dropping out, their disengagement was, nevertheless, a serious concern and potential hindrance to their academic and social success in school.

ANALYZING THE PROBLEM

Talking With Students and Teachers

I wanted to better understand how students were experiencing a sense of belonging within their classrooms. To do this, I conducted empathy interviews with students and staff. The purpose was to gain insight into how students perceived a sense of belonging, as well as to understand classroom teachers' perceptions of how to create a sense of belonging for students within the classroom setting.

During empathy interviews with students, I asked questions such as "What does feeling like you belong mean to you?," "Tell me about a time when you felt like you belonged at school, specifically in your classroom setting," and "Do you think it is important to feel like you belong in your classroom setting?" What I learned from students confirmed that some felt as if they belonged inside their classroom community, while others did not.

Students in fact had varied experiences with a sense of belonging, yet they all agreed that the teacher would be able to create a sense of belonging by either helping students create new relationships with their classmates or by helping them with a peer-related issue. They shared that when teachers made them feel like they belonged, they "want to go to school." They also explained that it is also easier to learn because they were "not nervous," allowing them to focus on learning.

Through the interviews with the teachers, and using questions such as "What does feeling a sense of belonging mean to you?" and "How do you go about creating a sense of belonging in your classroom for all students?," I noticed that teachers similarly defined a sense of belonging but were quite different in how each teacher went about creating it within the classroom setting. Generally, the teachers defined a sense of belonging as feeling comfortable, accepted, and safe. One teacher had a profound insight, noting that belonging is created by "being respected, vulnerable, and being seen by others." This interpretation expressed that someone could "simply be present but still not feel like [her or she] belongs." In addition, teachers who were interviewed suggested that the sense of belonging comes from the actions of others, including classmates and the teacher. When discussing how they, as classroom teachers, went about creating a sense of belonging within their classrooms, their responses were quite different: Their actions varied from daily activities to create a sense of belonging to only focusing on building a sense of belonging during the first week of school.

Reviewing Research

These student experiences speak to research on the sense of belonging as a psychosocial construct to describe the "sense to fit" or "feelings of acceptance that an individual feels to one's community" (Bouchard & Berg, 2017, p. 107). Goodenow (1993) explained that school belonging is "more than simple perceived liking or warmth, it also involves support and respect for personal autonomy and for students as individuals" (p. 25). It is both a "membership and a form of shared emotional connection" that plays a role in primary school children's sense of belonging (Sayer et al., 2013, p. 17). An overlap of the definitions implicates the importance of active personal relationships that include a level of respect and membership.

Identifying Causes of the Problem

To see how the system impacted the elementary school students' sense of belonging, a fishbone diagram was created to help sort out possible root causes that were contributing to the problem (see Figure 3.1). These overall root causes included the school's instructional focus and environment, the physical classroom, classroom teachers' focus, and the impact of virtual

Figure 3.1. Fishbone Diagram of School-Related Factors That Contribute to Variation in Students' Sense of Belonging

Classroom teachers

- Lack of attunement to all students' needs
- Inconsistent capacity to grow a sense of belonging with students
- Academic and content focused

Physical classroom

- Rug area not always large enough
- Learning space is teacher centered
- No space allocated for small-group work

Virtual learning

- Minimal time scheduled for building relationships
- Inconsistent use of Morning Meeting time
- Lack of physical proximity

School Environment

- PBIS is rule focused, not relationship focused
- Issues of race and racism are not discussed

Instruction

- Academic content driven
- ELA & Math score focused
- Small group instruction designed for academic, not social purposes

Students' sense of belonging varies

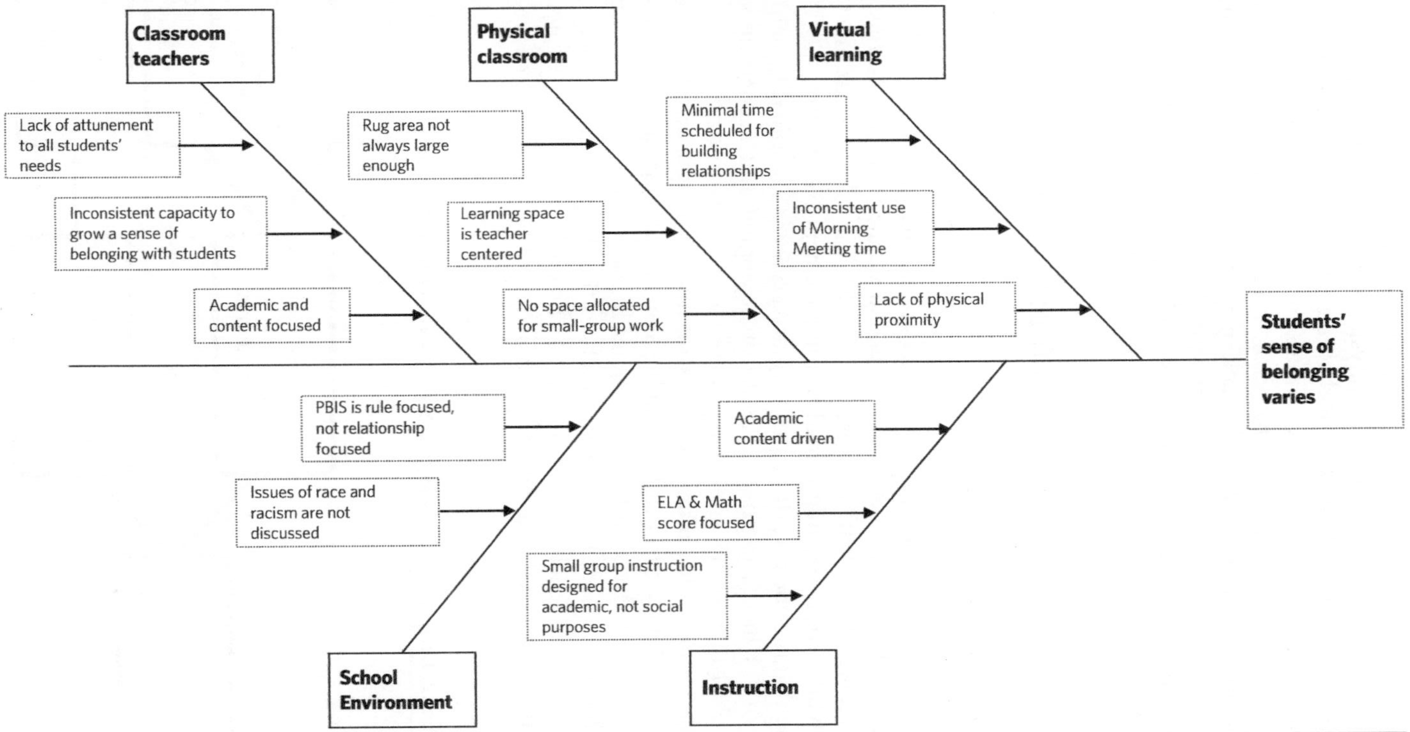

learning. In weighing the factors that contributed to disengagement, two primary "bones" were evident: physical space and teacher practice. The bones of virtual learning, physical classroom, instruction, and school environment caused students to lack a sense of belonging; however, the bone for classroom teachers appeared to be the greatest leverage point contributing to the problem. In this bone, the lack of attunement to all student needs was identified; classroom teachers were more focused on academic content than the social-emotional needs of their students. Furthermore, there was inconsistent attention paid to growing each student's sense of belonging.

DESIGNING THE SOLUTION

Forming a Theory of Action

Once I was able to identify the focus area of teacher practice, I needed to determine how my theory of improvement would work. To do this, I used a driver diagram to visually represent my thinking about what must change, and which strategies might lead to improvement (see Figure 3.2). As noted in the diagram below, three primary drivers were identified to help achieve the goal of increasing overall sense of belonging and decreasing variation among students: (1) enhancing school culture to prioritize the need for social-emotional learning in classrooms and a mindset shift that connects a sense of belonging to academic achievement and motivation; (2) increasing the amount of time that teachers engage in social-emotional learning in their classrooms; and (3) focusing on practices that help to build strong relationships between teachers and students. Therefore, my theory of action was that if teachers work together to implement research-based strategies that

Figure 3.2. Diagram of Drivers to Decrease Variation in Students Sense of Belonging

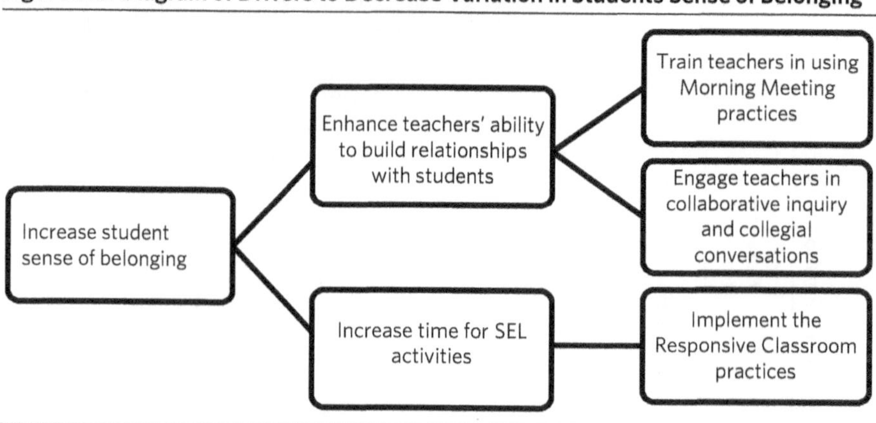

build a strong classroom community, then students will feel a strong sense of school belonging, motivating them to learn.

While all three of these primary drivers were important, as the school principal, I decided to focus on teacher practice so that teachers could build strong relationships with students. I was also hopeful that as teachers engaged in this work, the culture of the school would begin to shift and a mindset about the importance of creating a sense of belonging would change. Therefore, to focus on teacher practice, I needed to ensure that teachers had the proper training for implementing a research-based practice, as well as time to engage students in the practice and time to work together and become reflective about their practice.

Reviewing Available Research-Based Solutions

I wanted to find research-based strategies that teachers could use to build a strong classroom community so that students felt a strong sense of school belonging, motivating them to learn. I found that the Responsive Classroom practice of Morning Meeting incorporated the various practices into a single model, providing opportunities for student voice, fostering trust between peers, promoting inclusion of all students, and acknowledging the responsibility of the group to build on individual strengths (Baroody et al., 2014). Further, Baroody and colleagues found that providing teachers with training did not change the quality of teacher-to-student relationships, but teacher examination of the use of those practices did. Therefore, taking into account how teachers learn as a way to deepen and sustain their practice was important to incorporate into the design process. In addition, the research of Nelson and Slavit (2008) and Shulman and Shulman (2008) stressed how teacher reflection coupled with discussion in critical inquiry groups led to effective and long-term changes in teacher practice. Desimone and Garet's (2015) research added how school or district leadership support motivated others to apply newly learned practices and sustaining change over time. With these findings, I then designed my approach to the proposed change.

Designing the Proposed Change

My plan was to begin by using Responsive Classroom training to implement the practice of Morning Meeting daily in selected K–5 classrooms and to dedicate teacher meeting time for teachers to work with one another in critical inquiry groups on planning and refining this practice. These two efforts were tested by running two PDSA cycles in tandem over an 8-week period of time. One cycle assessed the implementation of Morning Meeting in the classroom and its direct impact on students. The second cycle tracked how teachers' work in a critical inquiry group with their colleagues strengthened their practice. Table 3.1 highlights the work that took place in each component of the PDSA cycle.

Morning Meeting

Over the 8-week period, nine participating classroom teachers from grades K–5 began each day by engaging their students in Morning Meeting, during a fixed scheduled time.Each day, teachers started their Morning Meeting with a greeting, had students engage in a shared topic, and ended with a whole-group activity. All students and the teacher sat in a circle and moved through the different components of Morning Meeting.

After the Morning Meeting was completed, the classroom teacher reflected in a journal on which of its components helped deepen connections with students and which did not, and added other thoughts they may have had about their own practice. The teacher used these journal reflections when they met with their critical inquiry group.

Critical Inquiry Groups

The nine participating teachers were divided into four small critical inquiry groups by grade level or department to maximize time for them to share personal experiences with one another. These small groups met biweekly for about 45 minutes, and teachers were provided with instructional coverage so that they could meet during the school day.

When the teachers met in the groups, they shared their journal reflections about their Morning Meetings. As a group, they then completed a Rose, Thorn, Bud Protocol to capture strengths (Rose), challenges (Thorn), and new modifications or new learnings (Bud) they wanted to try. This protocol was a mindful way to guide group reflections and structure conversations so that everyone in the group had an opportunity to share and remain on-topic.

Together, the teachers in each inquiry group helped one another modify the practice that was a challenge and create a plan for something new to try before the next meeting. The protocol had an exit question for teachers, to complete after each session, to reflect on whether the protocol and process of working together was helpful or not, and why. This exit reflection, which they shared with me, was especially important to help me understand how the groups were perceiving their own work and whether the protocol was useful.

IMPLEMENTING THE CHANGE

The proposed change integrated two efforts—adoption of Morning Meeting and teacher participation in critical inquiry groups—and operationalized them through concurrent PDSA cycles, as explained below.

Table 3.1. Elements of Two Plan-Do-Study-Act Processes

Cycle Phases	PDSA Cycle #1: Implementation of Daily Morning Meeting	PDSA Cycle #2: Participation in Critical Inquiry Groups
Plan	• Teachers attend Responsive Classroom training to learn how to implement Morning Meeting. • Administer the Sense of Belonging survey to students.	• Collect baseline teacher perception data from teachers. • Facilitate a meeting with teachers to unpack the data and create a vision for increasing a student's sense of belonging. • Set inquiry group meeting dates and establish group norms.
Do	• Teachers implement Morning Meeting daily with their students. • Teachers write in their reflection journal daily about the greeting and activity and share student reactions. • At the end of the 8-week cycle, students will complete the post–Sense of Belonging survey.	• Teachers meet biweekly in their critical inquiry group to share their reflections and experiences and work together to make modifications. • Teachers capture their reflections and learning in the Rose, Thorn, Bud Protocol. • Teachers reflect on the exit ticket whether the protocol and process of working together was helpful and why. • At the end of the 8-week cycle, teachers complete a teacher perception post survey.
Study	• Students' sense of belonging data are analyzed to determine improvements.	• The reflection journal entries, Rose, Thorn, Bud Protocol sheets, and exit tickets are analyzed to evaluate the process of reflections and critical work with colleagues and impact on teacher practice and mindset shifts. • The teacher perception survey is analyzed to determine teachers' mindset regarding t the importance of and their capacity in creating deeper connections with students.

(*continued*)

Table 3.1. Elements of Two Plan-Do-Study-Act Processes (*continued*)

Cycle Phases	PDSA Cycle #1: Implementation of Daily Morning Meeting	PDSA Cycle #2: Participation in Critical Inquiry Groups
Act	• If there is an increase in the sense of belonging of students, then daily Morning Meeting will be adopted as the framework for building positive relationships with and between students and the classroom teacher. • Without an increase, the Morning Meeting may be modified or abandoned.	• If teacher practice improves and they value how they work and learn with their colleagues, then this becomes a framework for how to work with all teachers in the school. • If there is not a change to teacher practice implementation or mindset or if working together is not determined to be helpful, then the process will be modified.

Plan Phase

Prior to starting, all nine teachers were trained in the Responsive Classroom practice of Morning Meeting. Through informal student conversations and informal observations, I noticed that not all teachers were implementing Morning Meeting the same way. To track how the Morning Meeting impacted students' sense of belonging, all students in the nine classes completed a baseline survey of their sense of belonging. I then shared the data with the teachers so they could see the differences in initial Morning Meeting implementation. Together we created a vision for how we wanted the sense of belonging to be in our classrooms.

I then met with the teachers initially to create their small critical inquiry groups, and to establish norms for our meetings and set dates and times for the individual critical inquiry groups to meet. To assess how participation in a critical inquiry group could change how teachers perceive their own impact on students' sense of belonging, all teachers completed a pre-test survey.

Do Phase

As the school principal, my role during the do phase was to ensure a protected time in our master schedule for teachers and students to engage in Morning Meeting each day. I also provided teachers with a protocol for reflection and a guide for their critical inquiry group conversations. Finally, I created a schedule for teachers to meet in their critical inquiry groups and found coverage for teachers on a biweekly basis, so that they could meet together during the school day. I did not meet with teachers during this time, as I wanted to ensure that they would have open and honest conversations with their colleagues without fear of evaluation. My main role was in ensuring protected time to engage in Morning Meeting with students and ensure that teachers could meet in their critical inquiry groups and use the reflection protocols.

During this phase of our work, teachers facilitated a daily Morning Meeting with students. Since this was still during the COVID-19 pandemic, our class structure required half the students to be physically present in the class and spread out around the room in a circle, with the other half of the class participating in Morning Meeting virtually on the interactive TV. This was the only way that all students would be able to see one another. Therefore, the teacher could facilitate each component so that students who were in-person and virtual all had a chance to participate.

As one teacher explained, this was the one time during the day that "allowed me to get to know them [students] better," make connections with one another, and "not feel so isolated from one another." For students, Morning Meeting started with an opportunity to greet their teacher and classmates. Teachers in grades K–2 tended to keep the greeting the same every day, while the teachers in grades 3–5 changed the greeting daily, "so that students feel more comfortable being silly with each other" and so teachers could "keep them engaged." Examples of greetings included saying good morning in other languages accompanied by a silly movement that each child needed to mimic for the group. There were greetings like "Count Off" and "1 . . . 2 . . . 3 . . . Pop!" that required students to concentrate and really listen to one another.

Following the greeting, each class engaged in a shared topic. Teachers specifically acknowledged that the "share" component was where students were able to open up and let others learn more about each of them, helping to create a safe environment for conversation. Often the share asked students to share something simple, such their favorite ice cream flavor; other times, shares were more personal, such as sharing their favorite storybook character, the invention they had in their head, and what they thought they were really good at doing. As one teacher stated, "The share was successful because the students know that they are going to be listened to and not judged or put down for expressing their feelings. They feel safe to share what they consider to be personal."

The final component of the Morning Meeting was the group activity. When reflecting on the activity, most teachers highlighted that this was the time for the students to either (1) come together and work toward a common goal, or (2) simply have fun in noncompetitive ways. Examples included an activity called "Coseeki," where one student identified a leader who changed a movement that the whole class mimicked. Others included Five Questions, Three Clues, and a Guess, where students work together so that their group could identify a hidden picture. Again, "laughter" and "highly engaged" were words used by teachers to describe students during these activities.

Once the class engaged in the daily Morning Meeting, the classroom teacher would take some time to reflect on what had transpired. They were looking to determine if a particular greeting, shared topic, or activity created a deeper connection between the students; and what questions they wanted to process with their critical inquiry group the next time that they met. Since we were still working with COVID-19 restrictions, teachers wanted to learn: (1) "more activities that kept students socially distant, but still engaged with each other"; (2) "how to shorten the components of the greeting, share, and activity to fit within the confines of the hybrid schedule"; and (3) "what greetings and activities would have the same impact on the in-person and the virtual students, since they are not all in the same physical space."

The teachers used the Rose, Thorn, and Bud Protocol after each session and shared their exit reflections with me. In the reflection journal entries, the theme of creating strong connections between peers and between students and teachers was noted by all teachers; teachers also mentioned the joy and safety that comes from being part of a close community. The teachers made observations of their students during the greeting, share, and activity components, frequently listing words to describe their students like "laughing," "smiling," "engaged," and "participating." One teacher shared that they personally "feel the connection that Morning Meeting creates for my students. You can tell by their smiles and participation that it is their favorite time of day."

Study Phase

While the individual reflection journals highlighted what was happening in a particular classroom on a particular day, the Rose, Thorn, Bud Protocol provided time for the critical inquiry group members to share their own experiences with Morning Meeting. An analysis of their protocols showed a consistent throughline for the four groups. What was discussed by one teacher as a success often led to a change in practice described by another teacher at the following meeting. Identified challenges often led to modifications or learning for the teachers' practice and were noted the following week as a success. For example, in one of the groups, teachers noted that it was challenging to fit in all three components in the scheduled time. During that same meeting, they collaborated and planned for shorter greetings, shares, and activities. At the next critical inquiry group meeting, this group reported success in being able to fit in all three components in the allotted time.

An analysis of the exit tickets revealed that not only did all teachers show up for every meeting, but some of the critical inquiry group members even reported extending their meetings into their lunchtime so that they had more time to work together. Overall, the teachers noted that the meetings were useful, as the meetings allowed them to identify practices they could implement with their own students. They responded with reflection comments such as "working in the group helped us to build on our strengths," the group time "allowed us to share what was working and not working and help each other to make it better," and "we found it productive to exchange ideas and then put them into motion."

In addition, the meetings allowed the teachers to create coherence among themselves as collaborators and their work with students. One teacher reported, "The [critical inquiry] meeting allowed us the time to validate our feelings and observations about Morning Meetings and find ways to help our students feel more comfortable by being silly, or opening up more, as these were our common issues." Another characterized the critical inquiry group meetings as "a powerful use of time as we were able to recall something from our training we had forgotten and modify it to use in this COVID-19 environment." All teachers responded positively to meeting with colleagues in their critical inquiry groups as a way to improve their own practice.

In reflecting on our critical inquiry study cycle, I learned that the teachers found success in the iterative process of capturing their own reflections, sharing their experiences, and then working collaboratively in their inquiry groups to refine and adjust their practice of Morning Meeting. It is important to note that despite the changing models of in-person and virtual learning, the model of Morning Meeting provided consistency for both teachers and students.

To examine what we learned through the Morning Meeting cycle, I tried to determine whether there was a decrease in variation in students' sense of belonging in their classroom environment. Therefore, students were administered a pre- and post-assessment. While the results did show an increase in a sense of belonging among the students, it was not statistically significant. Further, they were inconclusive about whether the daily practice of Morning Meeting, the attention to increasing the use of all three components of the greeting, the share and the activity at each meeting, or the coming together of both the in-person and remote students contributed to that change.

Act Phase

As demonstrated in the student assessments, implementing Morning Meeting consistently with all students helped to create or increase their sense of belonging. Therefore, we agreed to continue using Morning Meeting as the framework to build positive relationships with and between students and the classroom teacher. Given the benefits of the critical inquiry groups in changing teacher practice and providing a structure for how teachers work and learn with their colleagues, the piloted structure and reflective protocol would become a framework for how all teachers in the school work with one another.

RESULTS

Impact on Students

As a result of working in the critical inquiry groups with their colleagues and the larger group to reflect and share and focus on Morning Meeting, the teachers reported a strengthened connectedness with one another and greater perceptions of trust and safety between students and between themselves and their students. Results from the student pre- and post-assessments confirmed improvements to student sense of belonging, although data analysis was inconclusive about whether it was the result of the intervention. Despite the time commitment, teachers valued Morning Meeting as a way to promote stronger student connections in their classroom communities.

Impact on Teachers

The inquiry group process enabled teachers to gain fluency in using all three components of Morning Meeting (the greeting, student sharing, and student activities). Teachers also affirmed that the use of critical inquiry groups with a focused protocol for collaboration and protected autonomy for teachers on how the process was carried out, coupled with support from building leadership, was successful in driving improvement.

Once our PDSA cycles were completed, most of the teachers who had participated wanted to continue their work together. They found value in their critical inquiry group and found the Rose, Thorn, Bud Protocol to be an effective way to guide their conversations. The teachers wanted to both continue to focus on their students' sense of belonging, and to use their critical inquiry group process to focus on academic content. It is important to note that after the PDSA cycles were completed, the participating teachers no longer had designated time during the school day to engage in this work and so turned to using their own personal time to work with their colleagues.

Impact on the School

Given the teachers' positive response to the collaborative inquiry group process, a new master schedule was created the following year that provided for daily common planning time for each grade level. This change allowed grade-level teachers to continue to engage in this work with dedicated time during the school day without needing instructional coverage.

Other teachers wanted to learn more about Morning Meeting. They had heard their colleagues informally discuss the improvement in their classroom and saw a need for change within their own classrooms. I was able to dedicate faculty meeting time and grade-level meeting time to talking about Morning Meeting and the components that made it so valuable, which many other teachers subsequently tried. When it came time to select a cohort of teachers for training the following year, those who signed up did so because they already valued the importance of creating a sense of belonging in the classroom as a prerequisite to engaging students in academic rigor.

A year after the implementation of the PDSA cycles and as the COVID restrictions started to ease up, several teachers who had participated approached me about setting up a process to observe each other implementing Morning Meeting with their students. Specifically, they wanted to target different ways to implement the share and the activity components of Morning Meeting with their own students. In that moment we had moved from the principal engaging teachers in a shared learning experience to teachers taking ownership of their own learning.

The newest school-based initiative that we are working on as a school is creating a sense of belonging for all staff members. We are taking the ideas of the importance of having a voice, the use of protocols during shared learning, and restorative justice circles (which is an approach that helps schools shift toward restoring relationships among all community members when harm has been done) to move our work forward for the adults who make up our school community. This is now co-led by me and one of the teachers from the initial inquiry groups. We use protocols to guide the shared learning experiences that the adults engage in to keep conversations focused and encourage all voices to be heard. The restorative circles are the adult version of our Morning Meeting circles and continue to encourage all voices to be heard.

Recently, district leadership visited each school in the district to ask how teachers define excellence. During the meeting in our school, staff were engaged in a dialogue and shared the importance of students' sense of belonging and the impact of this building block to academic excellence. Two years after the work on students' sense of belonging was begun with a small group of teachers in my school, I was now hearing how far our beliefs have traveled.

LEADER REFLECTIONS

As a leader, I learned through this process that creating a sense of belonging at school is all about developing and fostering the positive relationships students and teachers have with one another and other members of the school community.

Improving School Culture

There are proactive ways that teachers can create positive relationships in a classroom community that allow all voices to be heard, encourage cooperation, build empathy, and create a safe space to be oneself and take academic risks. Through use of the Responsive Classroom practice of Morning Meeting, I have seen this sense of belonging spread throughout my school as the use of the practice has expanded.

Using Inquiry Groups to Impact Practice

When I started, I was focused on learning how the inquiry groups would be received by my staff and what outcomes they would yield. However, after running them with the staff and seeing the positive impact they had on teacher practice, coupled with the teachers who were part of the study wanting to continue them in other areas, I began to think about how to implement the inquiry groups on a larger scale.

Gaining Insights Into Effective Professional Learning

I learned that it is equally important to understand how teachers learn and grow together in order to directly impact their own practice. I gained a better understanding of adult learning and how structures around that proved to be more powerful. I found that how we operationalized the critical inquiry groups created a sense of belonging and safe space for colleagues to take professional risks. Identifying a protected time for teachers to meet elevated the importance of the work and provided time to focus on one particular topic.

Very often we (leaders) have teachers work on a topic, but we do not always give them the structure to make their learning more efficient and to push their thinking. The Rose, Thorn, Bud Protocol encouraged and taught teachers to have critical conversations. This protocol provided the structure and was feasible enough to be efficient for teachers. It was through the biweekly dialogues that teachers were able to reflect more deeply about their own practice and work together to make an implementation plan to change their practice, while capturing and celebrating all that they had accomplished. Helen Keller is quoted as saying, "Alone we can do so little; together we can do so much." The use of critical inquiry groups, coupled with protected meeting time and a protocol for critical conversations, is a true testament to her words.

Focusing Professional Learning on a Problem of Practice

As a leader, I learned how to support teachers in learning from and with one another and to focus this learning to address a problem of practice. Training alone is not enough to change teacher practice. The use of active reflection around one's own practice, coupled with critical analysis in a collaborative forum, freed teachers from working in silos and encouraged learning from the sharing of experiences as they tried out new approaches. My role was to frame and share the problem, engage teachers to voluntarily try out new practices and collaborative inquiry groups to support their learning, document the teachers' efforts and reflections, and share the results with them to study what was learned and what worked.

QUESTIONS

1. How did pairing training on Morning Meeting and adoption of the collaborative inquiry group process accelerate adoption and diffusion of the Morning Meeting model among the participating teachers and across the school? How does this reflect best approaches in adult and professional learning, and why?
2. What leadership actions were most critical to the success of this change effort? What could be done to improve it?
3. How can the leader use this experience to address other problems of practice in the school or district?

REFERENCES

Baroody, A. E., Rimm-Kaufman, S. E., Larsen, R. A., & Curby, T. W. (2014). The link between Responsive Classroom training and student-teacher relationship quality in the fifth grade: A study of fidelity of implementation. *School Psychology Review, 43*(1), 69–85.

Bouchard, K. L., & Berg, D. H. (2017). Students' school belonging: Juxtaposing the perspectives of teachers and students in the late elementary school years (grades 4–8). *The School Community Journal,* 27(1), 107–136.

Desimone, L. M., & Garet, M. S. (2015). Best practices in teachers' professional development in the United States. *Psychology, Society and Education,* 7(3), 356–369.

Goodenow, C. (1993). Classroom belonging among early adolescent students: Relationships to motivation and achievement. *The Journal of Early Adolescence, 13*(1), 21–43.

Goodenow, C., & Grady, K. (1993). The relationship of school belonging and friends' values to academic motivation among urban adolescent students. *The Journal of Experimental Education, 62*(1), 60–71.

Nelson, T., & Slavit, D. (2008). Supported teacher collaborative inquiry. *Teacher Education Quarterly, 35*(1), 99–116.

Sayer, E., Beaven, A., Stringer, P., & Hermena, E. (2013). Investigating sense of community in primary schools. *Educational and Child Psychology, 30*(1), 9–25.

Shulman, L., & Shulman, J. (2008). How and what teachers learn: A shifting perspective. *The Journal of Education, 189*(1/2), 1–8.

CHAPTER 4

A Multipronged Approach to Improve Reading Instruction for Students With Disabilities

Shaundrika Langley-Grey

This chapter describes how a new principal of an elementary school for children with disabilities worked with her staff throughout COVID to improve reading performance. After surfacing the low reading performance of her students and teachers' lack of reading instruction skills, she undertook a three-pronged approach to improving learning, using improvement science to test out solutions. One was to redesign grade-level team meetings for weekly reading instruction and trauma-informed practice training; the second was to work intensively with a small group of volunteer teachers on trying out new practices with collective feedback; and the third was to provide schoolwide monthly professional learning on culturally responsive and trauma-informed practices. By the end of the year, students were showing measurable improvement, and more teachers wanted similar small-group instructional improvement support.

Brandon enrolled in Zion Elementary School in the 1st grade but lived in a neighboring district. Exposed to trauma in his neighborhood, he was removed from his home school because of behavioral concerns and classified by his local Committee on Special Education (CSE) as a student with an Emotional Disability (ED). In Zion's 5th grade, Brandon was in the protective timeout area of the support room, having gotten upset—again—during his English Language Arts (ELA) class. Frustrated with the reading lesson, he flipped over his desk. He averaged about six incidents per week, with four of them occurring during his reading periods. One thing became apparent throughout Brandon's time at Zion: Every time he had an academic period that included reading, he would act out, severely disrupting his education process.

When I became principal of a specialized elementary school for students with severe disabilities in 2019, I discovered that many students, like Brandon, experienced both poor reading skills and significant behavior problems.

CONTEXT

Zion Elementary School (pseudonym) is a specialized K–5 elementary school that is part of a Boards of Cooperating Educational Services (BOCES) school district in New York State. Zion is a tuition-based program reimbursable through state aid. As part of the BOCES mission, the school receives students from affiliated school districts for varying durations depending upon the capacity of the sending districts to serve them. Consequently, Zion has a fluctuating student enrollment of about 188 students with disabilities.

Due to the nature of our student population, Zion's staff includes three administrators, 13 full-time school psychologists, three full-time social workers, 36 teachers, and 100 classroom aides. A typical classroom has one teacher, one aide, and six students. The class size ratio and related services are determined by students' Individualized Educational Plans (IEP) developed by the Committee on Special Education (CSE).

The school is predominantly comprised of children of color, all of whom receive free meals as part of a state grant, and 15% of whom are English Language Learners (ELLs). All are classified as Students With Disabilities (SWD), most of whom (in 2019) were emotionally disabled, on the autism spectrum, oppositional defiance disordered, attention deficit hyperactivity disordered, or other health-impaired. In addition, the children have diverse cultural backgrounds and needs. Some students are strong and physically healthy; others have complex emotional, physical, and learning challenges. Some come from high-poverty backgrounds and homes impacted by trauma. English Language Learners struggle with English while learning to read and managing disabilities.

Prior to this effort, Zion teachers and administrators had looked at assessments, curriculum, schedules, and training to improve teacher skills and capacity, without considering the effect on student learning. Thus, the school lacked an improvement culture within which to work.

DISCOVERING THE PROBLEM

Zion's students' poor reading performance has been a persistent problem. Despite adopting a reading curriculum in 2015 with input from teachers and central administration, student reading performance remained low. Specifically, based on our 2018–2019 Renaissance Learning STAR Longitudinal report (https://www.renaissance.com/products/star-assessments), 71% of students were reading three to four grade levels below, 7% were reading one to two grade levels below, and only 22% were reading on or above grade level. Given this low performance, the school staff and I knew that something needed to be done, and not just by selecting a new curriculum.

Many Zion students have experienced multiple traumatic events with varying degrees of intensity, which have shaped their young lives. The National Child Traumatic Stress Network (NCTSN) describes complex childhood trauma as "the simultaneous or sequential occurrences of child maltreatment—including emotional abuse and neglect, sexual abuse, physical abuse, and witnessing domestic violence—that are chronic and begin in early childhood" (NCTSN, 2003, p. 4). The outcomes of such maltreatment can lead to biological, cognitive, and behavioral impairment and other consequences. Yet the staff was ill-equipped to handle how the students coped through acting out or disengaging.

ANALYZING THE PROBLEM

I decided to use an improvement science approach to tackling the reading challenges of our vulnerable children. This entailed looking at the problem differently, particularly from the student's perspective and through a systems analysis. Improvement science would also center us on continuous inquiry, collaborative learning, and incremental change (Bryk et al., 2015).

Looking at our student performance data, coupled with the disproportionate number of behavioral incidents occurring during ELA instruction, the staff and I decided to explore alternative reading curricula and strategies. But before jumping into a new reading curriculum, I wanted to better understand our students' needs and how to better support them instructionally.

I began by exploring the problem first with my leadership team, holding multiple conversations about why students were making such little progress in reading and analyzing available performance indicators. Next, we conducted empathy interviews with students, teachers, and a parent to begin to understand the problem from multiple viewpoints. I reviewed available research about the problem to gain new insights. Using this information, the leadership team and I conducted a root-cause analysis, resulting in a "fishbone" diagram of the factors we perceived as contributing to the problem of practice. These findings are summarized below.

Empathy Interviews

I held roundtable discussions with all the teachers, in their grade-level teams, to gain insight into the root of the school's low reading performance problem. The teachers were very introspective regarding their thoughts and defined several stumbling blocks to increasing students' reading proficiency. They shared their opinions and identified specific reading challenges and related issues, and they also identified specific systems, structures, and lack of resources that inhibited their reading instruction.

Research Review

I reviewed available research on students who exhibit severe reading difficulties in the primary grades and learned that they often continue to struggle with reading throughout their schooling (Denton et al., 2006; Martin et al., 2008). For students with disabilities that compromise their reading success, the risk for dropping out of school, unemployment, and incarceration increases, suggesting that negative consequences for poor reading outcomes have far-reaching effects (Leone et al., 2003). While most students with disabilities are capable of meeting regular diploma requirements, their graduation rate remains 20% below their nonclassified peers, making early identification of, and intervention for, students with reading problems critical (Snyder & Golightly, 2017).

Given that many of our students have experienced trauma, I explored what is known about the effects of trauma on learning. Trauma is defined as an experience that threatens life or physical integrity and overwhelms an individual's capacity to cope with and regulate their emotions (National Child Traumatic Stress Network, 2017). Available research shows that early childhood trauma hinders school success.

System Analysis

To better understand why our students were not making adequate progress, my leadership team and I brainstormed possible factors that might contribute to students' low reading skills, given what we learned from our empathy interviews and understanding of the school's systems and structures. We organized them into a fishbone diagram, as shown in Figure 4.1, with each bone representing a set of causal factors, each of which is discussed below.

Lack of Reading Instruction Skill

Through conversations with our teachers, we learned that very few were licensed reading teachers, and all had difficulty teaching reading to students who were struggling readers. Out of our 36 teachers, just three had certifications in reading/literacy. Of those three, each teacher reported having taken only one class on reading within their undergraduate or graduate education program. While all teachers were licensed to teach SWDs in the elementary grades, they lacked the skills necessary to teach students reading two to four levels below grade-level standards.

Figure 4.1. Fishbone Diagram of the Factors Contributing to Insufficient Reading Gains

Lack of reading instruction skill
- Few teachers are licensed reading teachers
- Few teachers had teacher training in reading instruction
- Few teachers knew how to teach low level readers

Poor use of grade level meeting time
- Used for information sharing
- Not used to study student needs and progress
- Not used for professional development

Lack of trauma informed practice
- No professional learning on trauma informed practice
- Teachers lacked an understanding of students' trauma

Limited sense of teacher responsibility
- Limited capacity to use culturally responsive practices
- Teachers do not see teaching reading as their responsibility

Student behavior incidents
- Students frequently referred for behavioral incidents during ELA and math

Insufficient reading gains among SWD

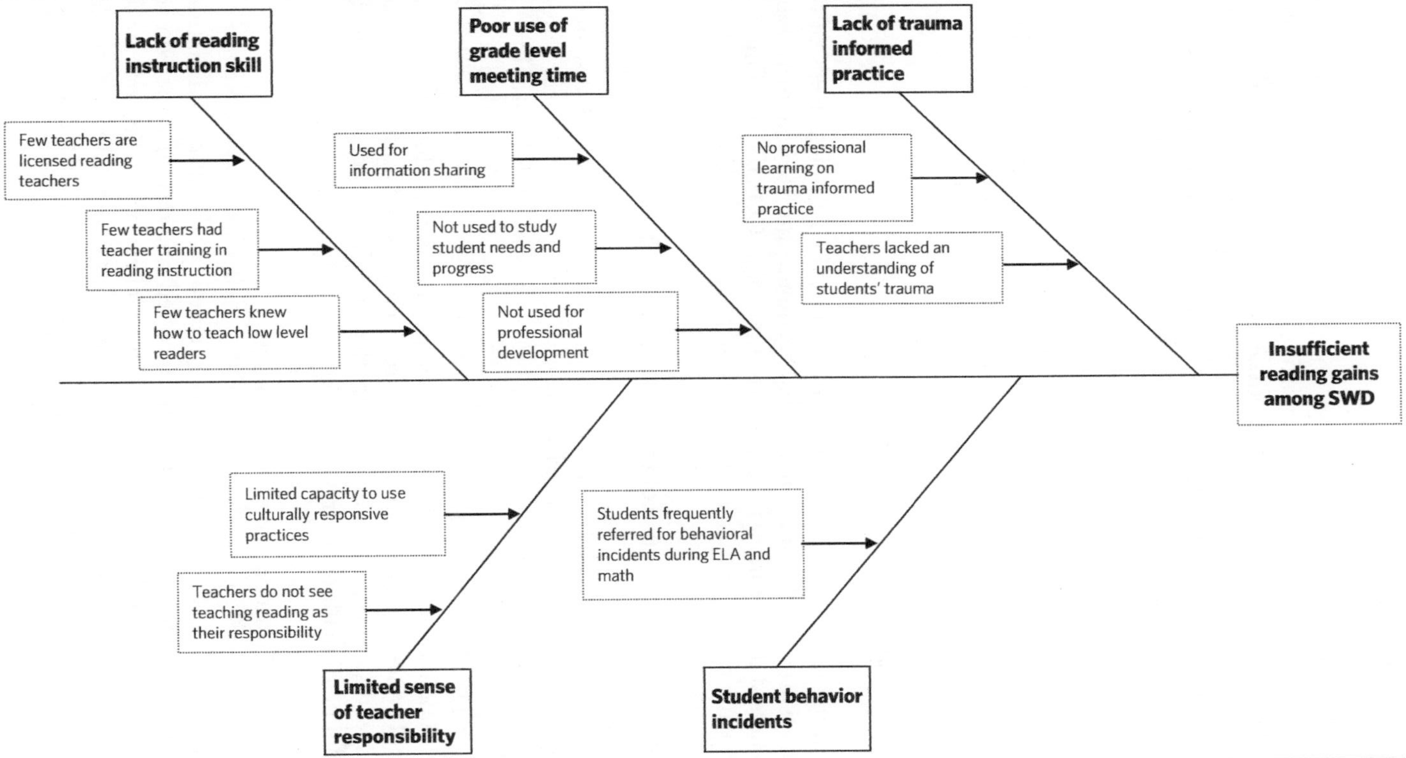

Student Behavioral Incidents

While examining our Technology for Assessing Student Conduct (TASC) data (our tracking system for reporting behavioral incidents) in the 2018–2019 school year, we found that out of the 63% of behavioral referrals during academic instruction time, 26% occurred during ELA and 20% during math. This suggests that learning to read may be particularly stressful for students, leading to acting-out behavior during instruction.

Poorly Used Grade-Level Team Meetings

The teachers typically met in grade-level meetings weekly. But these meetings were used solely for weekly information-sharing and not for the purposes of building capacity and professional development.

Lack of Trauma-Informed Practice

From my discussions, I learned more about the complex needs of our students who came from traumatic backgrounds and the extent to which the teachers did not understand how trauma (e.g., COVID and family-related traumatic events) impacted student learning.

Limits to Teachers' Sense of Efficacy and Responsibility

During this time Brandon was asked to leave our school because many staff believed that his needs exceeded what we could provide. In reflecting on this situation, I came to recognize deeply held values in our school culture that interfere with his and other students' success. Based on my analysis of the multiple referrals for out-of-classroom support areas and relationship to why our students with disabilities were having significant challenges learning to read, I concluded that challenges were in part rooted in the intersectionality of race, disability, and trauma biases that staff held. Such deeply held values would be difficult to address.

Inadequate Curriculum and Assessments

In 2019–2020, the district adopted a new curriculum, Fundations, for grades K–1. That year, all teachers received one day of in-person training by a Wilson consultant. Until fall 2019, teachers only relied on our district-wide assessment tool and other informal classroom assessments. We then adopted Running Records as a means of assessing students' progress, but the teachers were inconsistent in using this tool.

DESIGNING THE SOLUTION

In analyzing the factors that contributed to poor reading performance at Zion school, my team and I concluded that simply changing the curriculum, assessments, or schedules would be insufficient. There also needed to be a shift in mindsets, beginning with an overarching vision for and approach to improving practice. The plan for Zion going forward was to act on that vision. I wanted to dispel the idea that we were changing because we were broken. Instead, we would be working to close the gaps in educating struggling young readers with disabilities in order to improve their reading ability so as to be able to succeed to their full potential. To do this, we would need to challenge some core staff beliefs to move in the right direction, using as our guiding question: "Of all we care about, what must we give up to survive and thrive going forward?" (Heifetz & Linsky, 2002). We would also need to build the staff's capacity to continuously improve by trying out new practices, using iterative inquiry into practice and identifying the grade-level teams (GLT) as a structure within which to shift practice. Finally, we needed to create a safe space and means to engage staff in pursuing this journey of critical change.

After spending time examining and discussing the fishbone diagram, doing preliminary research, deeply contemplating the data available to me, and discussing the problem with my leadership team, I developed a theory of action: If teachers learn, through a supportive community of practice, to plan their reading lessons tailored to individual student needs and use culturally relevant and trauma-informed practices, then students will improve their reading proficiency.

This theory of action incorporates two drivers of change: (1) teacher training in differentiated reading practices, disability critical race theory, and trauma-informed practice; and (2) teacher engagement in inquiry and continuous improvement practices. To activate these drivers, I designed our work as concurrent cycles of Plan-Do-Study-Act (PDSA) to test these ideas in rapid cycles, with feedback and monitoring to assess progress.

Research Literature Review

I turned to research literature for ideas about how to best teach reading to low-skill readers and to support teachers' learning and improvement. Particularly useful for our work was Austin et al.'s (2017) synthesis of intensive reading interventions for grades K–3. The work of culturally responsive pedagogy and trauma-informed schools circles the idea of developing stronger teacher-student classroom relationships. Similarly, Duncan-Andrade's (2005) research encouraged school leaders to "put a system in place" to support the professional growth of teachers while also using them as resources. Finally,

Vaughn's (2016) case study research demonstrated that when teachers engaged in discussions using collaborative inquiry practices and culturally responsive pedagogy, they began to incorporate these theories into their curriculum, contributing to student learning. According to Vaughn, an inquiry group affords a space where teachers reimagine "teaching as a set of critical practices to disrupt the normative patterns of school and open spaces for new voices to be heard" (p. 18).

Design Components

Operationalizing our theory of action required three nested interventions, as shown in Figure 4.2.

The first was to embed professional learning about teaching reading and writing and trauma-informed instruction into weekly GLT meetings (6 teams for 36 teachers) that included all classroom teachers. The second was an intensive inquiry experience for four K–1 teachers (termed "focus teachers"). The third was to provide professional learning about differentiated reading instruction, disability critical race theory, and trauma-informed practice into monthly faculty meetings for all faculty, including the 36 teachers.

Redesigned Grade-Level Team Meetings

I redesigned the GLT meetings as collaborative inquiry groups in which teachers would learn to unpack data, discuss problems, and explore scenarios around dis/ability and race. During their meetings, the teachers would

Figure 4.2. Diagram of Proposed Drivers to Improve the Aim (Students' Reading Proficiency)

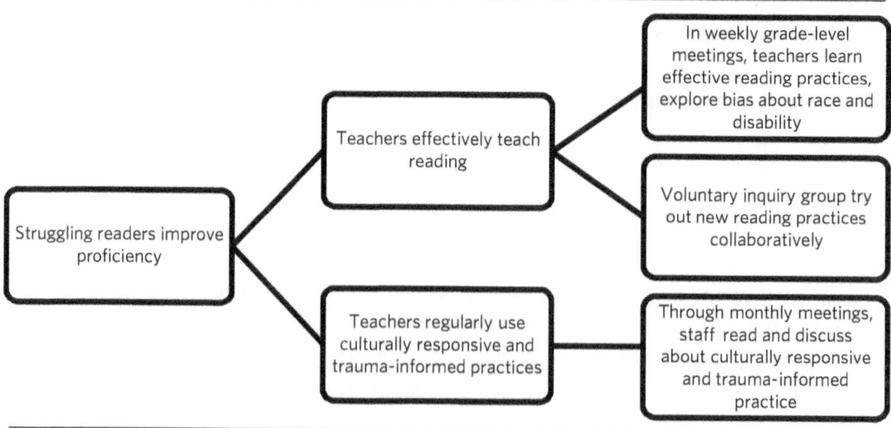

focus on setting goals, planning, and developing lesson plans and strategies to improve reading instruction to be tried out and then reviewed collectively to adjust practice. Using readings, discussion, reflections, protocols, and collaborative planning, I hoped to create opportunities for teachers to look at their practice and plan lessons tailored to their students' unique needs. The aim of this approach was to build the collective capacity of GLTs regarding trauma-informed practice (TIP) and culturally relevant teaching (CRT) as it related to dis/ability and race, while helping the teachers become proficient in inquiry, collaborative planning, and revising lesson plans using data.

I initially planned to lead 15 weekly 30-minute learning sessions that incorporated collaborative learning, application experiences, and journal reflections. I would set the agenda, provide readings, and work collaboratively with the teachers to develop plans to incorporate the material into classroom instruction. The leadership team would provide support strategies and resources for classroom reading instruction. I was to collect feedback from the teams to inform subsequent session plans.

Inquiry Group

Recognizing that we did not know enough about how to shift practice to improve student reading, I decided to form an inquiry group with four volunteer K–1 teachers to develop and test out ideas about how to improve reading support for their students. This gave us an opportunity to intensively focus on developing reading skills in the early grades. By working intensively with these teachers, through iterative cycles, we could learn how to help all teachers improve reading instruction. With the assistant principals, I also created a modified equity rubric on culturally responsive teaching practices, using Aguilar's (2020) equity rubric, for teacher observation and feedback.

Professional Learning Embedded Faculty Meetings

The third intervention was to enhance monthly faculty meetings with teachers and other staff to focus on culturally responsive and trauma-informed practices. Typically, these were monthly, hourlong information sharing sessions. During the first half of the year, we included one culturally responsive practice activity and added in monthly discussion of a children's book that addressed either social-emotional learning or culturally responsive practice. During the second half of the year, based on teacher reflections, these meetings were adapted to incorporate equity- and trauma-related conversations with the other teaching staff (i.e., special area teachers, school psychologists, social workers, and other specialists).

To prepare for these monthly meetings, I met weekly with an eight-member team that included two psychologists, two social workers, two teachers, and the assistant principal. This began the process of aligning our faculty meetings with the conversations around trauma-informed approaches, equity and inclusion, diversity, and growth recognition. This helped engage the nonteaching staff members to understand the goal of supporting our students at the intersections of disabilities, race, and trauma. This alignment also supported our district's Diversity, Equity, and Inclusion (DEI) initiative.

IMPLEMENTING THE CHANGE

This change effort was launched with the onset of the COVID pandemic. Zion School was among a small number of schools in the greater NYC area to open to full in-person learning, in 2020–2021. The return to school that year was met with many challenges: the ongoing pandemic, national racial unrest, and trepidation from staff and students alike. To ease our transition, the staff schoolwide, parents, and I began our professional development with Santat's (2017) book *After the Fall,* and we had many conversations at our parent meeting, staff meeting, and related services staff meeting about unpacking our fears about returning to in-person learning. The themes we centered around were those of courage and determination to overcome adversity. As one teacher reflected, "I initially didn't feel prepared to come back to school, but thank you for hearing my fears."

Although 25% of our student population had initially chosen to remain virtual (which was an option for them), scheduling and learning became even more challenging, with 11% of the teachers electing to take a leave of absence and 8% working virtually. We had to be flexible and place students in classroom groups for all-in-person or all-remote classes. I encouraged special area teachers and related service providers to push into classrooms and not to mix groups of students, if possible.

A Culturally Responsive Vision

To launch our improvement work together under these challenging conditions, I chose to articulate a strong vision for the school that centered on looking at our students and working to understand their voices, visions, and values. I urged teachers and staff to see each student, to hear them, and to genuinely value who each student was and what the circumstances were from which they walked into our school. The mission of our work for that year was to validate students' uniqueness, embrace their culture, and honor their diversity while acknowledging one's own preferences and expectations. This became our guide to test our resolve for teaching students at the intersections of disability, race, and trauma amidst the pandemic.

Grade-Level Team Meetings

This first intervention entailed embedding professional learning about reading instruction, culturally responsive practice, and trauma-informed practice into the weekly GLT meetings. These meetings were redesigned to engage teachers in collaborative work to develop and apply plans to incorporate new ideas and related material into classroom instruction. The new format of the GLT meetings was unfamiliar to the teachers, as were many of these learning strategies that were being taught. I used the PDSA cycle in Table 4.1 as my guide for trying out this new approach.

Do Phase

We launched the redesigned grade-level team meeting structure and process in fall 2020. Part of the grade-level team meeting time focused on effectively using the reading curriculum and strategies. All of these were new practices and tools that had never been used before.

Reading Instruction. Consequently, our weekly GLT meetings centered on sharing and discussing what reading instruction worked and what could be improved. For example, teachers recorded their students reading and used STAR assessments and Google Forms to analyze and interpret the students reading and responses.

We also identified the skills students needed in order to learn to read, such as phonological and phonemic awareness and letter–sound mastery. When interviewed at the end of the year, the teachers reported that they had learned to use strategies such as implicit instruction to support reteaching, phonological and phonic awareness, letter–sound correspondence, repetition, and engagement in multisensory instruction.

Table 4.1. PDSA Cycle for Grade-Level Team Meetings

Phase	Action
Plan	Unpack data
	Work with leadership team to plan grade-level team meetings
Do	Implement revised weekly grade-level meetings
	Teachers conduct empathy interviews
	Collect teacher reflections and survey feedback
	Observe teacher practice
Study	Review reflections and survey results
	Review student STAR and Running Records to determine student growth
Act	Made decisions about next steps for grade-level teams

In addition, the reading specialist began to pull out "jewels" from the new Fundations reading hub to provide targeted support in Fundations to teachers throughout the year. As teachers were transitioning from the Journeys reading program, many were using both in fall 2020. By January, teacher support in the grade K–1 teams focused only on Fundations, while all other grade-level teachers continued to use the Journeys curriculum.

During the informal observation process, teachers and I discussed relationships, culture, and class environment as an indicator of equity. We pushed the envelope for teachers and specialists to create conditions for students to see themselves in these lessons, creating an intellectually and socially safe learning environment as well as creating space for student voice. We added more diverse books and materials to help students see themselves in their resources.

Assessment. We used the GLT meeting time to retrain teachers on how to complete the assessment consistently, including testing remotely with students. Teachers were to complete Running Records three times that academic year—during the fall, winter, and spring. During the GLT meetings, we discussed the results for each assessment period, identifying the changes we observed, and identified strategies we could use differently and what we needed to reteach.

Empathy Interviewing. We also invited all classroom teachers to learn from their students' perspectives on how difficult it was for their focus students to read. Using an empathy interview guide, each teacher had conversations with one student about what was challenging about reading and how they, as classroom teachers, could support the student's efforts. They shared their varied summarized reflections during the GLT meetings. Through this experience, many teachers began to realize that they were the one person in the school that students felt were their safe zone. The teachers also shared the struggles that their interviewed students felt when they tried to read. One student shared that "learning the right letter sounds is the hardest thing to do." Another student said, "It's like my brain is acting crazy." These interviews gave teachers new perspectives for reworking how they were teaching their students, how they called on them in class, and how they could use their relationships to support student learning.

Collaborative Lesson Planning. Throughout the GLT meeting times, the teachers engaged in collaborative lesson planning and sharing activities that went well and pitfalls to avoid in future iterations of the lesson they planned. The meetings became a vehicle for teachers to share their work weekly. Consequently, they grew willing to take risks, engaged with assessment data, and reflected on their new learning. The meetings became more productive when they moved from developing readiness in the first semester to becoming more hands-on and teacher-learner-centered in the second semester.

Study and Act Phases

Initially, the school year began with me planning and leading all six GLT meetings. In response to initial participant feedback, I adapted the process and began scheduling weekly meetings with two out-of-classroom teacher leaders to discuss the reading instruction for the GLT meetings, review teacher feedback, discuss student data, and identify teachers who needed extra support.

Toward the end of the second quarter, I shifted the GLT meeting structure further, enabling teachers to engage in hands-on experiences and take a more active role in planning and leading meetings. The reading teacher and the out-of-classroom teacher took more active roles to support other teachers, particularly those who were becoming disheartened as a result of the pandemic. It was apparent that the teachers were then ready to become active in presenting their work to their colleagues and providing feedback to one another. This shift started first as a way to plan support around teacher reflections on the feedback survey and continued until the end of the academic year. Ultimately, the GLT meetings became the avenues whereby they supported one another around results, differences, similarities, and strategies for working with students.

Inquiry Group

In the second intervention, I, as the principal, and other out-of-classroom specialists in the school collaborated intensively to support four K–1 teachers who volunteered for additional support, using the planning described above, and a similar PDSA cycle to guide this work.

Do Phase

In addition to the weekly GLT meetings, these four teachers had additional formal and informal meetings for support on reading instruction. They met together during their daily prep periods to plan and share lessons and applications based on what they were learning about reading, culturally responsive pedagogy, and trauma-informed practice. They received several one-on-one coaching sessions with the reading specialists and out-of-classroom curriculum teachers on using the new reading curriculum and shifting their practice to better support student learning. The teachers also worked with me on their culturally responsive practices, based on my observations and feedback using the modified equity rubric.

The four teachers were adaptive as they restructured the curriculum to meet the specific learning needs of their students. They began the school year by collaboratively defining equity and developing their GLT mission as their compass for the academic year. Doing so guided their decision to use culturally relevant practices and to ensure that their students could see themselves, thereby giving value and voice to their lessons.

The four teachers took steps to foster stronger teacher-student relationships and better communication with parents and guardians. They wanted students' parents and guardians to trust them, so they worked hard to communicate in students' home languages, and provide additional resources to support homework and enrichment, along with proactive feedback to parents.

Study and Act Phases

Two new developments emerged as a result of this more intensive work. In the second half of the year, the four teachers began to lead their GLT meetings with other teachers around these new practices. These teachers also adapted their instruction to intentionally make space for teaching literacy in a different way, centered on cultivating relationships, culture, and mindsets. Developing trust became the cornerstone of their work together. It appeared that the intensive support that these teachers received was critical to how they changed their practice, and instrumental in creating teacher leaders who wanted to share what they learned with others.

Enhanced Monthly Faculty Meetings

We began our first fall 2020 meeting with a culturally responsive activity, but, unfortunately, subsequent faculty meetings returned to information-sharing, given COVID conditions. Using a similar PDSA cycle and based on the work we were doing schoolwide in the first semester, we made some shifts for the second semester.

Do Phase

In January 2021, the faculty meeting content shifted to incorporate equity- and trauma-informed practice conversations with all classroom teachers, special area teachers, school psychologists, social workers, speech teachers, and occupational and physical therapists. We began to share topics from the GLT meetings with the whole faculty for more extended, schoolwide discussions that built on but did not duplicate what was discussed at the GLT meetings. This began the process of aligning our faculty meetings with the conversations around trauma-informed approaches, equity and inclusion, diversity, and student growth recognition. The process helped bring into line the nonteaching staff members to understand the goal of supporting our students at the intersection of disabilities, race, and trauma. Developing an equity lens became a consistent theme in both weekly GLT and monthly faculty meetings.

Study Phase

These discussions helped to shift the culture of the school to become more student-centered, particularly in understanding the intersection of disabilities, race, and trauma in promoting student learning. Staff members began working together to address the needs of their students while engaging in their own professional growth. Investigating their own bias, activating an equity lens, and encouraging out-of-the-box thinking allowed them to develop their capacity to reflect and reinforce their ability to reimagine what it means to work with students at the intersections of disability, race, and trauma.

Act Phase

As a result of these meetings, staff members created and led various equity subcommittees across multiple disciplines; they created bulletin boards based on cultural themes and purchased culturally responsive books for our school library. Our faculty meetings became learning-centered and ran parallel with the GLT meeting content. The school culture shifted from a one-size-fits-all approach to a culture of seeing individual students and tailoring services to meet their needs. This alignment created coherence in our school culture.

RESULTS

Impact on Students

Sadly, Brandon himself didn't benefit from our improvement work. For a myriad of reasons, he was unable to leave our school with the tools needed to support his desire to read. Due to the changes in our program, however, other students now have teachers who have aligned their teaching with effective ways to teach reading and an understanding of family dynamics.

In our first year, we found measurable student gains. Between the fall and spring Running Records assessment periods, 80% of K–1 students ($n = 24$) increased their reading scores, and 20% remained the same. We found that these results varied based on whether the students participated remotely and had support available at home. In addition, we had 19 kindergarten and 1st-grade students who met the criteria for STAR testing for the 2020–2021 academic year by being physically in person, taking at least two tests, and scoring initially between 7 and 99. Prior to this year, only 43% of our students made our district's threshold in the 2018–2019 academic year and even fewer in 2019–2020. In contrast, 84% of our kindergarten and 1st-grade students scored above the district's 35 SGP threshold score for the 2020–2021 academic year. This was an extraordinary result given the ongoing pandemic and the implementation of several new strategies to improve student learning.

Impact on Teachers

Through periodic feedback surveys, I learned how professional learning benefited teachers. Ninety percent of surveyed teachers agreed or strongly agreed that the grade-level professional learning they received helped them meet the learning needs of their students and improved their teaching practice in several ways.

Working Collaboratively

One goal of our improvement efforts was to strengthen the teachers' capacity to improve practice collaboratively. Through this work, teachers began to lead their grade-level team meetings around the new practices they employed. After developing their own readiness, the teachers began to take ownership, accelerating their learning and practice changes. Once classroom teachers began to actively participate in grade-level meetings, the sense of belonging with their colleagues helped create the environment for them to grow and thrive. In the end-of-year survey, 87% of teachers agreed or strongly agreed that these teams felt like a community that was always trying to improve and get better at meeting the learning needs of our students.

They also learned how to collaborate differently to meet the needs of all students. Nelson and Slavit (2008) describe teacher inquiry as a collaborative process grounded in the willingness to wonder, ask questions, and seek understanding to answer questions. The teachers began to adopt this form of collaborative inquiry and became risk-takers and learners. They learned to allow other teachers in their meetings to challenge their stereotypes and deficit thinking.

The four inquiry group teachers reflected on the fact that their classrooms and grade-level teams now had a familial culture: "We are all in this together, we care, respect, and love each other." This was a new sentiment and shift that was shared across each classroom and interview. One teacher noted, "This is what was missing at my old school." Another said, "I never felt this support before." They were guided by their mission as a grade-level team and translated that into classroom rules and shared responsibility with their students. Their continued interest in collaborative inquiry will sustain this growth beyond the area of struggling readers.

Improving Reading Instruction

A second goal of our work, by adopting the new curriculum and discussing instructional strategies in GLT meetings, was for teachers to adapt their instruction to teach literacy in a different way, centered on cultivating relationships, respecting diverse cultures, and adopting more open mindsets. Through our work together, they began to try new strategies, share them across grade levels, and learn from one another. In the year-end survey, 90% of teachers agreed or strongly agreed that they had actively tested out new teaching practices that year to meet the learning needs of all their students, and 90% agreed or strongly agreed that they could effectively model reading strategies. The GLT structure seemed to accelerate this because 95% of teachers shared new teaching strategies with their colleagues and 95% reported learning a new teaching strategy from their colleagues. Examples of these new teaching strategies include building classroom relationships, creating a safe learning environment, translating materials for bilingual families, creating homework assignments where the first few answers are completed as examples, using data to help bridge student gaps, supporting lessons with hands-on activities, and adapting lessons using multiple modalities and scaffolding. In addition, with regard to reading instruction, many teachers used repetition, visual aids, identifying sound–letter correspondence, tapping out sounds and letters, technology, short and concise directions, student-centered learning, and student-led learning.

Becoming More Culturally Responsive

The teachers gained a greater understanding of the role of teaching reading, the socioeconomic factors influencing students, and the impact of trauma on students and the classroom. As we unpacked the problem of effectively teaching reading, the teachers became aware that just below the surface were some beliefs that were hindering better teaching. We surfaced that there had been a shared culture and level of comfort that expecting more from students with disabilities would be an "injustice" to them. They learned that this belief was actually holding back student learning and had to be confronted. By establishing an overarching vision and holding regular conversations through our faculty meetings, we were able to set a new direction of high expectations to meet the needs of our students and community. In the year-end survey, 90% of teachers agreed or strongly agreed that they could confidently meet the learning needs of their struggling readers at the intersection of disabilities, race, and trauma. Our concurrent work on culturally responsive and trauma-informed practices was critical to the teachers' change in practice for reading, and it created teacher leaders who wanted to replicate the work with other teachers, current and incoming.

Impact on the School

The improvement work began with our collaborative grade-level groups looking at the school's vision and mission as we completed the Back to the Future protocol (from the Center for Leadership and Educational Equity) for planning to achieve one's vision (Curtis & City, 2009). By the end of the year, many faculty were interested in expanding our collaborative approach and focusing on culturally responsive and trauma-informed practices. Moreover, other grade-level teachers requested switching to kindergarten or 1st grade in the next school year to become a part of the more intensive working relationship that the focus teachers had. Several teachers voiced that they wanted other teachers to be similarly prepared and to screen new teachers for their interest in learning to teach reading to struggling readers and willingness to teach students at the intersection of trauma, race, and disability. Not surprisingly, our end-of-year DEI scores were significantly better than other schools within the district, suggesting the positive benefits of our yearlong faculty meeting discussions on culturally responsive practice.

LEADER REFLECTION

Learning to use improvement science to guide our improvement work shaped my leadership approach. In my role as the new building principal, I was responsible for creating a culture of continuous learning and growth within our school and for ensuring that teachers had the resources and support they needed to improve their practice. The foundation of this work was laid when I was the assistant principal and increased as I took the lead as principal to continue to create systems and structures to support their investigations and work.

Navigating Challenges

Improving the school environment was challenging work, especially because our school was among a few schools in the greater New York area to open to full in-person learning in the fall of 2020–2021. Teaching under these conditions had many challenges, and I used our various meeting formats to discuss these challenges while striving to improve reading instruction and create a culturally responsive learning environment.

Piloting Strategically

Providing special support to a group of four teachers was a valuable means for me to better understand the needs and perspectives of the rest of the staff. Starting with the pilot group gave me an avenue to ensure that these meetings were tailored to the specific needs of the faculty. It helped me to learn how to support teachers so they in turn could support their students. The four teachers underscored the need for more time for collaboration and conversations to learn how to support students' mental, social, and emotional health so they could learn to read, particularly, as one teacher reported, to become "more aware of the large role trauma plays in how her students learn."

Creating Psychological Safety Strategically

Throughout every step of this process, I needed to ensure that I was increasing psychological safety and reducing the stress of teachers' learning anxiety and the external barriers to change through the norms and practices we developed. I shared the vision that we completed during the visioning process, provided the training needed to support students who are affected by trauma, and used evidence-based strategies for dealing with trauma, as well as provided evidence-based professional development practices for teaching students how to read.

Modeling a Learner Stance

In order to offer a model to staff, I researched articles and videos of schools that had become trauma-informed and used the strategies they presented to teach students with disabilities. I knew my staff needed to see what it looked like before they saw themselves doing it, so it was important that my leadership team modeled and encouraged this (Schein, 2016).

Articulating a Vision

Through Brene Brown's (2012) writing I was introduced to a quote from President Theodore Roosevelt that has become part of my mantra:

> It is not the critic who counts; not the man who points out how the strong man stumbles, or where the doer of deeds could have done them better. The credit belongs to the man who is actually in the arena, whose face is marred by dust and sweat and blood; who strives valiantly; who errs, who comes short again and again, because there is no effort without error and shortcoming; but who does actually strive to do the deeds; who knows great enthusiasms, the great devotions; who spends himself in a worthy cause; who at the best knows in the end the triumph of high achievement, and who at the worst, if he fails, at least fails while daring greatly. (p. 1)

Educating students with disabilities is my mission. Teaching those who have difficulties with reading and are affected by trauma is at the core work of educators. I need to have my heart meet the hearts of my staff so that they see the risks of simply moving students along versus changing their practice to meet students' needs and teach them more effectively. Is it worth it? Absolutely. I may not please everyone, but my greatest fear is being in the same place next year. So with that, I leaned forward.

QUESTIONS

1. The principal had an intensive role in designing and implementing three concurrent interventions—meeting weekly with each GLT and the inquiry group separately and planning and co-facilitating the monthly faculty meetings. What would have been gained or lost with less hands-on involvement?
2. Developing an equity perspective and gaining culturally responsive practice were critical to this improvement work. How did the principal's approach incorporate these in reshaping the school's culture?
3. The principal and her staff planned for sustainability of their approach to reading instruction, GLT meetings, and faculty meetings. How can she and her staff track the impact of their work over time?

REFERENCES

Aguilar, E. (2020). *Coaching for equity*. Jossey-Bass.

Austin, C. R., Vaughn, S., & McClelland, A. M. (2017). Intensive reading interventions for inadequate responders in grades K–3: A synthesis. *Learning Disability Quarterly*, *40*(4), 191–210. https://doi.org/10.1177/0731948717714446

Brown, B. (2012). *Daring greatly*. Avery.

Bryk, A. S., Gomez, L. M., Grunow, A., & LeMahieu, P. G. (2015). *Learning to improve: How America's schools can get better at getting better*. Harvard Education Press.

Curtis, R. E., & City, E. A. (2009). *Strategy in action: How school systems can support powerful learning and teaching*. Harvard Education Press.

Denton, C. A., Fletcher, J. M., Anthony, J. L., & Francis, D. J. (2006). An evaluation of intensive intervention for students with persistent reading difficulties. *Journal of Learning Disabilities*, *39*(5), 447–466. https://doi.org/10.1177/00222194060390050601

Duncan-Andrade, J. (2005). Developing social justice educators. *Educational Leadership*, *62*(6), 70–73.

Heifetz, R., & Linsky, M. (2002). *Leadership on the line: Staying alive through the dangers of leading*. Harvard Business School Press.

Leone, P. E., Christle, C. A., Nelson, C. M., Skiba, R., Frey, A., & Jolivette, K. (2003). School failure, race, and disability: Promoting positive outcomes, decreasing vulnerability for involvement with the juvenile delinquency system. *EDJJ: The National Center on Education, Disability, and Juvenile Justice*, 1–46.

Martin, D., Martin, M., & Carvalho, K. (2008). Reading and learning-disabled children: Understanding the problem. *Clearing House*, *81*(3), 113–118.

National Child Traumatic Stress Network. (2003). *Complex trauma in children and adolescents* [White Paper].

National Child Traumatic Stress Network. (2017). *Creating, supporting, and sustaining trauma-informed schools: A system framework.*

Nelson, T., & Slavit, D. (2008). Supported teacher collaborative inquiry. *Teacher Education Quarterly, 35*(1), 99–116.

Santat, D. (2017). *After the fall: How Humpty Dumpty got back up again.* Macmillan.

Schein, E. H. (2016). *Organizational culture and leadership* (5th ed.). Wiley.

Snyder, E., & Golightly, A. F. (2017, Fall). The effectiveness of a balanced approach to reading intervention in a second-grade student: A case study. *Education, 138*(1), 53–67.

Vaughn, M. (2016). Re-envisioning literacy in a teacher inquiry group in a Native American context. *Literacy Research and Instruction, 55*(1), 24–47. https://doi.org/10.1080/19388071.2015.1105888

CHAPTER 5

Cultivating a Schoolwide Approach to Integrate K–5 Students With Significant Disabilities

Tashia Brown

This case study describes how I, a new elementary school principal, made it a priority to reverse the district practice of outplacing students with severe disabilities. I worked with my school and district to design an in-school class for these students and integrate them into special area classes and schoolwide experiences. Despite the onset of COVID, I was able to launch a class for five students with autism and worked iteratively with a consultant, staff, and special area teachers to design the students' class experiences and participation in special area classes. Through regular collaborative meetings, the special area teachers learned to adapt their instruction to meet the students' needs. Broader efforts to shift the school culture to be more inclusive yielded mixed results. By the end of the second year, however, the school was serving eight students with severe disabilities, all of whom were making academic progress.

Cultivating schools that are welcoming and affirming, where access to a high-quality education is afforded to all students—regardless of zip code, race, ethnicity, class, socioeconomics, language, and ability/disability—remains one of the most urgent civil rights issues of modern education. As school leaders we are expected to foster environments where all students, especially those from historically marginalized groups, can meet their full potential, so they can live a quality life and contribute to our society in productive ways. As a school leader for 19 years, I know how challenging this work can be, particularly if the system is not designed to produce the results we seek, which in this case is to serve students with significant impairments in the least restrictive environment.

This chapter focuses on the inclusion of students with significant impairments in a highly resourced suburban district where, historically, students with this learning profile were educated in out-of-district settings.

I arrived in this district in July 2019, as the new principal at one of their elementary schools and with extensive experience and background knowledge in working with students with disabilities from my former school district. My experience with this population, coupled with the district's goal to bring students who were placed in out-of-district settings back to our district, was the catalyst for change. As a result, my school staff and I embarked on a mission to create a new self-contained special education program for students with significant impairments.

Using the tools of improvement science (Bryk et al., 2015), I designed a special education program to integrate students with the most significant impairments into our school so that they could make adequate individual progress. I purposely used this approach because I knew that developing and implementing such a program involved many unknowns that we would need to tackle through trial-and-error effort. We collected multiple data from different constituent groups: the classroom team that supported the students in the class, the special area teachers, and the faculty at large.

I began by conducting empathy interviews with a cross-section of teachers in the school to understand their worries and fears about the integration of the students into our school community. I also utilized other tools to collect data, such as surveys, observation of special area teachers, and semistructured interviews. The goal was to determine if we were building schoolwide capacity to provide more inclusive opportunities for students with significant disabilities to be served well in the least restrictive environment.

CONTEXT

District Context

This was a wealthy, high-performing school district located in the suburban Northeast in a large metropolitan region. The district consisted of five elementary schools, one middle, and one high school. Its student population of 4,700 students (in 2019) was predominantly White, with Asian students as the next dominant ethnicity. Only 10% were classified as students with disabilities. Students performed well above the state average on state assessments, and the graduation rates typically were 98–99%, with graduates usually attending high-ranking colleges and universities.

School Context

The elementary school for this case was K–5, with about 380 students. While the school's student population was predominantly White, it was the most diverse elementary school in the district, both socioeconomically and racially/ethnically, with on average a 17% Asian student population. It was a neighborhood school where most students walked, biked, or were transported by their families to school. It was a tight-knit community where the families valued diversity, as evidenced by the many cultural events that the school sponsored during the school year. The faculty and staff also professed to value diversity and so, by all accounts, this school had the basic ingredients to be the setting to integrate a new class of special needs students.

Prior to the launch of this new program, students with severe disabilities were outplaced into specialized public and private schools. There were no prior attempts to design a program that could support them onsite.

DISCOVERING THE PROBLEM

Although most of the school's students performed well above the state's average, the school did not always meet New York State's target for the percentage of special education students being educated in the least restrictive environment. In two consecutive years (2017–2018 and 2018–2019), the school was cited for not meeting this state target. The majority of elementary students who were placed in an out-of-district setting were classified with autism or were multiply disabled, often requiring intensive school-based support and therapies. Without a district or school program to meet the needs of these students, the school's Committee on Special Education (CSE) was left with no choice but to place them in specialized out-of-district programs, which was contrary to state standards.

As a high-performing school district, we were accustomed to students who performed at very high levels, and the system was not as skilled at meeting the needs of students with significant disabilities. The lack of an in-district program for our students with significant impairments resulted in a lack of instructional readiness and system preparedness not only to meet the needs of these students well, but to provide schools with the tools necessary to effectively integrate them into the school community.

As a new principal, I was facing a daunting task to address this need by designing and implementing this program, less than a year into my principalship, on the eve of the COVID pandemic.

ANALYZING THE PROBLEM

Given the state's analysis, I knew there were several students with severe impairments who were not being served by my school or the district. Consequently, my problem became one of figuring out how to design a program for them and how to fit it into the school's operations, and fit the students into the broader school culture. Analyzing this problem entailed understanding why such a program did not exist and what implementation considerations would be necessary. Thus, in summer 2021 I conducted a series of interviews with teachers and analyzed the existing school operations and culture for teacher receptivity and readiness to integrate these students into the school generally; and identified the resources, curriculum, and programming that the special area teachers would need.

Empathy Interviews

To begin, I talked with six teachers: three classroom teachers (grades K, 1, and 5) and three teachers who taught specialty subjects (art, library, music, physical education, and technology). The results from the empathy interviews revealed that most of the teachers were unfamiliar with this profile of students and felt unprepared to support and meet their needs. One of the specialty teachers expressed a desire to do the best job possible but was uncertain if her instructional approach would match the needs of the students. The teachers stressed that they would need professional development and training. Yet all six teachers agreed that our school was the best site for such a class to be successful in our district.

System Analysis

Next, I did a system analysis using a fishbone diagram to sort out the factors that contributed to our school's and district's problem of not educating our students with significant impairments in the least restrictive environment, and that would hinder the creation of a special class for them if not addressed (see Figure 5.1). In doing so, I identified four factors: unsupportive district/school culture, inadequate systems and structure, insufficient curriculum and instruction, and weak staff professional knowledge and skills.

Due to the lack of experience educating students with significant impairments within the school district, there was not a clearly defined profile of the type of student who had such impairments that our district's Committee on Special Education (CSE) could use to appropriately place students into a school-based program if we created one. Also, faculty and staff had no experience working with students with this profile. No teachers had the knowledge or skills to teach students with severe impairments. Without prior experience with severely disabled students, the district lacked expertise in selecting staff or curricula and assessments that were appropriate to meet the students' needs, particularly given that the educational and social/emotional learning needs of these students were very nuanced and required specific teacher expertise, curricula, and assessments.

Figure 5.1. Fishbone Diagram of Factors Contributing to the Problem

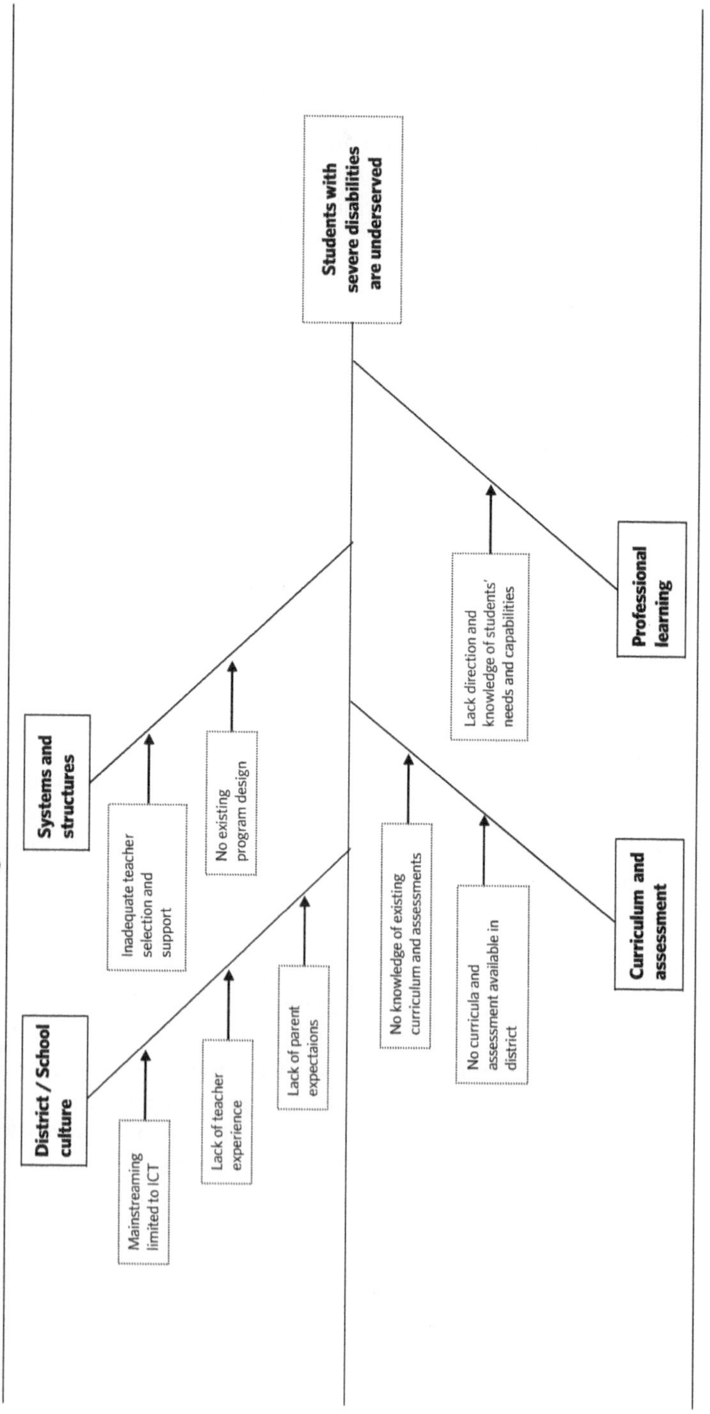

District / School culture

Mainstreaming limited to ICT

Lack of teacher experience

Lack of parent expectaions

Systems and structures

Inadequate teacher selection and support

No existing program design

Curriculum and assessment

No knowledge of existing curriculum and assessments

No curricula and assessment available in district

Professional learning

Lack direction and knowledge of students' needs and capabilities

Students with severe disabilities are underserved

From my system analysis, I recognized that whoever we hired as the classroom teacher and teaching assistants would require specific training and coaching. Also, the special area teachers (art, library, physical education, technology and music) would need training on how to effectively implement and adapt the curriculum to be most appropriate for each student. Such training was not available in the district.

Research Review

I explored available research literature on this problem to expand my understanding of the complexity of the challenge ahead. I found that the problem we were facing was not unique to our district, and was actually a national problem (Kurth, 2015). The Individuals with Disabilities Education Act (IDEA) serves as a legal safety net for millions of children with disabilities (U.S. Department of Education, n.d.); however, the research paints a grim picture of the slow progress the field has made in guaranteeing all students with disabilities their civil rights to be educated in a least restrictive environment (LRE), particularly students with substantial or significant impairments (Morningstar & Kurth, 2017).

In principle, most educators subscribe to the idea of least restrictive settings, but the reality is that some educators believe that students with significant impairments receive more benefits in a separate setting where they have access to individualized instruction from faculty with specialized training to meet their needs (Agran et al., 2020). There is a general presumption that students who present with these significant or profound disability characteristics should be educated in accordance with the stereotypes of their limitations (Agran et al., 2020). Thus, the available research only confirmed the challenge we were facing.

DESIGNING A SOLUTION

Given my analysis of the problem and the current system, and available research on solutions, I developed a theory of action and identified key drivers for change.

Theory of Action

I hypothesized that if a high-quality program were designed within our school where the faculty were adequately trained to support the developmentally appropriate integration of students with special needs into the larger school setting, then students with significant impairments would make adequate individual growth.

Figure 5.2. Diagram of Drivers of Change to Impact the Aim

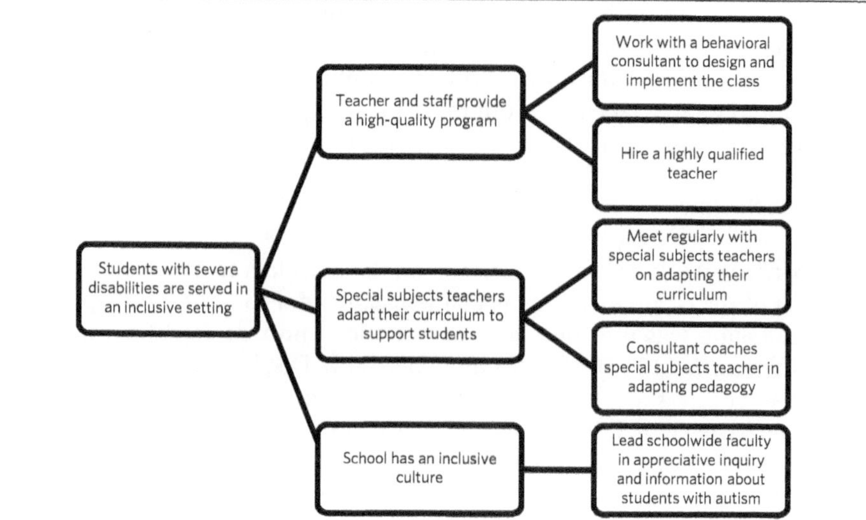

Drivers for Change

Given the lack of school and district expertise in serving this population, we engaged a Board Certified Behavioral Analyst (BCBA) consultant, a specialist in autism and cognitive disorders, to help us plan and provide professional development. During summer 2020, I worked with her and the assistant principal to determine what we would need to work in three primary areas (our drivers for change): (1) create a high-quality research-based program within a school, (2) address how to developmentally integrate the students into related school programs and services, and (3) develop the capacity of all teachers to integrate students in the special needs class into the larger school community. These areas represent our three drivers of change (see Figure 5.2).

Recruitment of Staff for the Program

Once the program was approved, district officials quickly took steps to recruit and hire a new teacher that spring. In addition, two existing assistant teachers volunteered to be part of the new class.

Recruitment of Students for the Program

Even before we had approval for the program, we began to identify students who could be recruited, employing a profile instrument used by another school district. Using the list of students who had been previously outplaced, we visited their programs and observed the students to determine their fit for this class. In April 2020, despite COVID, we continued to recruit parents to enroll their students using the available list. By early July, we had five students whose parents had agreed to place them in the school-based program.

Design of a High-Quality Program

In the meantime, the school psychologist, assistant principal, and I engaged in planning the new program that spring and throughout the summer. The success of our effort (and arguably the sustainability of the program) was predicated on the design and implementation of a highly effective, well-designed class. Our first step was focused on how we would design a high-quality program. Hehir and Katzman (2012) maintained that in order to educate students with significant disabilities, schools could not just offer a standard program. Instead, a customized program must be "invented" for each child on site by knowledgeable professionals, parents, and caregivers working together in an *ad hoc* manner. After receiving the green light from the district in spring 2020 to move ahead with procuring an outside expert, I entered into a contract with a consultant firm I had previously worked with in another school district. The work was led by a consultant who was a PhD, Board Certified Behavior Analyst (BCBA).

During the summer, using another district's program as a model and working with the consultant, my team and I designed the class by working within the classroom to design the space. We ordered furniture for 1:1 instruction, and ordered sensory items, curriculum based on students' IEP, and other related materials and equipment. We set up binders for each child with relevant data sheets and goals. We also began professional learning for the team (myself, the assistant principal, the newly hired teacher, and the two assistant teachers) in the class with the consultant. During the professional learning, we covered each student's IEP goals, the principles of Applied Behavior Analysis (ABA), and strategies for handling problem behavior, and planned for future integration into schoolwide activities. We also helped the new teacher unpack the new supplies and equipment and set up the room.

Preparations to Integrate Students into Special Area Classes and Schoolwide Experiences

During the latter part of the summer, we took steps to develop the capacity of the special area teachers and the faculty at large to successfully integrate these new students into the special area classes, as well as to enable their participation in regular school life, including lunch, recess, schoolwide assemblies, and other related school services and programs. We wanted to ensure that we considered each student's readiness, socially and cognitively, to be integrated into settings with their neurotypical peers, while simultaneously building special area teachers' knowledge of how to work with this new profile of students in particular. Our initial planning was limited, however, in part because of COVID. Each special area teacher took the lead in planning how to integrate these students into their subject area classes, using trial-and-error efforts.

Development of an Inclusive School Culture and Climate

A third strategy for program success was to simultaneously develop an inclusive culture and climate in the school by focusing on systems and structures and professional learning. It was evident that since the school staff had limited knowledge about how to integrate these students, I, as principal, had to prioritize their learning. My aim was to cultivate a staff mindset focused on inclusivity to integrate these students, as fully as possible, into all aspects of school life, particularly lunch period, recess, and schoolwide assemblies. My plan to develop this culture was to use a series of faculty meetings to educate the staff about this student profile and build empathy for and acceptance of these students.

The COVID pandemic thwarted our plans to integrate the students with the broader school community in the first year, 2020–2021, however, as the locally imposed health mandates prohibited large gatherings. As a result, there were no in-person schoolwide assemblies for a good portion of that school year. For the first half of the school year, the other students did not eat lunch in school, as they attended school for only half a day of in-person learning.

In the meantime, we made plans to have the students scheduled for lunch and recess at the same time as the other students, as well as attend schoolwide assemblies for the following year. To develop the other teachers in the school's readiness to support the new students' integration into the large school community, I planned for a series of learning activities, including appreciative inquiry, as part of our faculty meetings.

IMPLEMENTING THE CHANGE

To implement these changes, I used separate Plan-Do-Study-Act (PDSA) cycles to develop, test out, and improve each strategy as they were implemented. Below is a summary of the implementation and revision of each change strategy.

The New Class

The new class was launched in the 2020–2021 school year, using the PDSA cycle in Table 5.1 as our guide. As part of our plan, we identified key measures to track the quality of implementation and program effectiveness.

Table 5.1. PDSA Cycle 1: Design and Implementation of the 8:1:2 Self-Contained Class

Phase	Action
Plan	Designed and implemented a self-contained 8:1:2 program with the proper resources and support
Do	Implemented the initial class as designed Provided feedback on coaching observations, meetings, resources, and support Collected the program measures of program quality (APQI) Observed effective classroom practice
Study	Evaluated the observations of practice Analyzed the results of the APQI
Act	Made decisions about next steps

Do Phase

Despite COVID, we were able to begin the new class as planned. All five new students were scheduled to come in person every day (while the rest of the school was split between 50% in person and 50% online). The students' typical day comprised their arrival, unpacking, participation in a morning meeting, listening to a story, and then engaging in 1:1 instruction with the teacher or assistant teacher (on rotation). These activities were followed by a late-morning snack and a special area activity pushed into the classroom. In the afternoon, the students had lunch in their classroom, followed by math instruction, choice time, recess at the end of the afternoon, and then dismissal. Overall, the class functioned well following this schedule.

In the meantime, we gave the teacher and assistant teachers additional support. The classroom teacher received weekly intensive coaching from the BCBA consultant. It focused on supporting classroom instruction, creating individual student programs, implementing behavior plans, making student assessments, and modifying the classroom environment. I held monthly team meetings with the classroom teacher, assistant teachers, classroom aides, speech teacher, and occupational therapist to provide feedback and support to this newly formed team of professionals.

Study Phase

To evaluate program quality and effectiveness, the BCBA consultant and I created a walkthrough observation tool, based on the elements of an effective class, and conducted informal walkthrough observations of the class.

We found that the class was functioning as planned, but that the instruction was not being customized sufficiently for each student. We also found that the teacher struggled with documentation and data collection, and did not manage the assistant teachers well in supporting the students. Finally, we noticed that she struggled with handling problem behavior and reinforcing positive behavior, particularly with one nonverbal student.

Act Phase

We took what we learned in the first year of the program to make some necessary changes. First, we replaced the first teacher and recruited a new teacher for the class who had extensive experience working with this profile of students, was a certified BCBA, and had experience with a start-up program in a nearby school district. I provided her with coaching from our BCBA consultant. We also had to replace one of the assistant teachers.

Second, we made several curricular changes based on recommendations from the new teacher. During the summer, the new teacher led the training with the team, including the assistant teachers.

We had some student turnover. Three students left the program for various reasons, and we successfully recruited three new boys and one girl, all of whom were students with autism. The second year followed the same schedule as the first year, except recess now was scheduled during the regular school lunch/recess period. By the end of the second year, we retained four students and added two more students and another assistant teacher. For the third year, we split into a grades K–2 program and grades 3–5 program and hired a new teacher for the grades 3–5 class.

Special Area Teacher Program Adaptations and Supports

Our second intervention was to enable the special area teachers to provide instruction for the new students. Table 5.2 shows the PDSA cycle for this work.

Do Phase

As first adopters of this class of students, the special area teachers were responsible for providing instruction in their respective content areas (art, library, music, physical education, and technology), and we collectively recognized that their existing programs of study would not meet the needs of the students of the class. Unfortunately, we were not able to plan sufficiently to help them adapt their instruction for the new students initially, so we worked on these adaptations iteratively through the year. During this first year, the teachers took steps to adapt their curriculum on their own, using

Table 5.2. PDSA Cycle 2: Special Area Teacher Program Adaptations and Supports

Phase	Action
Plan	Prepare the special area teachers' instruction for inclusion of students in the 8:1:2 class
Do	Implement inclusion in special area classes Document and collect feedback on coaching, observations, monthly meetings, resources, and support Observe the students and evaluate their engagement
Study	Evaluate the observations and monthly meeting notes
Act	Make decisions about how to further support special area teachers

trial-and-error strategies based on reviewing the children's IEPs and goals. They had the freedom to experiment in order to determine how to adapt instruction for these children and had varying degrees of success. The students' specials were scheduled on a 6-day cycle (except for PE and music, which were twice during the 6-day cycle). The physical education teacher and art teacher found that their curriculum was easier to adapt to the students' needs, while the library, music, and technology teachers were finding curriculum adaptation to be more challenging.

To support the adaptations needed as the fall semester progressed, I consulted with each teacher individually, and all of them as a group, about what they thought they needed to feel prepared to meet the needs of this student group. I met with the special area teachers weekly and learned over time that they needed more support to improve their efficacy and plan for their curricular adaptation.

Study Phase

Generally, the consultant and I found that this was a talented, skilled, well-intentioned group of professionals who desperately wanted to meet the needs of these students but lacked the knowledge and teaching experience to adapt their programs to meet the students' needs. Nonetheless, our coaching observations suggested that teacher willingness and expectations varied somewhat. Two specialist teachers (library and technology) collaborated most closely with the classroom teacher in planning their lessons and the classroom teacher remained with them and the students during these special area sessions. Because of this collaboration, they had the greatest student growth. In contrast, student growth varied by student interest and teacher expectations in the other three areas of art, music, and PE.

Act Phase

By the following summer and throughout the second year, I provided these teachers with BCBA consultant customized coaching and scheduled regular opportunities for them to work in person together to plan and share what was working to learn with and from one another. They received job-embedded coaching and feedback from the BCBA consultant to improve their instruction and classroom management approaches to meet the needs of the students. They were provided with in situ modeling and coaching on differentiated curriculum, effective academic instruction, behavior management procedures, and positive behavior supports. Together, the BCBA consultant and I worked with the five special area teachers on the appropriate instructional approaches to incorporate into their lesson plans and instructional practices.

Inclusive Schoolwide Culture

The third intervention was to create an inclusive schoolwide culture. This plan was thwarted in Year 1 due to the COVID pandemic. That year, these students had limited movement within the school building; hence, most other faculty and staff did not have the opportunity to interact with them. We used this delay to prepare teachers to integrate the students into schoolwide functions and mapped out a PDSA cycle to support this work (as shown in Table 5.3).

Plan Phase

All students and staff returned in person in 2021–2022 That fall, I took steps to work with the rest of the faculty members on their knowledge and understanding and acceptance of the new students and build an inclusive culture. I planned for five professional learning sessions (four led by me and one led by the BCBA). I began by using an appreciative inquiry process (Cooperrider & Srivastva, 1987) to surface and build on the school's foundation for inclusion practices and, by most teachers' accounts, identity as an inclusive school, as the most ethnically diverse in the district. My intent was to capitalize on our inclusive mindset and ask the staff to broaden their perspectives on inclusion, to integrate the students in the new class into the whole school, by leveraging the staff's strengths and helping them envision their future. If I were to gain the buy-in and support of the faculty who had limited to no experience with these students, they had to be a part of the plan to integrate them. I also planned to use the lessons from the special area teachers to inform our work with integrating the students in the special needs class, as well as continued professional learning topics.

Table 5.3. PDSA Cycle 3: Creating a Schoolwide Culture and Supports

Phase	Action
Plan	Create a plan to develop a schoolwide inclusive culture and a series of schoolwide professional learning experiences.
Do	Provide a series of professional learning experiences during faculty meetings on creating a schoolwide inclusive culture.
Study	Analyze findings of inclusive climate survey and our experiences in leading the faculty meetings.
Act	Make decisions about adaptations for future work.

Do Phase

For the first session, I had the classroom teacher make a video of the students' day and show the video at a faculty meeting. The classroom teacher, school psychologist, assistant principal, and I then introduced the appreciative inquiry process for us as a school community to envision what integration would look like at our school. The faculty had previous experience using the appreciative inquiry as an approach to a problem of practice, so the process was familiar to them. We described each cycle of the appreciative inquiry, and then posed the design challenge: How, or in what ways, can we provide integration opportunities for the students in the 8:1:2 class? We shared some guiding principles for the integration of the students into the larger school community. The work paused there until the next faculty meeting, where we would engage in the "dream phase."

Rather than engage in this discussion, however, raw emotions surfaced as faculty members expressed discomfort with the timing of the work to envision a future of integration for these students. They focused instead on the rising COVID cases due to the new Omicron variant, and competing district priorities: a new math program and shifting from Response to Intervention (RTI) to Multi-Tiered Support System (MTSS). The faculty was frustrated and used the inquiry space to articulate their feelings.

Study and Act Phases

In response to the faculty's frustrations, I acknowledged their feelings of frustration and overwhelmedness and declared that we would pause the work on envisioning integration at our school. Nonetheless, the whole school began interacting with the class students more regularly. The class students had recess and lunch on the same school schedule and attended schoolwide events with the other students.

RESULTS

Impact on the In-School Program

We successfully designed and implemented a high-quality program from the ground up, based on the New York State's Autism Program Quality Indicators (APQI; New York State Education Department, 2001). To nobody's surprise, the indicator that was scored the lowest among all the participants was "inclusion." With the COVID restrictions, we did not collect these data in the second year.

Impact on Students

The greatest student impact was on the students whom the program was designed to serve. At the end of Year 1, we retained some of the students who were members of the inaugural class and recruited four more students for the second year. The class started in the second year with six students, and by the third year, had seven students. All students in this class made significant progress on their IEP goals, particularly starting in the second year, with the support of the new, more experienced teacher. Finally, we received many inquiries about the program by families with students in out-of-district programs. Those were important metrics, as most families were initially quite reluctant to bring their children back to the district.

Impact on Teachers

The primary teacher impact was on the special area teachers, who worked to adapt their curriculum to support each student's individual needs from the beginning. All five teachers became more effective over the first 2 years of the new class, based on their own experimentation, support from peers, and training by the consultant and me. According to monthly meeting discussions, the special area teachers identified that the most significant experience contributing to their self-efficacy was their collaboration and partnership with the second teacher of the special class. The teachers also credited the various collaborative structures I created for them to meet and exchange ideas. The permission they were given to experiment with new instructional approaches was a strength that contributed to their overall self-efficacy.

With increased support in the second year, the special area teachers' ability to meet the needs of these students increased dramatically. Based on discussions and observations, I learned that they were also generalizing what they were learning into their practices with the general student population (e.g., station teaching). They also became informal ambassadors for the children with other teachers, informally contributing to an inclusive culture.

Impact on the School

The work with the broader faculty, beginning with appreciative inquiry, did not have the same success as the other two goals. Nonetheless, through discussions and observations, I became aware that the teachers and other students schoolwide were becoming more accepting of the children, particularly when exposed to their nontypical behaviors. The class teacher and school psychologist collaborated with some classroom teachers and started a peer buddy program in Year 2 between their students and the class students.

Impact on the District

The final impact was on the district as a whole, as it now supports two classes (K–2 and 3–5) for students with significant disabilities. The district (and school) now has the structures and protocols to recruit and select students for the program and evaluate their progress.

LEADER REFLECTIONS

The work to create inclusive schools is rather complex and requires school leaders to take into consideration their local context, resources available, and of course staff (and my own) dedication and commitment to seeing the change through despite challenges that arise.

Being Flexible and Adaptive

My primary leadership lesson was the importance of being flexible and adaptive, while maintaining a commitment to the goals of this effort. From the onset, I recognized that I had set ambitious goals for myself and the faculty. The design and implementation of a high-quality program for students with significant impairments, in a place with limited knowledge on how to educate these students well, was a tall order. As the saying goes, I was definitely "building the plane while flying it." I was actively designing the program utilizing the tools of improvement science, revising and refining as I went along, while simultaneously providing professional learning and coaching to the special area teachers as they also began to provide instruction. I sought to expand the entire school community's experience of inclusion. I sought to integrate the students of the special class into school life in authentic ways that did not feel imposed and, of course, were aligned with the students' developmental readiness. All three goals (creating a new class, developing the special area teachers, and creating an inclusive school-wide culture) worked together to help us achieve our overarching goal, which was to design a high-quality environment where each individual student would make adequate growth.

Creating Supportive Systems and Structures

Through this work, I learned the importance of creating appropriate systems and structures. I found three elements that were critical to the successful implementation of our work: creating structures that facilitate teacher learning and collaboration, creating structures for teacher voice and input, and targeting professional learning opportunities around inclusive practices. In this case, leveraging the talents of the experienced teacher of the special classroom by creating opportunities to collaborate with all the special area teachers was important in strengthening teacher capacity to positively impact individual student growth outcomes.

I also had to be creative with how I allocated and managed time with the master schedule, grade-level meetings, and faculty meetings. What is most important is that teacher collaboration be prioritized by providing the time and the necessary resources for them to be able to meet and work together. I made it a priority to seek out and provide opportunities for teacher voice through each of the interventions. Teacher voice is critical, as I learned from the appreciative inquiry work with the faculty, as is adequate time for sense-making of new ideas, opportunities to reflect, grapple, and ask questions, before being invited to "dream" about new endeavors.

Using Improvement Science

I adopted the principles of improvement science to support this work, helping myself and others learn to plan, try, evaluate, and redesign (as PDSA cycles) iteratively in each phase. The staff, consultant, and I intentionally adopted a collaborative, risk-free learning stance: that we were learning as we designed and implemented each component, that we would share what we learned as we did so, and that we would design and use relevant assessment tools and observation protocols to measure progress in meeting our design goals. This process enabled greater risk-taking, particularly with the class teacher and special area teachers. By using the improvement science process, I was successfully able to create a safe space where they could try curricular and instructional solutions, fail and try again, and at the same time talk with others about what they were learning and help one another. Over time, these teachers took on greater leadership roles in the improvement process, particularly the new class teacher who served as a professional learning resource for others.

EPILOGUE

I left the district at the end of the school year in 2023. The fact that the program has been sustained and is flourishing is a testament to our success.

QUESTIONS

1. The principal started this school change effort by first creating a new class to serve students with severe disabilities. How different would the change effort have been if she had started first with schoolwide inclusion?
2. Because of COVID, the principal was limited to providing professional learning on site, using a consultant and the new teacher. How else could the change in the school's inclusive culture and the special area teachers work been developed? What other strategies, besides formal faculty meetings, could the principal have used to build greater whole-school support for inclusion of the students with severe disabilities?
3. The principal led this change effort with little apparent district involvement. How could she have cultivated more involvement, and how would that have been beneficial?

REFERENCES

Agran, M., Jackson, L., Kurth, J. A., Ryndak, D., Burnette, K., Jameson, M., Zagona, A., Fitzpatrick, H., & Wehmeyer, M. (2020). Why aren't students with severe disabilities being placed in general education classrooms: Examining the relations among classroom placement, learner outcomes, and other factors. *Research and Practice for Persons with Severe Disabilities*, *45*(1), 4–13. https://doi.org/10.1177%2F1540796919878134

Bryk, A., Gomez, L., Grunow, A., & LaMahieu, P. (2015). *Learning to improve: How America's schools can get better at getting better.* Harvard Education Press.

Cooperrider, D. L., & Srivastva, S. (1987). Appreciative inquiry in organizational life. In R. W. Woodman & W. A. Pasmore (Eds.), *Research in organizational change and development* (Vol. 1, pp. 129–169). JAI Press.

Hehir, T., & Katzman, L. I. (2012). *Effective inclusive schools: Designing successful schoolwide programs.* Wiley.

Kurth, J. A. (2015). Educational placement of students with autism: The impact of state of residence. *Focus on Autism and Other Developmental Disabilities*, *30*(4), 249–256. http://dx.doi.org/10.1177/1088357614547891

Morningstar, M. E., & Kurth, J. A. (2017). Status of inclusive educational placement for students with extensive and pervasive support needs. *Inclusion*, *5*(2), 83–93. https://doi.org/10.1352/2326-6988.5.2.83

New York State Education Department. (2001, August). *Autism program quality indicators*. https://www.nysed.gov/sites/default/files/programs/special-education/autism-program-quality-indicators.pdf

U.S. Department of Education. (n.d.). *About IDEA*. https://sites.ed.gov/idea/about-idea/#IDEA-History

CHAPTER 6

Supporting English Language Instruction for All Through a Nested Learning Experience

Christopher Keogh

This chapter details how a new district curriculum director collaborated with general education teachers at an elementary school to address the needs of Multilingual English Language Learners (MLL/ELLs). Together, they investigated and implemented instructional strategies to support MLL/ELLs. Through a series of professional learning community (PLC) meetings, the director and teachers examined a problem of practice and explored potential instructional solutions, piloting an intervention of their choice and sharing the outcomes. The case highlights both the successful steps and the challenges encountered in this initial instructional improvement effort. It concludes with the improvement results and the director's reflections on using improvement science to enhance learning outcomes.

Stepping into a new role as Director of Curriculum, Instruction and Technology within a new district, I understood that leadership required actively fostering a culture of continuous growth. Committed to lifelong learning, I wholeheartedly embrace the principles of improvement science as a means of inspiring meaningful transformation. In this case, the tenets of improvement science enabled me to drive positive organizational change while also communicating my values and engaging in professional development myself. The case described below demonstrates my development as a leader as I designed a professional learning community (PLC) for general education teachers to investigate and implement instructional strategies to support Multilingual English Language Learners (MLL/ELLs).

Using improvement science in a learning organization has a nested quality: I engage in my own personal form of continuous improvement while the staff participates in their own form of networked continuous improvement. While this is all happening, students are learning and growing. This experience activated multiple levels of my own learning, including familiarizing myself with the culture of my new district, leading organizational change, and growing as a leader. For our teaching staff, continuous improvement required reflection on their practices through a structured model. We all organized around a problem of practice, analyzing data and developing action plans. One teacher ultimately commented, "Isn't this the type of learning we want for students in our classrooms?"

CONTEXT

The Marblehead School District (pseudonym) a suburban district, has a relatively small enrollment of approximately 1,100 students, where 4% of students in the district receive English as a new language (ENL) services, and 16% have an Individualized Educational Plan (IEP). Unlike its wealthier neighbor districts, one in every five students in the Marblehead District identifies as economically disadvantaged. Within the boundaries of Marblehead's socioeconomically diverse community are affordable housing complexes and multimillion-dollar homes. Some of the most sought-after school districts in the country share our borders.

Marblehead largely employs experienced teachers. The faculty is predominantly White, female, and almost exclusively English-speaking. Teachers identify compassion as one of their collective strengths, citing a commitment to the social and emotional needs of the whole child. They speak knowledgeably about families in the community and the lengths they would go to for their students.

I arrived at the school district amid the COVID-19 pandemic, when schools nationwide struggled to reopen. Our district was one of the first in the country to close in early 2020 and, in 2021, mobilized to be among the first in the region to reopen its doors to full-time in-person instruction for all students who wanted it. Faculty and staff were flexible and nimble, demonstrating their commitment to quick thinking and responsibility to students. Working with them during these challenging times was a privilege.

DISCOVERING THE PROBLEM

The work began with the discovery of a problem of practice rooted in inequity. Specifically, the district's special education director sought my help in addressing the overclassification of MLL/ELLs with speech and language disabilities (SLD). While only 2.0% of students of other races in the district were identified as having an SLD, 9.0% of students with disabilities who are

Hispanic (most of whom were identified as ENL) were classified as having an SLD, nearly five times the rate of the others.

ANALYZING THE PROBLEM

Given the severity of the overclassification problem, the other district leaders and I needed to analyze its root causes to reverse the practice. Early on, I narrowed our focus to the district's elementary school, where most referrals to special education were taking place.

System Analysis

I conferred with the superintendent, director of special education, elementary school principal, and ENL specialists about the potential contributing factors to this issue. All were generous thought partners, considering how we were differentiating instruction and setting students up for success. They shared data, anecdotes, and historical context for this problem. Together, we identified several contributing factors across six main areas that potentially led to the overclassification of MLL/ELLs in our elementary school, represented in the fishbone diagram below (see Figure 6.1).

Using this diagram as a discussion aid, my district-level colleagues and I agreed that classroom instruction was a high-leverage point for intervention, an area where the overclassification practice could most easily be reversed. We posited that if classroom instruction were more differentiated and responsive to the needs of MLL/ELLs, then there would likely be a reduction in referrals of MLL/ELLs to special education.

Research Review

I reviewed available research for guidance on strengthening differentiated instruction for MLLs. One study highlighted a disconnect between the findings of school-based instructional support teams and a panel of university-level experts when classifying Multilingual English Language Learners as needing special education. In a longitudinal study of Spanish-speaking MLL/ELLs identified as learning-disabled, Wilkinson et al. (2006) found that the expert panel's decisions significantly differed from those of an instructional support team in an urban district in central Texas. In some cases, the expert panel believed that the students had been misdiagnosed with the wrong disability or that there were insufficient data to validate eligibility for special education.

Another study found that having an understanding of what made MLL/ELLs different from their peers as learners helped to mitigate overreferrals. Fernandez and Inserra (2013) found that teachers who demonstrated

Figure 6.1. Fishbone Diagram of Factors Contributing to Overrepresentation of ELLs in Special Education

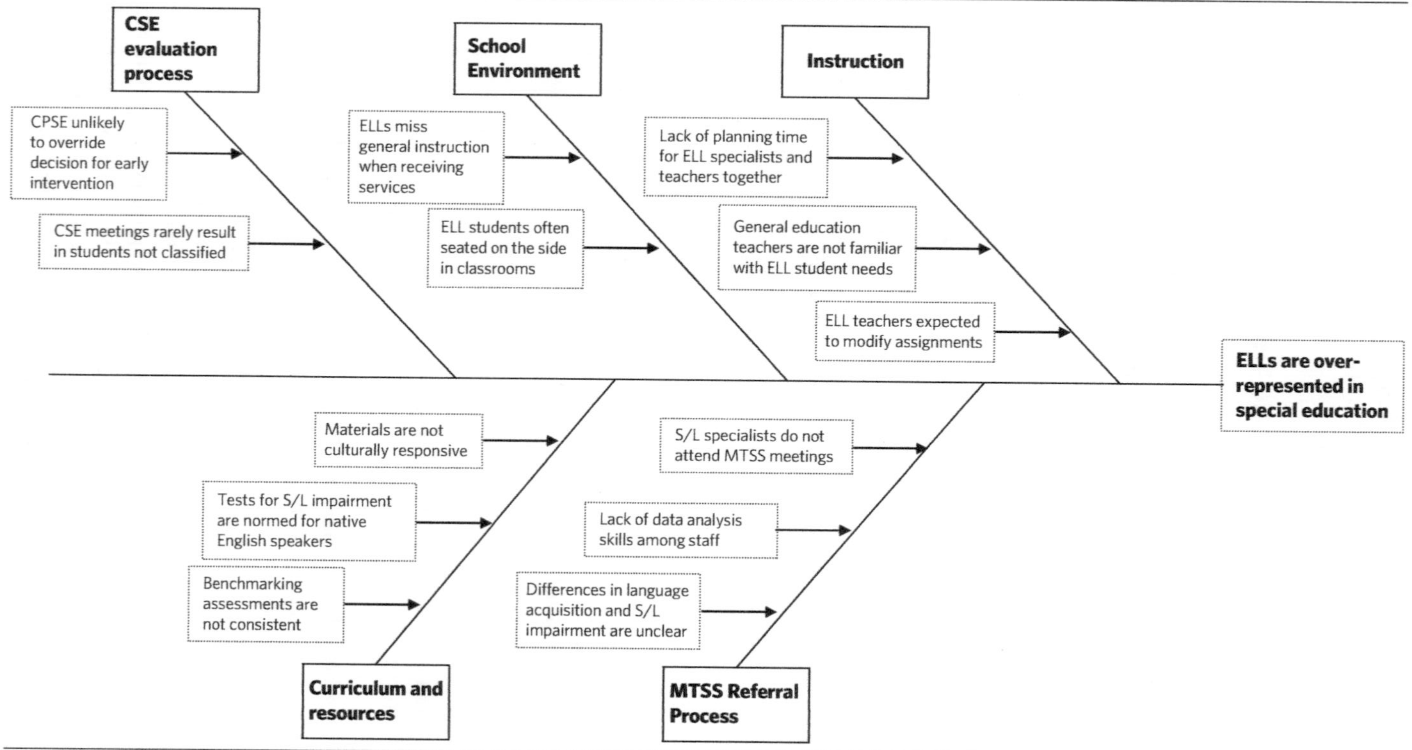

a strong sense of the differences between a Multilingual English Language Learner's social and academic language referred students to special education less frequently.

DESIGNING THE SOLUTION

Given these findings, I reflected on the type of professional learning currently provided to staff in MLL/ELL language acquisition and recognized that this would need to be embedded in our solution. I wondered if teachers were being given opportunities to build capacity in this area.

This reflection led my district colleagues and me to focus on strengthening Tier I instructional practices in the general education classroom setting. Tier I includes the curriculum, instruction, and assessments provided to all students in a grade level. My district colleagues and I agreed that by using improvement science, I could lead a group of teachers who were closest to the problem in analyzing and strengthening instructional practices through iterative cycles, ensuring that all learners receive a high-quality, evidence-based Tier I general education experience.

The available research informed my thinking about designing a professional learning community (PLC) to address this problem of practice head-on by working through possible instructional strategies with teachers. I chose to organize our work as a PLC because it provides a long-term structure for meetings and collaborative inquiry. I would facilitate the learning of a group of teachers, uniting their efforts around a problem of practice while they engaged in a series of Plan-Do-Study-Act (PDSA) cycles, where they planned, implemented, studied, and acted on new practices, ultimately learning and evolving together.

Forming a Theory of Action

In designing these structures, I developed an early theory of action that I shared with my district colleagues. If I could create a PLC in which teachers boosted their self-efficacy in supporting ELLs with Tier I strategies through a series of data inquiry cycles, referrals to special education would be reduced. Teachers would become more confident in their abilities and would be more likely to tackle the problem of supporting MLL/ELLs independently without a referral to special education.

Thus, I focused on two primary drivers of teacher practice: implementing effective instructional strategies for MLL/ELLs in the general education setting and collaborating around data-directed dialogue. Both included secondary drivers to activate the primary drivers, specifically, developing the professional learning community (PLC), training around data use, and

Figure 6.2. Diagram of Drivers to Decrease Special Education Referrals of ELLs

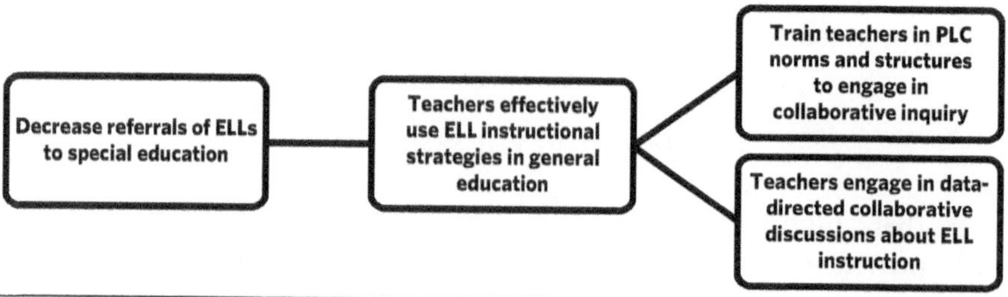

Decrease referrals of ELLs to special education

Teachers effectively use ELL instructional strategies in general education

Train teachers in PLC norms and structures to engage in collaborative inquiry

Teachers engage in data-directed collaborative discussions about ELL instruction

refining the building's Response to Intervention (RTI) processes, as shown in Figure 6.2.

Designing the Proposed Change

My plan was to organize a PLC of six elementary school teachers and two English as a New Language (ENL) specialists around addressing this problem. As a first step in launching this PLC, I organized an initial meeting of this group to garner buy-in and interest, during which I shared data demonstrating the overrepresentation of MLL/ELLs in special education. We discussed what might lead to a student being referred to special education and the negative outcomes associated with being improperly identified as needing special education.

In leading this conversation with teachers, I considered the perceptions identified in the research literature. This was a complex problem, not unique to our district. One interesting finding in my research was that this problem of practice was typically not perceived as a problem by teachers. Many teachers in the studies suggested that students needing help should be expeditiously classified so they could receive the support they needed to succeed. For example, in one study (Skiba et al., 2006), interviews with teachers revealed that most saw special education as the only resource for struggling students.

I could sense similar attitudes in the initial meeting with teachers and specialists. Throughout my career, I have seen examples of teachers advocating for the classification of a student, believing a smaller class ratio or specialized reading instruction was critical for a student's success. This ardor often involved overlooking the benefits of a less restrictive educational placement, where the general education setting is made more amenable to a diverse population of learners. While classifying students for special education is an integral part of a school's work and critical to ensuring that a student's civil rights are honored, we also need to recognize our capacity as educators to differentiate, scaffold, and meet the needs of all learners.

Having presented the problem of practice to our newly formed PLC, I outlined my plan to lead teachers through cycles of improvement aimed at enhancing instruction for MLL/ELLs in the Tier I classroom. Through our PLC meetings, I would host a series of learning experiences and facilitate improvement cycles. Together, we would unpack the problem of practice, review strategies, implement instructional changes, and study their impact. Teachers would discuss their learning, thereby networking their collective improvement. By addressing the problem collaboratively, we would all contribute to the solution.

To enhance teachers' self-efficacy in providing general education support to MLL/ELLs in the Tier I setting, I selected a survey to be administered at the beginning and end of the process. This would help measure any improvements in their confidence and effectiveness in these areas.

The nested nature of this work meant there were two layers to this PDSA approach, as shown in Table 6.1, one for me as facilitator and one for the teachers.

Table 6.1. Plan-Do-Study-Act Cycle for the Facilitator and Teachers

Role of the Professional	Plan	Do	Study	Act
Facilitator	Develop the PLC to investigate Tier I instructional strategies for MLL/ELLs Administer an efficacy survey to general education teachers	Implement and facilitate a PLC and support teachers through their own PDSA cycles	Review teachers' reactions to the new process Re-administer teacher efficacy survey and review results	Reflect on the findings and continue to support teachers as they initiate future PDSA cycles
Teachers	Learn PLC structures, review data, study problem of practice, and consider new instructional strategies	Implement a strategy of their choice in the Tier I general education classroom	Teachers reflect on the implementation of their strategy and review student-level results	Teachers incorporate their learnings into their practice and look ahead to future inquiry cycles

Table 6.2. Meeting Schedule, Focus, and Teacher Actions

Meeting	Focus	Teacher Actions
November (Plan Phase 1)	Overview of the problem, introduction of the PLC and the PDSA cycle Developing group norms Unpacking the data on the problem	Conduct empathy interviews
December (Plan Phase 2)	Discuss empathy interview data	Consider possible solutions
March (Do Phase)	ENL teachers lead a workshop on effective instructional strategies for MLL/ELLs	Try out at least one new strategy and track using the lesson plan template
May (Study, Act Phases)	Study the results Propose next steps	Reflect on process and think about next year

The work was to be structured around four monthly meetings, each focused on one of the four PDSA phases, as shown in Table 6.2.

IMPLEMENTING THE CHANGE

November Meeting (Plan Phase 1)

As noted above, I used our first meeting as a PLC to define the problem and establish the PLC structure, which was new to the Marblehead staff. In addition to introducing the problem of practice, I also provided an overview of the tenets of improvement science, shared referral data, and walked the staff through Figure 6.1, the fishbone diagram that illustrated how the district leaders and I unpacked the problem and its causes.

In hindsight, these early stages of defining the problem included far too much "facilitator talk." The PLC teachers should have been more involved in analyzing the problem rather than simply receiving a presentation of what the district leaders thought. Given the demands on teachers at the time—revamping their instruction to accommodate videoconferencing and cohorting their classrooms due to the COVID pandemic—I tried to do the legwork for them. This was a mistake that became clearer as the meetings continued.

However, the potential for collaborative design was fully displayed when teachers helped develop norms for working together. Here, the group came to life. Participants reflected on how they learned best and emphasized the importance of recognizing and affirming one another's contributions. They suggested "giving hearts" by holding our thumbs and forefingers in the shape of a heart rather than applauding. This became a trademark of our conversations and a welcomed source of levity.

In defining the problem, the teachers and I reviewed the referral data and discussed the importance of exploring the problem qualitatively and capturing our students' voices in our work. The teachers agreed to conduct empathy interviews with their MLL/ELL students using open-ended questions designed to learn about the students' lived experiences. The teachers were encouraged to be mindful of their responses to what students shared and to explore inconsistencies to understand the students' experiences better. I developed a template for the empathy interview questions and note-taking and distributed it to teachers. An ENL teacher later emailed a suggested revision to use more kid-friendly language. This insight and update were welcomed, and we made sure to give hearts. Following our first meeting, the teachers conducted their interviews almost immediately.

December Meeting (Plan Phase 2)

In our second meeting, the teachers came ready to share the results of their empathy interviews. Teachers reported that students enjoyed the opportunity to share their feedback. Interestingly, much of what the teachers reported that the students shared aligned with what I learned from the research literature. Students had explained that they appreciated when concepts were explained with expression, such as when teachers pointed to visual aids or acted out terms. Students also mentioned that visuals, such as posters and signs around the classroom, were very helpful. However, they explained that they found the class speed challenging at times, struggling to keep up with instruction or move from one activity to the next. These insights, coupled with data showing discrepancies in the performance of MLL/ELLs compared to students for whom English was their first language, spurred our next steps to tackle the overrepresentation of MLL/sELLs in special education.

March Meeting (Do Phase)

With the problem identified and defined, the teachers and I now moved on to instructional improvement. We faced several challenges in getting this phase off the ground, including schedule disruptions due to the ongoing COVID-19 pandemic, which negatively impacted time for professional development. This unexpected delay, however, allowed me time to work more closely with our ENL teachers on planning the learning experiences for the PLC group. To prepare, the ENL teachers and I discussed the data gathered on the problem of practice and reviewed the discussions from previous sessions. We also considered the current focus on vocabulary instruction in the lower grades and how our work with the PLC could better align with the work of other general education teachers. We were mindful of ensuring that this work did not feel like an "extra" burden.

The ENL specialists planned an interactive workshop on instructional strategies that research showed were especially effective for teaching vocabulary to MLL/ELLs. They included examples of strategies already employed in Marblehead classrooms. For example, one of our ENL specialists recalled using a vocabulary notebook that had students draw images of words and write synonyms. Additionally, a professor I worked with suggested clarifying the different levels of language acquisition, which we incorporated. The ENL specialists prepared an overview and handout for the teachers.

During our March meeting, the ENL teachers' presentation was lively and engaging. It included simulations, such as having teachers try to read a statement in a different language, and the subsequent conversations were inviting. Teachers built on one another's comments and asked how certain strategies could be applied. Unsurprisingly, exit tickets and reflections from this session were the most positive so far.

With a sense of what the quantitative data on referrals and student progress established, an understanding of what the students communicated, and knowledge of effective instructional strategies, the teachers were ready to plan and launch their own PDSA cycles. They would try one or more new strategies and monitor the results. Provided worksheets allowed teachers to share which strategy they planned to implement, how they would determine a baseline, and how they would analyze the impact of the strategy. Most teachers selected previous assessment data to help determine a baseline. Teachers planned to employ different strategies, including vocabulary notebooks, act-it-out activities, explicit pre-teaching, and increased visuals. Teachers at the same grade level, for the most part, agreed to implement the same strategy (e.g., both 1st-grade teachers selecting vocabulary notebooks).

As their intervention cycles kicked off, I received many questions from teachers about using data and whether the data they selected were "right." There were several questions, for example, about the pre- and post-test. I encouraged teachers to find an approachable way to integrate the data into their practice. "Think of feasibility and all the data you already collect," I advised.

With the question in mind, "What data will help you track the effectiveness of your intervention?" I later realized I should have provided clearer support and guidance. While I focused on efficacy around instructional strategies for MLL/ELLs, perhaps a better place to start would have been building the teachers' self-efficacy around data collection, analysis, and inquiry. My driver diagram was due for an update.

April Meeting (Study and Act Phases)

As we entered the final phase of the cycle—studying—I had already anticipated issues with data. Only half of the teachers collected data as planned, but used a pre-test in which most the students scored as "highly proficient," limiting its use as a formative assessment tool. Some teachers only collected data for their MLL/ELLs, others administered their student assessments too late, and a few did not bring any data to the final meeting, citing schedule changes or extended student absences. This inconsistency around data impacted our ability to focus on quantitative analysis during the reflection phase.

Before the meeting, I asked two teachers who had done a thorough job with their data collection to share their experiences with the group. They presented their data on an interactive whiteboard, highlighting changes from baseline to final assessments. While MLL/ELLs did not experience uniform growth, with some scores even decreasing slightly, their presentations opened the floor to conversation.

One teacher mentioned that during implementation, one of her MLL/ELL students unenrolled from the school, leaving her with only one MLL/ELL in her classroom (whom she identified as a "strong student"). She observed that the vocabulary notebook helped her student, but she wished to see the intervention's impact on her other student, who had been struggling.

Her grade-level colleague shared that her MLL/ELLs seemed to "get it" due to the intervention, providing an example where students recalled the word "gnaw" in an unexpected context. Another teacher chimed in with a similar experience, noting how exciting it was for her and the students. She explained how the visuals were helpful and shared an example of a book with the group.

Another pair of teachers from a different grade level shared their surprise at how students struggled to develop sentences for the words provided. They shifted to cloze sentence activities, where students fill in blanks, and conducted a pre-test with students matching the words. From early observations, they saw benefits to using this approach with all students, especially with their MLL/ELLs, who now engaged in conversations more confidently.

Throughout the discussion, it was clear that teachers were more comfortable discussing anecdotal observations around student enthusiasm and excitement than they were around more formal assessment data. While we reviewed the available data, it often led to qualitative stories, reflections, and anecdotes rather than in-depth quantitative analysis.

Hearing from the teachers as they reflected on these processes was insightful. I appreciated being able to step back and facilitate their connections. Elements of my driver diagram came to fruition—teachers became more familiar with instructional strategies that benefited MLL/ELLs in their Tier I general education environment and saw how some of these interventions were universally helpful. Hearing directly from the teachers also provided me with meaningful anecdotes about successful Tier I strategies that could be disseminated to other teachers. This was my favorite conversation.

At the conclusion of the meeting, participants set goals for their next steps in their exit tickets and worksheet reflections. One teacher stated she would "continue to explicitly teach vocabulary with each unit and explore additional strategies for the children who continue to struggle." Another shared that "moving forward, I will begin this type of journal activity earlier in the school year, starting with our first unit. In doing so, I hope that this immersive vocabulary technique will help students use vocabulary learned in everyday life."

RESULTS

The nested nature of the learning process resulted in all participants learning at various levels, including students, teachers, and school.

Impact on Students

At the center of our work were the students. By the fourth session, half of the teachers submitted worksheets with completed assessment data, providing insights into the type of learning students experienced. Benchmark and final assessments demonstrated that most classes saw benefits for both their MLL/ELL and their non-MLL/ELL population. Additionally, teachers described increased enthusiasm: Students were eager to practice vocabulary, design their notebooks, or play the "act-it-out" game. They observed students excitedly encountering new vocabulary words and integrating terms into different activities, such as designing greeting cards for holidays.

I learned that to better track the impact on students, there should have been two assessment pieces in this cycle. First, the schoolwide benchmark assessment could have served as an indicator of students' vocabulary ability. While these assessments provided a launchpad, they may have served better as an outcome measure. Additionally, formative assessment data should have informed our more targeted interventions.

Impact on Teachers

An important improvement I tracked was teacher efficacy changes based on survey and interview results.

Self-Efficacy

I administered the TELLS Efficacy Scale (Carney, 2012), which asked teachers to reflect on their self-efficacy in areas related to teaching MLL/ELLs before our first meeting and then again at our final meeting. Comparing the results (see Table 6.3), I found increases in teacher efficacy across the board. Below is a sample of items illustrating these improvements.

Notable increases in teachers' self-reported efficacy stood out in this comparison related to work we had done in the PLC. Teachers reported growth in their efficacy in identifying ELL students' individual English proficiency and their ability to conduct assessments at an appropriate level for ELL students' current language proficiency. There was a substantial increase in reported efficacy in teachers' ability to identify students' individual English proficiency.

Survey items related to collaboration around teaching MLL/ELLs also evidenced teacher growth. Teachers reported an increased ability to use community members as resources for working with MLL/ELLs. Teacher responses indicated that they were more comfortable reaching out for assistance or seeking outside resources to support their learners, reflecting the increased value they placed on their ENL colleagues and community partners like families.

Table 6.3. Teaching English Language Learners (TELLS) Scale Responses

TELLS Measure	Pre- ($n = 6$)	Post- ($n = 5$)	Change
Identify ELL students' individual English proficiency.	5.25	8.17	2.92
Perform assessments at a level for ELL students' language proficiency and current teaching.	6.8	9.33	2.53
Post common expectations in the classroom in English for ELL students.	8.25	10.6	2.35
Plan evaluations that accommodate individual differences among my ELL students.	8.2	9.83	1.63
Use mechanical aids, real objects, music, art, games, and hands-on experience to reinforce ELL students' learning.	9.4	10.83	1.43
Use ongoing assessment for ELL students.	9.0	10.33	1.33

Note: The scales are based on a 10-point scale rating system from 1, "Certain Cannot Do At All," to 11, "Certain Can Do."

Areas where teachers initially reported high efficacy also saw improvements, including their efficacy in modeling classroom tasks and their ability to learn new teaching and learning strategies for MLL/ELLs. These areas of reported strength were leveraged as part of the teacher-led interventions.

Differentiating Practice

I conducted interviews with teachers where they reflected on their experiences. In these conversations, teachers spoke about "reconnecting" with learning or strategies they had engaged in earlier in their careers, which may have been lost in the shuffle of new classes, curricula, and initiatives. They also reconnected with lessons they had learned in college about differentiating for Multilingual English Language Learners, reminding them of the value of visual aids. Additionally, teachers remarked on the value of reflecting on their practice with others. One teacher, despite having over 15 years of teaching experience, mentioned that speaking with teachers outside her grade level exposed her to new strategies. This experience broke down some walls in the school as well. This insight into teaching and learning in different grades prompted her to think about the journeys of her students and how she could better meet them where they are.

In follow-up interviews and the feedback surveys, teachers responded positively to the act of working collaboratively. They felt comfortable taking on different leadership roles such as when the ENL specialists led the learning sessions or when classroom teachers redesigned the empathy interview protocol.

Impact on the School

At the end of the year, teachers outside of the initial PLC showed an increased interest in learning in a PLC as well. A professional needs survey at the end of the year fielded schoolwide indicated that many teachers had not previously used this structure, but they were interested in participating in the structure as a form of professional growth. The district PLC represented a cultural shift around professional learning as well, and I was heartened to see the broad interest in continuing to learn in a similar structure. Moving forward, capitalizing on this interest, teachers participated in data inquiry cycles at each grade level.

After a building-wide data team of teachers and administrators reviewed school-level benchmark assessment data in math and reading, all teachers were grouped into grade-level PLCs. These PLCs were provided with data briefs highlighting areas of strength and concern. The data team presented the assessment data to each grade level in context, explaining trend lines and discrepancies among demographic subgroups. Each grade level considered these global data in conjunction with their classroom-level data. Once teachers had time to review the data, I led a workshop on the PDSA cycle for the entire faculty, using the work of the ENL PLC as an example and calling on participants to help explain the steps in the process.

This implementation of the PLC model represents a building-wide shift. Rather than bringing in outsiders to present on our professional development days, staff worked collaboratively on areas of inquiry and tracked the success of their interventions. After all grade-level PLCs had completed the first PDSA cycle, teachers shared mixed results. Similar to the ENL PLC, some teachers noted positive changes while others saw little impact. However, reports led to lively discussions. Teachers reflected on their processes but were more eager to begin the next phases of their PDSA cycles.

Scaling up, while exciting, has also been difficult to manage. With so many different PDSAs happening in one building, tracking their progress was challenging. Moreover, similar to my experience facilitating the first PLC with our MLL/ELL teachers, demands on teachers' time and schedule shifts posed a challenge to momentum. Schedule disruptions were not merely a function of the global pandemic; a snow day, a schoolwide incident, or a single teacher's absence could disrupt a critical PLC meeting.

This Plan-Do-Study-Act cycle structure has tremendous potential for building capacity and school culture. As we look ahead to incorporating more research findings into our early literacy program, the PLC structure, with its PDSA cycles, will ensure thoughtful implementation of strategies. Teachers have a voice and a hand in their learning. Meanwhile, since these PDSA cycles were presented to the entire faculty, our RTI team cultivated a list of effective Tier I strategies, with evidence based in our building. Educational research will not just be undertaken outside our building in institutions of higher learning; rather, the Marblehead faculty will be actively involved in contributing to a body of local research that can inform our best practices.

Since this initial PLC experience, our PDSA meetings schoolwide have been scheduled around the administration of diagnostic, nationally normed assessments to ensure that we include objective data in our conversations. Data briefs from the building-wide data team led teachers to develop their own areas of inquiry around topics such as sight word recognition, geometry, and text features. Formative assessments in these areas helped teachers determine their next steps and served as a pre-test for our PLC conversations.

Our organizational culture has begun to embrace a common language regarding instructional improvement built on readiness and trust. At recent meetings, when teachers in different grade levels came with data that did not show marked improvement, they felt comfortable sharing this information with their teams and the larger school community. The conversation focused on how we can make small adjustments to improve.

LEADER REFLECTIONS

While students and teachers were experiencing the impact of the improvement science cycle, I experienced deep learning as a district leader on how to design for and lead continuous improvement.

Coherence

The PLC could not thrive as a separate initiative, and in implementing it as a change strategy, I learned much about the importance of coherence. For a PLC to be successful, it needed to be woven into the school's systems, structures, and procedures. Changes to the Response to Intervention (RTI) referral process and training were critical elements that needed to occur alongside our shift to a PLC model of problem-solving and professional learning. Starting small and scaling up meant that some of the necessary cultural shifts were not yet in place. In implementing this work across the entire building, I saw how coherent structures supported shifts in teacher practice.

Collaborative Practice

In leading this change effort, I learned that I should not shoulder all the work on my own. While I thought I was being helpful by taking on the labor of getting this project off the ground, collaboration in the design of the PLC was essential. Going it alone meant that I missed out on valuable perspectives and deprived teachers of the opportunity to craft something relevant to their practice. My work with the ENL specialists highlighted this. Initially, I was concerned that I was putting too much on them. Like my efforts to downplay the design of assessments, I tried to eliminate any additional work for team members. However, doing so was to the group's detriment because I spent so much time leading the sessions in the early stages. Sessions where teachers took greater leadership roles were received far more positively than those where I led the presentation.

As a new district administrator, collaboration with the principal was another critical component. This partnership was important for scheduling sessions and aligning our goals. Competing priorities made it difficult for the two of us to co-facilitate sessions; however, the principal effectively communicated the value and essential nature of this work. This aligns with recent findings analyzing the role of building and district leaders in leading instructional change.

Data Literacy

In reflection, I realized that I had not spent enough time defining the role of formative assessment in our improvement efforts. While teachers selected benchmarks and post-assessments, these tools were not sensitive enough to capture change effectively. The fact that most students scored "highly proficient" on the pre-tests should have informed our selection of assessments and interventions. This confusion around the role of assessments in our work contributed to inconsistent worksheet submissions and limited our ability to let data drive our instructional planning.

Continuous Improvement

Ultimately, I have found the use of improvement science and professional learning communities to be powerful tools in facilitating meaningful change in instruction at our elementary school. By focusing on collaborative problem-solving and committing to continuous improvement, our educators work together to identify and address the root causes of challenges, implement evidence-based interventions, and monitor progress toward their goals. Learning happens on many different levels. This has been a particularly meaningful learning experience for me as a new leader. It is an exciting initiative to lead, and I have found it an even more exciting initiative in which to participate.

Developing these continuous improvement structures has had a positive impact on our school and district culture around professional learning. Moreover, implementing them as an administrator new to the district communicated that I did not see the staff as "broken," requiring outsiders to come and repair them with workshops and training. Instead, I communicated improvement science almost as a personal value, further operationalizing what I meant by being a "lifelong learner." This process helped me establish my identity as both a leader and a learner and continues to do so and helped to engage the staff as co-learners with me.

QUESTIONS

1. The curriculum director engaged the teachers in three simultaneous change experiences: tackling a problem of practice collaboratively, working as a professional learning community, and trying out solutions using a PDSA cycle process. How well did he lead each change effort, and how might he have structured these changes differently, rather than simultaneously?
2. The curriculum director noted learning how to support the learning and engagement of others in improvement work (particularly through collaboration and improved data literacy). What other leadership practices are noteworthy in his case?
3. This problem-solving experience seems to have been beneficial as a model for district change, as the district is now scaling up from this experience. Why do you think that occurred?

REFERENCES

Carney, M. S. (2012). *Teaching English Language Learners Scale (TELLS): A study of validity and reliability* [Doctoral dissertation, University of Missouri–Columbia].

Fernandez, N., & Inserra, A. (2013). Disproportionate classification of ESL students in U.S. special education. *The Electronic Journal for English as a Second Language, 17*(2), 1–22.

Skiba, R., Simmons, A., Ritter, S., Kohler, K., Henderson, M., & Wu, T. (2006). The context of minority disproportionality: Practitioner perspectives on special education referral. *Teachers College Record, 108*(7), 1424–1459.

Wilkinson, C. Y., Ortiz, A. A., Robertson, P. M., & Kushner, M. I. (2006). English language learners with reading-related LD: Linking data from multiple sources to make eligibility determinations. *Journal of Learning Disabilities, 39*(2), 129–141.

CHAPTER 7

Engaging Middle School Teachers in Improvement Cycles to Increase Achievement

Gail Joyner

In this case, a 3–8 school principal is faced with turning around a persistently low-performing school. In talking with staff, she learned that they were unaware of their school's performance data and were unaccustomed to working together on examining practice. The principal adopted the improvement science principles and tools as the means for staff to learn to examine data in their grades and content areas and try out standards-aligned solutions through iterative problem-solving cycles. The staff worked in grade-level teams and as a whole school to learn collaboratively and support one another's efforts. Over a 3-year period (with the COVID interruption), the teachers gained a strong collaborative inquiry capacity, supported by new organizational systems and structures, and the students made learning progress, particularly in the classes where the teachers were most engaged in this process. Along the way, the principal learned how to support change and share leadership while maintaining a strong focus on the school's improvement needs.

During my first year as principal in 2019–2020 at We Can Do It Academy (WCDIA), a pseudonym, located in Westchester County, New York, I was faced with the challenge of determining the most effective way to improve student learning and achievement. The school was designated a Comprehensive Support and Improvement (CSI) school by the New York State Education Department (NYSED), which defines CSI schools as those that perform at Level 1 (which is the lowest performing level on a scale of 1–4) on a combination of Every Student Succeeds Act (ESSA) indicators (NYSED, 2019). WCDIA had been designated as a struggling or priority school since 2010. WCDIA had to show student improvement in both English Language Arts (ELA) and math in the next 2 years or the state would take over the school. While our goal was to improve student performance in ELA and math, I found that I needed to develop the teachers' capacity for continuous improvement as a central change strategy. Thus, I undertook a nested improvement approach, trying out various strategies to help them to bring inquiry into their own improvement approach.

CONTEXT

When I became principal, the campus consisted of two schools, serving, respectively, Pre-K–2 and grades 3 to 8. The upper school, which I lead, served 329 students, of whom 85% were considered low-income and 87% were black or Hispanic. The school included 22 teachers, most of whom were experienced. The school's vision was, "[We Can Do It Academy] will engage and empower socially conscious, responsible citizens in a student-centered environment that will prepare all students for college and careers."

The school is one of 40 schools in an urban-like school district outside a major metropolitan city. The district was designated by the NYSED as a target district based on its large number of CSI and Targeted Support and Improvement (TSI) schools in 2018–2019. The district and school were required to create an improvement plan and identify initiatives to positively affect student learning and address the accountability measures for which they had been identified. Only in recent years had the district begun to actively use data for planning, improvement, and accountability purposes, but data usage remained extremely limited in this school.

Through informal conversations and feedback at initial meetings, I had learned that the existing school culture was one in which teachers were typically introduced to a plethora of improvement initiatives with little staying power. Over the years, they had experienced a variety of consultant-driven change ideas (such as Journeys, Eureka Math, and different Positive Behavior Intervention Strategies [PBIS]) to improve student learning. Over the previous 19 years there had been four principals, and their 22 programs were tried and quickly discarded. Initiatives changed with each administration, so teachers were left wondering how long any new framework or curriculum might last. Among the multiple initiatives were various protocols for data analysis and data review sessions at the beginning, middle, and end of each school year. But with little or no expectations about what to do after the data were analyzed, the impact that teacher practice had on student outcomes remained underexamined.

Consequently, the life cycle of a school building or district leader at WCDIA often did not align with that of teachers who would spend 30 years in the same building. There is a comment that I heard many times from staff members: "I was here for the last seven principals or superintendents, and

I will be here for the next one." Their willingness to wait out the existing mandates and do little to change practice had become a cultural norm and a barrier to change.

DISCOVERING THE PROBLEM

Despite the school's ambitious vision and mission, the staff had been unaware of their low performance and had not seen the data as indicators of their performance. Although there has been an increase in the district's use of data over the years, the quality and extent of data use varied from school to school. It was evident, given the school's persistent underperformance, that data use and practice improvement were not part of the school culture and routines.

Continuous improvement is described as undertaking initiatives that involve multiple iterative cycles of activity over extended periods. In working to promote continuous improvement as a new principal at WCDIA, I learned that teachers lacked the skills needed to use data for problem exploration, problem-solving, and solution-testing. Although teachers had used data before, they had not been asked to use it for the purposes of continuous improvement. For example, after the first few grade team meetings, I asked teachers to enter student performance data into a Microsoft Excel spreadsheet, and some struggled with even this task. This gap in data use and improvement practices became my focal problem of practice.

ANALYZING THE PROBLEM

To analyze this problem further and find solutions, I had to engage the staff in a learning journey by unpacking the presenting problem of practice. Equipped with travel references and puns, I led my staff through a series of exercises and professional learning around data and its use. In my first faculty meeting in the fall, I invited teachers to join me on a 182-day "cruise" into the new school year. The use of the cruise theme was intentionally symbolic to create a different culture, while being centered on addressing the problem. The idea of a cruise invited teachers to join in a shared adventure; it represented movement, togetherness, fun, and excursions, but also the need to negotiate rough water, manage new experiences, and overcome unexpected challenges. The presentation's theme also brought some levity to a very serious issue. The reality was that the school was in danger of closing if we did not make progress, which helped most of the grade-level teams understand why we had to increase student achievement.

Unpacking State Performance Data

My first step was to create a sense of urgency and an understanding of the problem. During the opening faculty meeting, I presented data that outlined our current reality. In ELA, 81% of the students were not proficient in 2018, and 79% were not proficient in 2019. In math the numbers were quite similar: 82% not proficient in 2018 and 78% not proficient in 2019. I highlighted how the percentage of those not proficient rose with each increased grade level. While sharing these bleak figures, I emphasized the modest improvements: the 3.0% decrease in the number of Level 1 students and the 2.0% increase in the number of Level 2 and Level 3 students in ELA, and the 4.0% decrease in the number of Level 1 students and the 5.0% increase in the number of Level 3 students in math.[2] I intentionally wanted to show the teachers that they had the capacity to make a difference because they were beginning to impact student scores, but that more work was needed.

During the meeting, I then formed the teachers into five grade-level teams for grades 3, 4, 5, 6, and a combined team for grades 7–8. The teams were then sent on a data dive excursion, stopping on the "island of instruction" as we discussed instructional expectations for the year. We engaged in a process of piloting teachers' use of improvement science principles. In the grade-level team meetings, each team added additional items to the fishbone diagram that were specific to their grade level. Each team identified a problem of practice that the members were willing to address by engaging in a Plan-Do-Study-Act (PDSA) cycle over the next few weeks.

Collecting Formative Performance Data

Our work was interrupted in spring 2020 due to the onset of the global COVID pandemic in March 2020, and the school closed and switched to remote learning. We were preparing for a third cycle when the pandemic hit. We continued to meet virtually, and our teachers were able to shift to Microsoft Teams with ease due to the structures and systems that were put in place prior to the pandemic.

Despite continuing to work remotely in fall 2020 (Year 2), we used the disruption to learn more about student performance and adapt to the changing conditions. We administered diagnostic assessments virtually in September 2020 and placed students in instructional groups. By winter, while we were operating with both hybrid and fully remote learners, we administered midyear assessments to all students as part of our new assessment practices. During this time, the state suspended state assessments and

2. Student levels are defined by NYSED as follows: Level 1 is considered not proficient, Level 2 is partially proficient, Level 3 is proficient, and Level 4 is advanced proficient.

Figure 7.1. Fishbone Diagram of Factors Contributing to Poor Student Performance

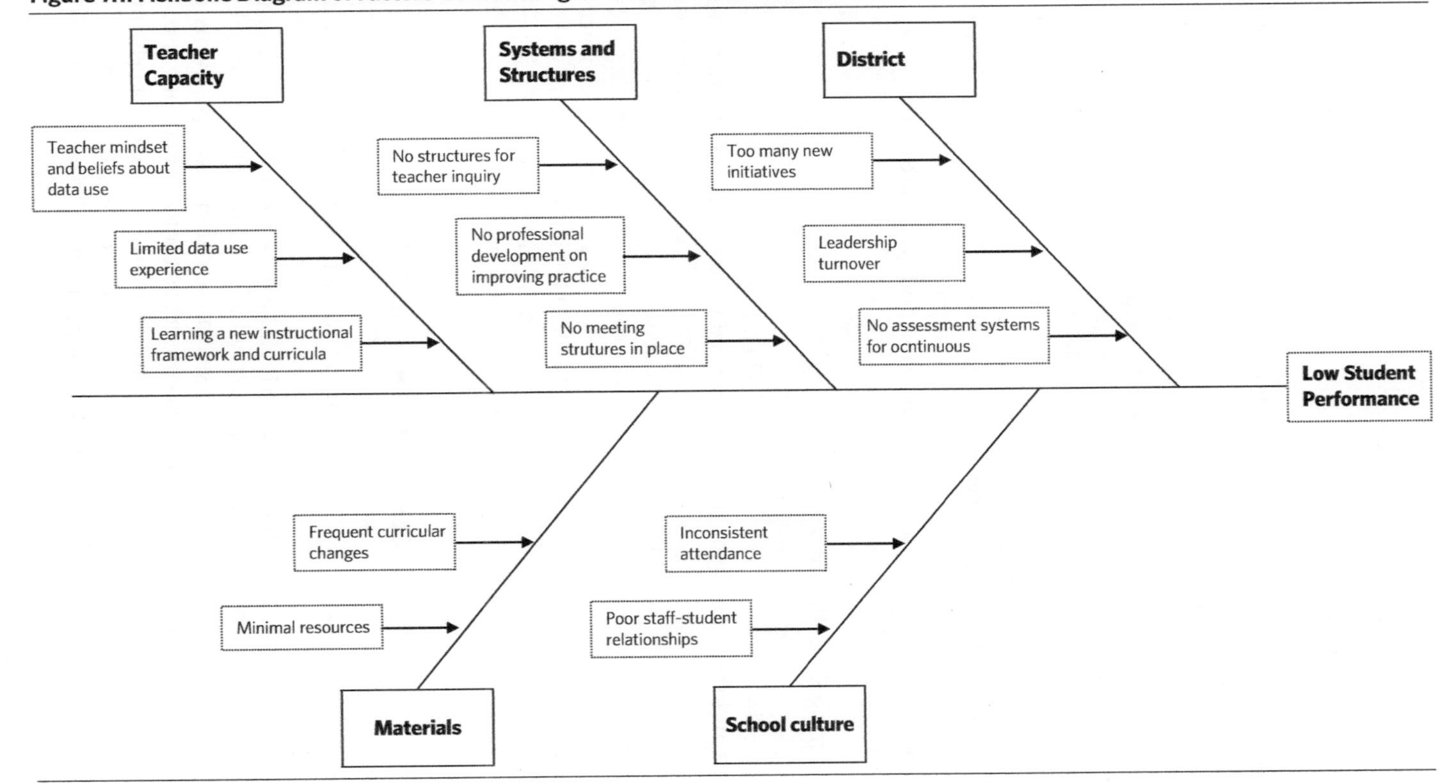

the school's status remained unchanged, and with all the disrupted learning, we paused our work on improving data use.

Analyzing the System

During Year 2, I invited the teachers to explore the nature of and causes for their poor student performance, using a fishbone diagram to organize the identified factors and causes that influenced this outcome. Some of the factors identified, as shown in Figure 7.1, were the environment, which included poor staff and student relationships; students' social-emotional needs; and insufficient parental support. In addition, materials, lack of resources, and frequent changes to the curriculum (including learning a new instructional framework and two new curricula required by the district) were placed on the diagram. They and I concluded that these factors impacted the teachers' mindsets and beliefs around data use and their limited experiences using data. Finally, the multitude of initiatives imposed by the district, coupled with the lack of systems and structures to support them, were other identified factors that contributed to low student performance.

Conducing Empathy Interviews

During the spring of Year 2 (2020–2021), I interviewed two assistant principals and three teachers about current data use skills and practices, to prepare to relaunch our work in the fall of Year 3. They shared similar thoughts about what data meant to them: facts, figures, graphs, charts, and the collection of information to be used for a purpose. I realized then that they and our other teachers did not perceive data use as an inquiry-based process for monitoring and problem-solving in schools. My challenge, therefore, was to find a way to encourage this and move staff from a static data use perspective to a more dynamic process-related perspective.

DESIGNING THE SOLUTION

Given what I had learned in working in the school for 2 years, I now understood that I had to design a solution that would work within the macrocultures of the state and district, which heavily valued test scores, while changing the microculture at (WCDIA), which initially placed less value on data and test scores and generally resisted change initiatives. Evans et al. (2019) argue that "although there is consensus that teachers ought to both examine and then act on this relationship between student performance data and their instruction, the critical questions are whether and how they actually do so in their daily practice" (p. 3). I used these questions to start my improvement work, focusing on current data use practice.

Following the analysis of the data and preliminary research into the problem, the staff and I selected the one factor to address that was within our sphere of influence and would have the most impact. We focused on a plan using PDSA cycles for using data to improve instruction, by taking a close look at what skills our teachers needed to effectively use data for problem exploration, problem-solving, and solution-testing. Without building this teacher capacity, we believed teachers would be limited in their ability to change instruction and impact student outcomes.

As we started back to school fully-in-person in Year 3, my leadership team and I planned to have the teachers continue to work in grade-level teams through six 3-week PDSA cycles, in which they used data to analyze specific student learning needs (based on standards), identify and test instructional solutions, and monitor the results. They would utilize Benchmark Advance/Ready Curriculum diagnostics, interim assessments, and end-of-year assessment tools. The instructional strategies for interventions were to be drawn from the suggestions from the Learner-Active Technology Infused Classroom (LATIC) framework and Benchmark Advance/Ready Curriculum or the teacher teams. In addition, the teachers would focus on a cross-section of 15 students in each class (their focus group) to test instructional differentiation strategies. Their work was supported through regular meetings that incorporated continued professional learning into improvement science practices. Thus, we integrated three drivers for change, as shown in the diagram below, by centering the cycles of improvement on the mandated curriculum implementation, using their PLCs as collaborative venues for inquiry about practice.

Figure 7.2. Diagram of Drivers to Improve Student Learning Through Continuous Improvement

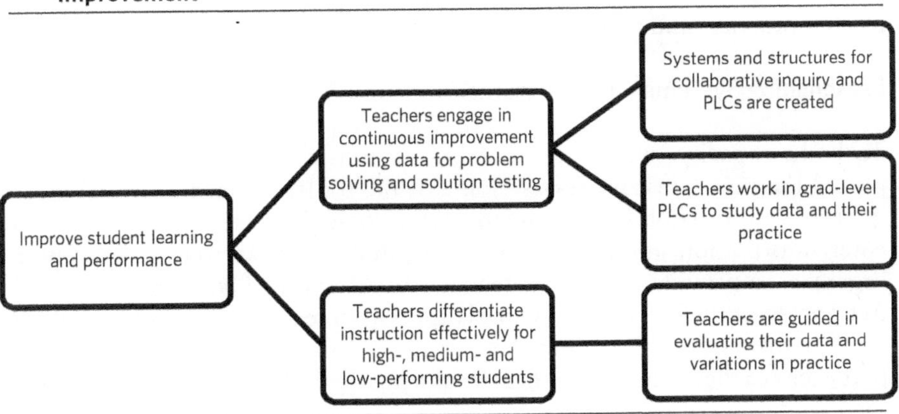

To accelerate our work and promote continuous improvement and urgency, I adopted another travel metaphor for the year. In September, teachers were invited to board Flight #2122. I shifted the metaphor from a cruise to a flight following the global pandemic, as there was a need to "take off" at a different pace.

IMPLEMENTING THE CHANGE

Accelerating Continuous Improvement

Our pre-departure was the preparation time in September 2021 before we conducted our first cycle of the year on instructional improvement in October. The focus of our work in teams revolved around the question, "What is it that we are going to do this year that was tied to the urgency that we discussed for the past two years?" During the session, teachers charted ideas, which included increased attendance, social-emotional learning, authentic learning units, and technology. All three groups included the use of data and PDSA cycles on their charts. As we prepared to "take off" in September, we discussed the structures, systems, and tools that would help us reach our destination: increase student achievement.

Throughout the academic year, the staff and I expanded our iterative problem-solving approach, by asking each grade-level team to identify a high-leverage instructional strategy to focus on. The leadership team and I provided further professional learning on the PDSA cycle itself: how to identify a problem of practice and interventions using the PDSA cycle as a vehicle. Together with the staff, we revisited our initial fishbone and driver diagrams. We identified new instructional strategies for implementation and helped the teams identify and analyzed pre- and post-assessment data for each cycle. We took a closer look at the instructional core and how the teacher, student, and content impacted student learning. We also looked at academic interventions, teacher practice, and their impact on student learning.

Establishing Systems and Structures

To build capacity, we created conditions and introduced tools that supported the new work processes. Some of the tools included an Excel sheet to record and maintain the student data, PowerPoint slides for groups to enter information about their problems, and a PDSA circle as a graphic organizer to provide a space for teachers to record the Plan, Do, Study, and Act phases of their work. These tools supported teachers in presenting their work to one another. We created a system for data collection and sharing so that each teacher could place their results in an Excel spreadsheet to compile their students' data in one place.

Incorporating Professional Learning Community Practices

During the PDSA cycle processes, from October 2021 to March 2022, we examined what conditions influenced teacher capacity to engage in continuous improvement and identified several practices to add. My leadership team and I provided teachers with professional learning to improve their capacity to work together in professional learning communities (PLCs) to engage in continuous improvement. We created a professional learning calendar for 2021–2022 so that everyone was aware of the common planning meeting topics, dates, and times. We established a schedule design that provided uninterrupted, dedicated time for teachers to meet in their PLCs. Teachers were not asked to cover classes during their PLC time, and a dedicated space was provided for their PLC sessions. We continued to focus on building the skills and capacities needed to use data for problem exploration, problem-solving, and solution-testing. We were guided by Love's (2009) assertion that collaborative inquiry works best when teachers have a model to follow, admitting that "we have all suffered in teams that flounder with lack of direction or simply recreate old patterns of thinking and responding" (p. 45). Finally, we helped each team to identify a problem of practice and create a driver diagram in order to articulate the drivers that would impact their aim.

As teachers engaged in these new work processes, I engaged in my own cycle of inquiry to ascertain the impact of professional learning in building capacity to use improvement science. Using the teams' data management tools and monthly reporting, I monitored their approaches, data use, and problem-solving efforts.

Tracking Variation

To develop teachers' data-use practices for instructional differentiation was to have teachers attend intensively to their focus groups. Many teachers had challenges in interpreting data and planning for differentiating instruction for their whole class. Learning by monitoring smaller numbers of students was thought to be more manageable for teachers. Using randomly selected students from three performance levels (i.e., top, middle, and lower third) enabled teachers to more easily evaluate different instructional needs and test the benefits of changes in practice.

Engaging Teacher Teams in PDSA Cycles

Throughout the third year, the teacher teams worked on standards-based problems of practice and solutions in the six 3-week PDSA cycles. This process allowed the teachers to work in small groups on a specific learning standard and focus on a single intervention.

Each team analyzed its own class data. Following this analysis, the grade team conducted a deeper analysis looking across the grade and identifying trends and commonalities. Although each cycle focused on a different topic or standard, teachers were able to determine when they should continue with a new approach to teaching a learning standard, shift to a different intervention, or proceed to a new standard. Working iteratively and using data, teachers became more able to make informed decisions on what a specific group of students needed. The analysis of the data within each cycle helped them and us determine the impact of their interventions. The expectation was that through this process, teachers' capacity to engage in continuous improvement using data for problem exploration, problem-solving, and solution-testing would improve.

Developing an inquiry approach to test PDSA cycles is an iterative process that allows for adaptation throughout the change process. This work is time-consuming, and we learned together as an organization to overcome barriers to this work and celebrate successes. The role of the leader in creating the conditions and supporting the work is to leave behind what Cohen-Vogel et al. (2016) describe as a "system of profound knowledge" instead of a program or practice. Teachers were able to make shifts in their practice that could continue to impact their pedagogy. An example of one team's PDSA cycle is shown in Figure 7.3.

Using this improvement science tool, we were able to measure change in each teacher team's practice and student learning as we compared the data that they shared throughout the six cycles. This generated a new way of working together as teachers made public their multiple iterations of PDSA cycles for problem exploration, problem-solving, and solution-testing, using data to guide curriculum and instructional change.

Figure 7.3. PDSA Cycle Example: ELA Phase One—Cycle One

Phase	Action
Plan	Plan a mini-lesson on elements of a story using a graphic organizer and an escape room challenge requiring student groups to answer four questions
Do	Teachers implement the lesson and activity
	Students complete the activity and an exit ticket that assesses learning
Study	Evaluate the assessment results and compare by instructional element and student skill level
	Evaluate student engagement
Act	Adapt the lesson to encourage individual effort

Organizing Monthly Faculty Meetings

We continued to meet monthly for the teams to share their progress and continue professional learning. Over time, this approach led to the creation of a standard meeting structure that facilitated participation and dialogue about processes and their experiences. Each meeting for the past 3 years (2019–2022) began with an opening activity or circle that encouraged discussion and team-building. Conducting a discussion circle with a specific prompt or providing an opening activity that required everyone to respond was one way that I was able to listen to their feedback; it helped me validate and affirm their practices around improvement. Teachers also had the opportunity to respond to one another during these circles or opening activities. Trust and openness allowed us to move forward together as we addressed concerns and revisited our goals. Out of our discussion grew a collective understanding that although this work was hard, it is work that we had to do to monitor student progress and plan meaningful instruction.

Conducting Appreciative Inquiry

Throughout the process, I periodically incorporated Cooperrider et al.'s (2008) appreciative inquiry model. An early meeting led to the introduction of the appreciative inquiry approach, highlighting the concept and value of taking a positive approach to change. This approach allowed the teacher teams to feel valued as they co-designed the work. These conversations led to a discernible shift in how teachers talked about their work and student learning. They were encouraged to assess the current reality and environment with a goal of minimizing initiative fatigue by aligning work processes and collaborating to co-design implementation processes.

RESULTS

Impact on Students

At the end of the third year, the staff and I evaluated the impact on student learning by PDSA cycle, focus group, and subject domain. Each cycle was unique in that it focused on a specific content area (i.e., ELA or math) and interventions targeted toward specific performance standards. The impact of the interventions within the cycles was assessed by analyzing the following: (1) the student data from interim assessments in October and January (within-cycles pre-post); (2) assessments in October and March from Benchmark, i-Ready, and DataMate; and (3) teacher-created assessments for the cycles.

To illustrate, the results from Cycles 1, 2, and 6 were analyzed and compared across all teacher teams. There was a notable increase in the scores from the pre-assessment to the post-assessment during each subsequent cycle; not surprisingly, Cycle 6 saw the biggest improvement (+20.56 points). This improvement suggested that the teachers were learning to be more strategic in using data to target instruction and provide support. In particular, the increase on the ELA DataMate post-assessment from the first cycle to the final cycle aligned with the interventions the ELA team put in place. Nonetheless, the wide variation in the scores for both the pre- and post-assessment suggested that more work was needed to develop standard practices that are effective for all students.

Students' scores from the beginning of the year and the end of the year were compared by assessment and subject. The mean improvement for ELA (23.03) was more than double that for math (9.06), with less variation for ELA. These subject-area differences paralleled differences in subject teachers' efforts to modify and differentiate instructional practice to support student learning. The greatest improvement in scores was for students rated by teachers as "average" (22.06), followed by students rated by teachers as "low" (16.30). Students rated by teachers as "high" gained the least (9.78), and their scores showed the greatest variation in improvement.

During our final reflection session, I asked all the teachers to share what they noticed about their student focus-group data across the cycles, across classes, and across grade levels. All teachers noted that all three tiers of students showed some improvement. Most teachers reported that the low-achieving students showed the least amount of growth over the cycles. They also noticed that scores for the high-achieving students declined from the diagnostic to the midyear assessment, wondering if inconsistent attendance attributable to the pandemic was a factor. Teachers also discussed whether the high- and low-achieving students required different levels of intervention.

We concluded by agreeing that there remains the need to engage students in the process of progress tracking. This will require building leaders and teachers to work together to identify processes and protocols for student engagement with the goal of strengthening students' ability to track their own progress and develop their own agency. Consequently, there is a need to include students as collaborators in this process.

Finally, the following fall of 2021, we were able to see how and in what ways these student performance improvements were reflected in the state assessment scores. What I learned from the analysis of the state ELA and math data results aligned with our interim findings. The ELA teachers' students showed significant improvement across the grades. The number of students whose scores increased was double that of their math counterparts. Math scores, however, declined across the grades, except for one of the math teacher's students, who showed some improvement. These improvements aligned with which teacher groups had actively engaged in cycles of improvement, showing the value of the improvement process for better student learning.

Impact on Teachers

Engaging in continuous improvement work over 3 years, and most intensively in the third year, substantively changed teachers' practice, both in how they approached learning and problem-solving, but more importantly, in their instructional practice, particularly in using data to differentiate student support.

Changing Teachers' Approach to Learning and Problem-Solving

The leadership team and I noted marked improvement in how the teachers engaged in learning. Initially, in the first year, teachers had struggled to complete basic tasks related to data, and they often came to meetings unprepared, not bringing a laptop or completing tasks prior to the meetings. By the third year, we had refined and created systems during the various cycles and noticed a difference when the grade teams presented their work. Moreover, their final presentations in June 2021 showed what they had done throughout the cycles, and the data were entered into the necessary document. They also shared what they learned about improvement science.

Using an inquiry approach encourages the problem-solver to slow down, minimizing the tendency to jump to improvement actions (Bryk, 2017; Marsh et al., 2015; Van Gasse et al., 2017). In addition, it increases teachers' ability to move from data improvement to meaningful discussions and decisions about their practice based on the data. It also provides opportunities for reflection on their practice and its impact on student learning outcomes.

Enacting Iterative Improvement

Through their end-of-year-3 presentations, I learned that teachers were able to engage in dialogue about their practice. They took ownership of their learning and were willing to make their experiences public, as demonstrated in our reflective discussion. The math teachers shared that they were able to discuss student progress with the other math teachers on the team. The teachers appreciated having the time to meet to dig into topics during a given cycle. The way they used data was different from previous years. A math teacher cited the impact of the pandemic, noting that the data "made us face the results right away. It had been difficult to learn and teach math remotely because we were unable to see students' faces or responses on paper. This process reminded the teachers to go back to prerequisite skills." Consequently, they could discuss things with peers who taught in grades 5 to 8.

Both ELA teams shared that working in small groups on a specific standard allowed them to focus on a single intervention. Based on the outcomes they produced within a short cycle, teachers were able to determine if they should continue to teach students with that standard, try a different intervention, or proceed to a new standard. As a result, many teachers were able to make informed, data-driven decisions on what their identified groups of students needed.

I observed that the ELA teachers and math teachers thought about, and approached, their iterative improvement work differently. Math teachers seemed to be a bit more linear in their thinking, like the subject matter that they teach. Traditionally, math teachers have students solve a problem with the mindset that there is a right answer. As the field of mathematics has started to lean toward the inquiry approach, the math teachers have begun the shift to allow students to discover multiple approaches to obtain an answer. English teachers, due to the nature of their discipline, have traditionally spent more time discussing and analyzing text to see what each reader thinks or feels. Perhaps this difference in practice accounts for some difference in ELA and math teacher engagement throughout the process, which was stronger among the ELA teachers than the math teachers.

Impacting Instructional Practice

As evidenced by observation notes and reflection sessions, many teachers, particularly in ELA, became more intentional in their planning of interventions to meet students' needs. They adjusted and modified lessons for their three tiers of students and were observed incorporating differentiated practices into their lessons.

During our final reflection session, the teachers shared that working with smaller groups allowed them to adjust the teaching methods and focus on the needs of that group. Teachers had to think about what they were doing for each group of students. As one ELA teacher shared:

> This process held me accountable because I had to meet with certain students at certain times. This helped with lesson planning, as the preparation for each [student] group was different. The students looked forward to the small-group time with teachers and the small-group activities. Those who did not have it wanted to know how they could sign up.

Impact on the School

Harrison et al. (2019), in reviewing existing research on continuous improvement, noted that "critical questions regarding our ability to implement these systems in the complex environment of schools, the best practices for facilitating their use, and the impact of doing so on outcomes of value remain largely unanswered by the literature" (p. 5). Some of the key lessons we learned at We Can Do It Academy (WCDIA) align with the findings of Harrison et al. (2019):

- The process of continuous improvement is slow; big change requires months of small change initiatives.
- There is a critical need for building a culture of improvement. Participating in this process requires being comfortable with the idea of the unknown and the potential for failure.
- Building a culture of improvement requires creating systems for identifying, acquiring, and deepening necessary principal and teacher capacities.
- The work of developing, adapting, implementing, and expanding innovations is tightly interwoven.

As this case shows, it took us 3 years (COVID pandemic notwithstanding) to develop the capacity to work together on iteratively improving student learning using improvement science principles. Along the way, we took steps to develop robust standard work processes that would yield predictable results, by engaging in continuous improvement through professional learning communities (PLCs) and utilizing PDSA cycles to link data to changes in practices. We tested this approach with a team of ELA and math teachers in 5th through 8th grades to examine the impact of this change approach on their ability to engage in continuous improvement.

Operationalizing the idea that schools or districts must take the time to explore the problem, identify potential interventions, and then test solutions for impact would be a game-changer in education, especially in light of a myriad of post-pandemic needs. It is not solely about the data; it is about creating a culture where they persevere.

LEADER REFLECTIONS

In shifting the school capacity toward continuous improvement, as a leader, I also had to shift my current practices in intentional and research-informed ways. I wanted to reinforce that the teachers and other staff had the capacity, with support, to improve student outcomes. As principal, I had to show that the old way of thinking and the existing work processes and structures must and could be altered. I needed to show staff that with new learning, they could overcome this challenge. To do this, I needed to seek ways to build relationships with school staff and figure out the best way to leverage those relationships to support the change.

Using Metaphors to Set Expectations

First, to engage teachers, I used the metaphors of a cruise and an airline flight to signal that we were "on the move" with a sense of lightness and fun. I believe that a lighthearted approach, rather than a heavy-handed top-down approach, was particularly important, as this change initiative came to take place during the pandemic, when teachers were highly stressed personally and professionally.

Creating Psychological Safety

Second, I recognized that I needed to create a psychologically safe space for change, as it can be challenging, entail painful self-reflection, and require uncomfortable adaptations to new practices. Creating a safe space was especially important for me as a new leader taking on change while building relationships with my staff. I was guided by the advice of Heifetz and Linsky (2017), who contend that courage and vision are not enough to facilitate change. Rather, they argue, leaders must help staff with the challenging process of grappling with hard realities, which includes the creation of a psychologically safe space that enables change and risk-taking.

Ensuring Voice and Sharing Leadership

Third, I wanted to ensure teachers' voices, so I worked with staff to create general norms for discussion and design opportunities to incorporate teachers' voices throughout. Engaging teachers as a part of the process was critical, especially considering the initial apathy toward low student achievement. To that end, I was committed to promoting distributed leadership. This was an act of trust with an unfamiliar staff at a new school, but that trust paid off in the long run.

Adapting Leadership Practices

These changes helped create a balance in the feedback process and strengthen collaboration. The structures put in place, which included dedicated time for team meetings and the use of protocols, allowed for discussions that shifted teacher mindsets, as evidenced by data I collected from weekly PLC meetings, monthly faculty meetings, discussions, presentations, and Poll Everywhere responses. I engaged in and modeled restorative approaches to build relationships and community with teachers that they could use with their students.

I adapted the pace of change to promote maximum participation and engagement of teachers. Teacher feedback on the pacing of our improvement cycles was instrumental in agreeing to adopt the PDSA cycle as the means to support improvement. During the initial pilot, we conducted multiple cycles but did not leave adequate time between cycles to analyze our data. This prompted a reduction in the number of cycles from the previous year. We also added a week in between cycles to analyze data and plan for the next cycle. This modified timeline was the one we used in Year 3. As a leader, by honoring the teachers' voices and input, I created a safe and collaborative space to continue to improve. Teachers did not feel pressured to stick to an arbitrarily fast-paced schedule that could have led to additional burnout or turnover; instead, they could be honest about their perceptions and needs. In the long run, this led to improved outcomes for me as the leader, for teachers and their instructional practices, and for students and their learning.

Using PDSA Cycles to Build Capacity

I learned to use PDSA cycles as a practical approach to build teacher capacity to work in grade-level PLCs, because each cycle relied on using data for problem exploration, problem-solving, and solution-testing. It is particularly useful in helping teachers learn to differentiate their practice based on students' learning needs. Employing PDSA cycles is an effective practice to support exploration of how to differentiate effectively, by evaluating the experiences of different students. The use of short, iterative cycles provided an opportunity to develop and test targeted interventions and, ideally, improvement for these students during each cycle. The use of multiple cycles allowed for the exploration and assessment of a variety of interventions to impact student outcomes.

Providing a set of structures and processes to support teacher inquiry into practice using PDSA cycles was essential for the teachers to work together on improving student learning. These both enabled collaborative work and, when integrated, were critical supports of continuous school improvement.

Creating a Data Use Culture

I also learned that the leader's role is critical in developing a shift in culture and practices around data use. The systems, structures, tools, and professional learning around both can influence the impact of a team's effective use of data. Moreover, school leaders are key to the data use process, so it is incumbent upon the leader to create opportunities to engage in the learning with their teams as they create the conditions for data usage. Datnow et al. (2021) describe how system leaders encourage data use in schools by establishing norms and expectations specifically for it. According to Coburn and Turner (2011), making these connections is critical: "By emphasizing the nature of linkages between different facets of the data use phenomenon, this framework can inform the design of studies that are better able to connect different aspects of what has heretofore been a disconnected field" (p. 197). Coburn and Turner's desire to address the disconnect is aligned with my desire and commitment as an educator and advocate for meaningful data use and true differentiation of student learning.

EPILOGUE

Prior to the start of the 2022–2023 school year, I accepted a position (a promotion) in another district. After my departure, I learned that several teachers wanted to continue to use the PDSA cycles and use data for problem exploration, problem-solving, and solution-testing. I also learned that the school has been removed from the state list because of improved student performance. In my current role I am using improvement science principles with my current district's schools to explore a problem of practice around chronic absenteeism.

QUESTIONS

1. If it is the desire of schools and districts to create sustainable change, how can they create the conditions to support using data for problem exploration, problem-solving, and solution-testing? What data systems can be created for districts and schools to engage in this type of work?
2. Engaging in continuous improvement requires that teachers and other staff adopt an experimental approach to improving their practice, which is a significant shift in how teachers and other staff typically approach instructional improvement. What norms and practices are needed to help teachers and others make this shift and to follow through on more than one iteration when trying out a new practice?
3. The principal launched her improvement approach with the whole school, without piloting it first with a smaller group of teachers, such as one grade or subject area. What are the pros and cons of this decision? How might she have strengthened her efforts?

REFERENCES

Bryk, A. (2017). *Redressing inequities: An aspiration in search of a method*. Carnegie Foundation for the Advancement of Teaching. https://www.carnegiefoun

dation.org/resources/publications/redressing-inequities-an-aspiration-in-search-of-a-method/

Coburn, C. E., & Turner, E. O. (2011). Research on data use: A framework and analysis. *Measurement: Interdisciplinary Research and Perspectives, 9*(4), 173–206.

Cohen-Vogel, L., Socol, A. R., Cannata, M., & Rutledge, S. A. (2016). A model of continuous improvement in high schools: A process for research, innovation design, implementation, and scale. *Teachers College Record, 118*(13), 1–26.

Cooperrider, D. L., Stavros, J. M., & Whitney, D. (2008). *The appreciative inquiry handbook: For leaders of change*. Berrett-Koehler.

Datnow, A., Lockton, M., & Weddle, H. (2021). Capacity building to bridge data use and instructional improvement through evidence on student thinking. *Studies in Educational Evaluation, 69*(4), 100869. https://doi.org/10.1016/j.stueduc.2020.100869

Evans, M., Teasdale, R. M., Gannon-Slater, N., La Londe, P. G., Crenshaw, H. L., Greene, J. C., & Schwandt, T. A. (2019). How did that happen? Teachers' explanations for low test scores. *Teachers College Record, 121*(2), 1–40.

Harrison, C., Wachen, J., Brown, S., & Cohen-Vogel, L. (2019). A view from within: Lessons learned from partnering for continuous improvement. *Teachers College Record, 121*(9), 1–38.

Heifetz, R., & Linsky, M. (2017). *Leadership on the line: Staying alive through the dangers of change*. Harvard Business Review Press.

Love, N. (2009). *Using data to improve learning for all: A collaborative inquiry approach*. Corwin Press.

Marsh, J., Bertrand, M., & Huguet, A. (2015). Using data to alter instructional practice: The mediating role of coaches and professional learning communities. *Teachers College Record, 117*(4), 1–40.

New York State Education Department (NYSED). (2019). *School improvement*. New York State Education Department. http://www.nysed.gov/accountability/school-improvement#:~:text=Comprehensive%20Support%20and%20Improvement%20(CSI,performing%20at%20a%20level%201.

Van Gasse, R., Vanlommel, K., Vanhoof, J., & Van Petegem, P. (2017). Unravelling data use in teacher teams: How network patterns and interactive learning activities change across different data use phases. *Teaching and Teacher Education, 67*, 550–560. https://doi.org/10.1016/j.tate.2017.08.002

CHAPTER 8

Leading Principals Through Short-Cycle Improvement Work

Kris M. DeFilippis

This case demonstrates my approach, as an assistant superintendent, to improving underperforming schools in the Bronx by engaging school leaders and their teams. We used improvement science principles and tools, along with an equity framework, to address local problems of practice in their schools. Pairs of district administrators worked with six school principals to pilot an improvement approach that consisted of an 8-week cycle to investigate potential problems of practice, evaluate existing practices, and design and test an intervention through one or more Plan-Do-Study-Act cycles. All six schools made demonstrable gains in making progress in solving their targeted problems, and principals learned to adopt the practices for continuous improvement. The district team of 10 district administrators and I used this initial pilot to test out our improvement development approach, which, after modifications, subsequently scaled up to 130 additional schools.

School systems across the United States are struggling with continued disproportionality, segregation, and competing priorities for educational goals (Fergus, 2016). Disproportionality is defined as the over- and underrepresentation of racial/ethnic minorities in relation to their total enrollment (Ahram et al., 2011) As a Bronx district leader, I faced these challenges when assuming my position in 2019. Like elsewhere, several Bronx districts grappled with persistently low academic improvement progress and strong evidence of disproportionality-related problems.

This case study explores how my team of 10 district administrators and I developed a process to support multiple principals in learning and using improvement science while tackling problems of practice related to equity and disproportionality. Our approach engaged principals and their leadership teams in collaborative inquiry, and challenging longstanding assumptions often wrapped up in tradition and a system of confusion. This chapter shows the process and outcomes designed with group of six initial schools.

Consistently, school leaders and stakeholders reported expanded continuous improvement approaches that centered the experiences of students and community members.

CONTEXT

Student and Teacher Demographics

In fall 2019, 96% of students in the Bronx were Black, Indigenous, or Latino/a and 87% were classified as economically disadvantaged. Yet more than 60% of teachers were White. These contrasting statistics underscore the deep-rooted racial and economic divides that manifested in the Bronx schools and districts. Despite a myriad of programmatic shifts, initiatives, and readily available quantitative data, there remained pervasive racial disproportionality across multiple indicators. Black students were over twice as likely to be suspended as their non-Black peers. In addition, 23% of Black students and 24% of Latino/a students had an Individualized Education Plan (IEP), compared with 13% of White students and 7% of Asian students. Only 5% of Latino/a students and 7% of Black students were enrolled in advanced courses, compared with 19% of White students and 27% of Asian students.

Within this inequitable educational context were many schools with significantly underperforming specific student subgroups, as designated by New York State, in the areas of English Language Arts (ELA) and math. Many other schools were close to being designated as underperforming, based on marginal and variable achievement gains, and thus on the cusp of slipping into the state's lowest designated status.

Support Resources for Schools

For the lowest-performing schools in the Bronx there were a range of state-, city-, and district-based support and resources, as well as significant accountability and progress expectations. No similar funding or support existed for somewhat better-performing schools, even those at risk of dropping to the lowest-performing status. Almost all schools in these low performance categories also experienced persistent disproportionality based on race/ethnicity, Multilingual English Language Learner (ELL) status, or special education placement, compounding their performance problems.

The six Bronx schools were under the organizational umbrella of a Community School District (CSD), headed by a superintendent and district staff. Each CSD was under a Borough/Citywide Office (BCO), led by an executive superintendent, supported centrally from the citywide education chancellor's office. The Bronx BCO supported the districts in teaching and learning, procurement, student services, safety and transportation, and human resources. While support was helpful, it centered on crisis management and compliance. Additional support focused on low-performing schools or specialized services like those for gifted and talented students. When I was hired, the then–executive superintendent of the Bronx BCO had undertaken several steps to address the problems of disproportionality, as an outgrowth of her deep commitment to equity and her awareness of the impact on student achievement. Through her direction, Bronx BCO employees, district and school leaders, and teachers participated in a variety of equity-centered trainings and workshops, led by both internal staff and external experts. For example, BCO employees participated in an Equity in Action series, presented by colleagues. There was citywide implicit bias training for teachers and administrators, and external experiences such as the annual Courageous Conversations Summit. Advancing equity became central to all initiatives in the Bronx BCO, as reflected in borough goals and expectations for district leaders. District and school leaders were encouraged to expand equitable access and opportunity for all students throughout the borough. Yet none of this work helped leaders of lower-performing schools improve their schools' performance or address the effects of disproportionality on achievement.

Special Funding Opportunity

With an eye toward advancing student equity and opportunity, the First Deputy Chancellor's Office began to identify approaches to better support individual schools. One such initiative was the creation of Academic Response Teams (ARTs) (Bryant, 2020). Each borough was equipped with one or two ARTs responsible for providing rapid and intentional assistance to schools and districts that otherwise would not be supported. It was intended to close existing system gaps that led to academically underperforming schools. While the city's central administration outlined a desired approach, it granted wide flexibility in implementation, based on each BCO's needs.

Prior to my appointment, the Bronx executive superintendent recruited 10 educational administrators (EA) for the Bronx ART team. NYC's EAs are administrators who are not school leaders but instead support the system in other ways. Approximately half of the new ART teams in the Bronx consisted of veteran administrators who had either led schools or supported them in other ways for over a decade. The other half were new school administrators who had recently left the classroom.

I was hired as a Bronx assistant superintendent/ART director in September 2019. It was my task to design our team's approach and implement it rapidly. I quickly realized that supporting the designated schools would require a fundamentally different approach to school improvement and leader development, but that we needed to first identify our problem as it existed in the Bronx.

DISCOVERING THE PROBLEM

ARTs were designed to support those schools that were identified by the central office as underperforming, but not low enough to be eligible for low-performing school support. Each executive superintendent could leverage their ART support in the manner that was most contextually appropriate. In the Bronx, our executive superintendent had the foresight and deep system understanding to determine that the underlying problem that contributed to the gaps in student performance was rooted in a lack of leadership capacity to engage in continuous improvement practices.

Therefore, she asked me to design an ART process that would support underperforming schools through leadership development in continuous improvement. She also asked that, given the limited resources, the ART process be used to advance equity by addressing both disproportionality and low academic performance. Thus, the problem analysis became two-pronged—determining which schools met the ART criteria for support and had equity problems, and assessing in what ways leaders lacked the capacity for continuous improvement progress.

ANALYZING THE PROBLEM

To begin with, particularly as someone who was new to the Bronx schools, I had to learn about Bronx schools' performance and persistent racial disparities. Using an internal identification system, I examined data for approximately 45 schools identified as moderately at risk of being identified as needing support from New York State. These schools were persistently on the cusp of failing to meet state standards based on graduation rates or state assessment scores.

Inequitable Student Treatment

Using the ART initiative criteria, I identified several schools that were also struggling with persistent disproportionality. I used the Relative Risk Ratio (RRR), which measures the risk of over- or underrepresentation of a subgroup compared to others. In an equitable system, RRR equals 1.0. My analysis revealed that schools with elevated discipline and referrals to special education also exhibited persistent disproportionality in suspensions, special education identification, or advanced coursework. Using both criteria, I identified 23 of the initial 45 lower-performing schools as also having persistent disproportionality over the previous 3 years based on race, MLL/ELLs, or special education identification.

Problematic Leadership Processes

A perpetual lack of attention to the problem of disproportionality strongly suggested that school leaders did not or could not engage in continuous improvement. Next, I learned, after reaching out to principals and meeting with district superintendents and other district leaders, that school leaders often jumped from problem to problem. Their focus was on putting out proverbial fires and juggling competing and overwhelming compliance-driven demands and frequent day-to-day emergencies. Thus, it appeared that leaders did not know how to stay focused on a problem until resolution. They instead suffered from what improvement science calls "solutionitis," by applying solutions without sufficiently investigating problems and the systems that produce them.

Analyzing the System

In designing the Bronx approach for school support, I first wanted to understand the system in which I was working, particularly how system practices contributed to the problem. In my first month, through interviews (with school leaders, teachers and students), school-based observations, and data analysis, I identified four key challenges contributing to the problem of practice, as illustrated in the fishbone diagram (Figure 8.1) and as explained below:

- Lack of systemwide internal coherence: There was misalignment between central offices, the BCO, district offices, and schools in addressing even basic academic goals.
- Limited school leader capacity for continuous improvement: Principals reported feeling overburdened by competing demands and lacked skills to synthesize data, prioritize initiatives, and create actionable bridges from professional learning to practice.
- Culture of compliance: The system's longstanding hierarchical culture with praise for heroic individualism stifled innovation and risk-taking.
- Differential readiness to engage in equity work: While equity-focused professional development had increased, many leaders

Figure 8.1. Fishbone Diagram of Factors Contributing to Inequitable Student Outcomes

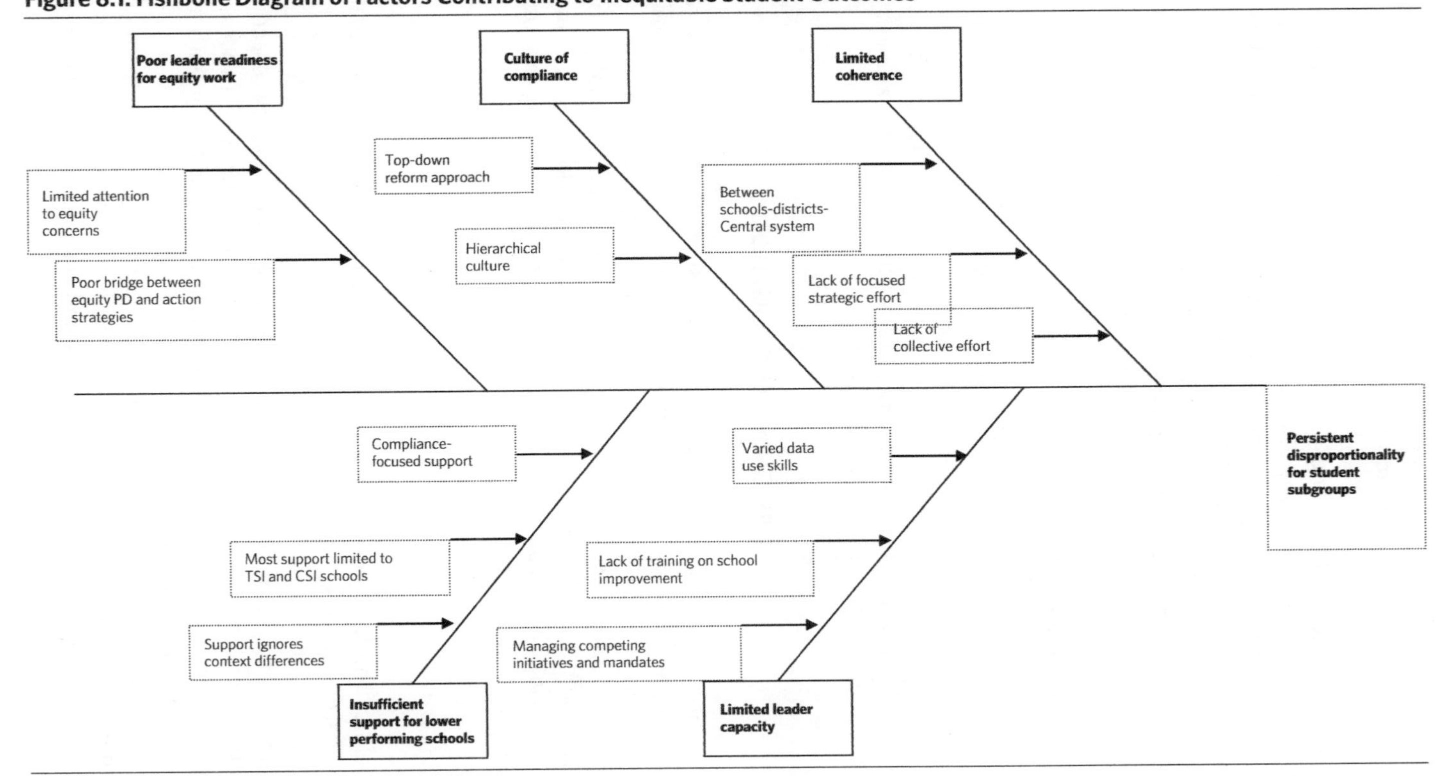

lacked foundational preparation in equity-based leadership and struggled to turn it into meaningful action plans.

After 2 weeks of meetings, my 10-member team and I identified the lack of school leadership capacity as the key leverage point for improvement. To increase equitable experiences for students, we proposed developing principals' ability to investigate problems, evaluate strategies, analyze data through an equity lens, and engage in adaptive problem-solving with their school communities. This approach prioritized the most effective and efficient solution for students and the system.

Determination of Eligible Schools

Following this analysis, I met with each community district superintendent to discuss whether they wanted ART support for their eligible schools, and to identify which ones. With their input, we whittled the 23 schools down to six, based on urgency, need, and willingness and readiness to receive support from a newly formed team.

DESIGNING THE SOLUTION

As the area of greatest leverage from our fishbone diagram was school leadership, we decided that our aim would be: "School leaders and staff regularly use an equity-based inquiry approach to improve student experiences." Given the six schools' varied learning and organizational problems, my team and I needed to create an approach for working with principals on improving their schools' performance and for how our team would be working together with them.

Change Drivers

To help us think through our approach, the team created a driver diagram to visualize our ideas and slow us down to prevent us from jumping to immediate solutions. Our primary driver became developing leader and staff capacity to engage in equity-focused inquiry. We identified two secondary drivers to activate this primary driver: implementing the ART process with school leaders and developing all support and implementation with an equity lens (as shown in Figure 8.2).

Implementing these drivers required the team to create three processes: the continuous improvement process that we would ask principals to engage in, our means of working with principals and their schools, and our means

Figure 8.2. Diagram of Drivers to Reduce Disproportionate Student Outcomes

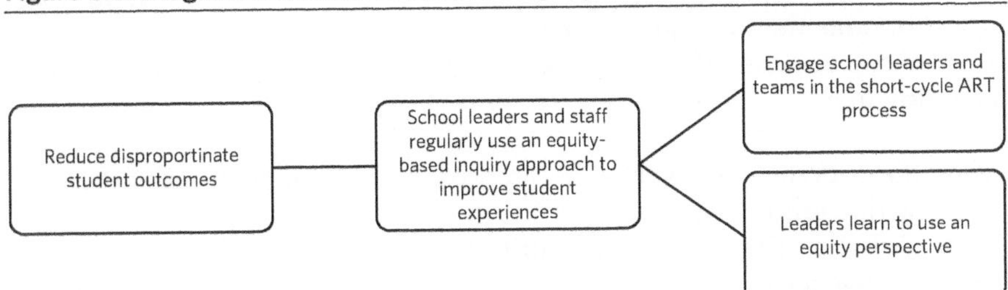

of working together as an ART team while working with principals and their schools.

A Continuous Improvement Model

As the team developed its strategy for operationalizing the drivers, we adapted a continuous improvement model first set forth in the Carnegie Foundation for the Advancement of Teaching's (CFAT) improvement science (IS) principles (Bryk et al., 2015). Improvement science provides a structured yet flexible approach to unpacking a persistent problem of practice and solving it through continuous improvement using iterative Plan-Do-Study-Act (PDSA) cycles. Importantly, it emphasizes starting by thoroughly understanding the system producing current outcomes before jumping to solutions.

For our proposed process, we wanted to build the capacity of school communities and building leaders to engage in equity-based inquiry to improve student experience. However, I knew that without strategic interruption, improvement science (IS) alone would be insufficient to address the deeply-rooted equity challenges (Irby, 2021). Without a critical approach, we had a high probability of merely layering solutions onto the same systems that caused the problems we were trying to address. To enact our theory of change, we needed an approach that would simultaneously center racial equity explicitly; build leader capacity for continuous improvement and self-reflection/system analysis from an equity lens; account for each school's unique context; and shift mindsets and behaviors, not just implement technical solutions.

To center our work on racial equity, we grounded our approach in critical race theory (CRT) and challenged dominant ideologies like meritocracy (Ladson-Billings & Tate, 1995). Crucially, we designed the process to be educative; we sought to build leader capacity to continue cycles of equity-focused improvement after our direct support ended. This IS–CRT hybrid became the foundation for our ART process.

Key components of our approach to working with principals included the following:

- Short cycles (4–8 weeks) of intensive focus on a problem of practice with a school team
- Collaborative inquiry to identify a problem of practice and test change ideas
- Emphasis on qualitative data and contextual understanding
- Root cause analysis of the system factors through tools like fishbone diagrams
- Creation of a driver diagram to map a theory of improvement
- Design and implementation of PDSA cycles to rapidly test and iterate on change ideas
- Sustainability planning for iterative improvement

The Academic Response Team (ART) Approach

As important as the technical aspects of our approach were, I recognized that our process of working with principals and how we showed up as a team would be equally critical to our success. We were asking principals to be vulnerable, take risks, and challenge longstanding assumptions and practices through an intensive collaborative process. We needed to model the collaborative inquiry, psychological safety, and willingness to learn that we hoped to cultivate in schools. I was highly intentional about forming our team culture from the start.

When I joined the district's central office staff in late August 2019, I devoted our first month to intensive team-building and norming our practice. We held 20 full-day meetings focused on crafting our collective "why" and vision, building relationships and trust; studying improvement science, critical race theory, and other foundational concepts; developing our specific model and protocols; and practicing difficult conversations about race and equity. I drew upon research and best practices around team effectiveness, emphasizing psychological safety to take risks and learn from failure, distributed leadership and flattened hierarchy, critical friendship and productive struggle, and celebration of learning over demonstration of expertise.

This intensive norming process diverged from typical district work culture. Skeptical colleagues urged stricter control, but I remained committed to fostering a collaborative, learning-oriented culture. Key elements included daily check-ins, "clearing" circles for emotional processing, weekly learning discussions on equity, appreciative inquiry, continuous improvement, consultancy protocols, shared leadership, and radical transparency about learning and struggles. This process built internal coherence, shared language, and relationships, enabling us to consistently show up as thought partners rather than compliance monitors or outside experts.

Support Process for the Schools

We also designed the steps of our support process with each principal that would be spread across 8 to 15 weeks, depending upon the schools' needs. We trained and assigned two-person teams to work with each school for this dedicated work, at times one-to-one with the principal and at other times, with a school team. These steps began with relationship-building and examination of the school's context and areas of low performance. It progressed to selection of a problem of practice and analysis of the system that produced it, followed by developing a theory of improvement and a PDSA plan for trying out new approaches to addressing the problem. These steps are described further below.

Step 1: Building Relationships and Understanding Context (2–3 Weeks)

We began with relationship-building and context understanding, by holding initial meetings with the principal and leadership team to establish rapport and alignment. We gathered and analyzed extensive quantitative and qualitative data, delving deep into school metrics and documentation. We conducted empathy interviews with students and staff and observed classes or other aspects of the school, seeking to understand the lived experiences of students, teachers, and staff. We analyzed each school's history and culture and its surrounding community, recognizing that current challenges were often rooted in longstanding systemic issues.

Step 2: Collaborative Inquiry to Identify Problem of Practice (1–2 Weeks)

Following our initial data gathering, we entered a critical phase of collaborative inquiry to identify a core problem of practice. This phase began with rigorous analysis and synthesis of quantitative and qualitative data to identify a particular problem of practice. We sought to paint a comprehensive picture of the school's challenges as they contributed to their persistent low academic outcomes and areas of disproportionality. Typically, the problem of practice was specifically based on its disproportionality (i.e., elevated discipline rates for Black students), or on continued academic underperformance (i.e., poor reading outcomes in the 2nd grade).

We then facilitated a collaborative root cause analysis using the fishbone diagram to enable school teams to explore and map out the factors contributing to their identified issue. This exercise was complemented by a force field analysis whereby we examined the driving and restraining forces influencing the problem, such as union resistance. This structured approach enabled school teams to move beyond surface-level symptoms and begin to grapple with the underlying systemic issues at play, setting the stage for more targeted and effective improvement efforts.

Step 3: Developing a Theory of Improvement (1–2 Weeks)

With a clear understanding of the problem of practice, its root causes, and the contributing system factors, each ART team worked with the principal and leadership team to develop a theory of improvement, often through several meetings. This step required crafting a concise and measurable aim statement, articulating the specific goal that they wanted to achieve, and creating a driver diagram, mapping out the primary and secondary drivers to achieve their aim. This process helped school teams identify potential leverage points for change and think systemically about their improvement efforts. Finally, through collaborative discussion, the ART team and school team identified a specific, high-leverage change idea to be tested. This change idea became the focus of their Plan-Do-Study-Act cycle, allowing the principals to map out how they would move from analysis to action in a targeted and strategic manner.

Step 4. Implementing the Plan-Do-Study-Act Cycle (3–6 Weeks)

The heart of the improvement process was the Plan-Do-Study-Act (PDSA) cycle, to be carried out over 3 to 6 weeks. Each school team picked a small intervention that could be piloted within their PDSA cycle. Each cycle began with developing a detailed plan for a change idea and its implementation of specific actions, responsibilities, and timelines. As their plans were operationalized, our teams provided ongoing support and monitoring to help school teams navigate challenges and collect relevant data. Once the implementation period concluded, we facilitated a thorough analysis of the results, examining quantitative metrics and qualitative feedback. This analysis became the basis for determining next steps, with teams deciding whether to adopt the change idea as is, adapt it based on learnings, or abandon it for a new approach. This cycle was designed to foster rapid learning and improvement while building the school leadership and team's capacity for ongoing cycles of inquiry and change.

Step 5: Planning for Sustainability (1–2 Weeks)

The last step in our plan was to dedicate time and resources for sustainability planning, ensuring that the improvement work would continue beyond our team's direct involvement. Our team crafted a comprehensive sustainability report for each school, documenting the process, key learnings, and recommendations for future work. Our team then collaborated with principals to plan for continued cycles of inquiry, helping them identify next steps and potential focus areas. We held follow-up check-ins at 4 and 8 weeks after the cycle ended to provide further guidance, troubleshoot challenges, celebrate progress, and gradually release responsibility to each school team. This sustainability focus was crucial in transforming our short-term intervention into a catalyst for long-term, continuous improvement within each school.

We captured our continuous improvement approach in a comprehensive *ART Guidebook* (https://sites.google.com/strongschools.nyc/bronxart/improvement-science-resources), as both a practical resource and an embodiment of our values and vision.

IMPLEMENTING THE CHANGE

We launched our first cycle of support with six schools across six CSDs in October 2019. This became our pilot for how we worked with schools and with one another, following our own overarching PDSA cycle, using our initial 8–15 week school improvement plan and process as our intervention (as outlined in Table 8.1).

Do Phase

We began working with six schools, each of which had elevated racial disproportionality in key indicators like suspensions, chronic absenteeism, or referrals to special education. Each cycle of support lasted from October 2019 to January 2020. We followed our initial implementation plan, assigning two-person teams to each of the six schools, which began with the initial steps to identify a problem of practice and the area of focus. The teams successfully identified them, as shown in Table 8.2, focusing on specific student subgroups (e.g., English Language :earners [ELLs], students with disabilities [SWD], and Black and Brown students), content areas (e.g., English language arts [ELA] and science), and teacher practice (e.g., discipline, instructional expectations, and culturally responsive practice). Using these problems, the ART teams narrowed the schools' focus on a specific dimension of inequality and turned these into aims, about which they designed specific change ideas and tested out through their PDSA cycle.

In the Do and Study phases in each school, we found that a strong focus on planning largely led to increased fidelity during implementation and progress monitoring. Five of the six schools were able to closely follow their initial plan during the Do phase, making only minor adjustments to prescribed dosages (e.g., shifting the number of times the afternoon huddle

Table 8.1. PDSA Cycle for the Academic Response Team's Approach and Process

Phase	Staffing	Process	Data
Plan	Assign two-person teams to work with six schools.	Plan out the five-step process. Select six pilot schools.	Identify data to be collected about the process.
Do	Work with two schools each, coordinated by the project director.	Follow the planned process using the *ART Guidebook*.	Gather data about the focal problem and the school's progress. Report, through weekly meetings, on implementation challenges and successes.
Study	ART team and director work collaboratively.	Study the data gathered to identify ways to improve support and the means of engaging principals and schools.	Base the analysis on the collected data.
Act	Make decisions by ART director and staff.	Propose revisions to the ART process that were identified and adopted.	

met in School B, or changing the number of questions in School C). The Do phase proved to be more challenging in School F, where the ART team had to move to the Act phase (abandoning our initial work) more quickly than initially anticipated. In this case, they went back to their fishbone and driver diagrams and developed greater buy-in from the school principal, to focus instead on creating a schoolwide data system.

Table 8.2 shows the schools' proposed change ideas, which often were strategies for teachers to work collaboratively (e.g., as a PLC, huddle, or NIC) on a narrow instructional strategy (e.g., applying vocabulary strategies for ELLs) or assessment (e.g., daily exit tickets, culturally responsive assessment) or to try out a new student support strategy grounded in shifting adult behavior. Working with the schools, the teams tracked progress toward the identified objective, finding that all six schools successfully adopted new practices as planned, with some showing immediate improvement in teacher practice and student performance. Through the follow-up

Table 8.2. Pilot Schools' Problems, Change Ideas, and Outcomes

School	Problem of Practice	Area of Focus Identified in Fishbone Diagram	Change Idea From Driver Diagram	Outcome (After 6–8 Weeks)	Sustainability
School A (Elementary School/ Middle School)	2.9% of ELL students are proficient on the NYS ELA assessment over the last 3 years	Instruction: specific to inequity in how language instruction occurs	Norm and implement language objectives in one classroom in each grade (n=5)	Each teacher creates a language objective in their classrooms	Adopt: Completed an additional PDSA on expanding the use of language objectives
School B (High School)	Elevated suspension rate for Black male students	Structures and procedures: specifically relating to hallway and cafeteria systems	Implementation of afternoon "huddle" with teachers, administrators, deans, and students to discuss daily situations and "vulnerable decision points"	21% drop in "serious" discipline for Black male students	Adapt: Made the afternoon huddle team permanent and created two PDSAs: teacher-led bias training and restorative practices
School C (Elementary School)	Limited questioning, reflecting low expectations for Black and Brown students	Instruction: specific to scaffolding of lesson	PDSA 1: Two mini-NICs formed in two grade levels to identify a bank of questions for shared lesson plans	Increased planned scaffolded questions by 200%	Adapt: Continued planned scaffolding questions, scaled cycle of inquiry approach, and shifted to common assessments

(*continued*)

Table 8.2. Pilot Schools' Problems, Change Ideas, and Outcomes (*continued*)

School	Problem of Practice	Area of Focus Identified in Fishbone Diagram	Change Idea From Driver Diagram	Outcome (After 6–8 Weeks)	Sustainability
School D (High School)	Teacher practice and assessment not reflective of a culturally responsive classroom	Leadership: specific to lack of building mission/vision coherence among the faculty	PDSA 1: Weekly professional learning conducted PDSA 2: Creation of culturally responsive common assessment for subject areas	Culturally responsive assessments created for each subject area by teacher team Student performance increased by 15% by second quarter.	Adopt: School created quarterly schoolwide Culturally Responsive sustaining education (CRSE) assessment fair for faculty professional learning Implemented schoolwide cycles of inquiry
School E (Middle School)	Inconsistency across the science department in implementing ENL strategies to foster language acquisition	Instruction: specific to science department as a lever for change, using Muhammad's Cultivating Genius Framework (2020)	PDSA 1: Agree on and apply vocabulary strategies to support transitioning ELL students grounded in identity	90% of students in science classes created culturally responsive visual representation of target vocabulary	Adapt: Implement continued inquiry cycles using IS process on Muhammad's framework through cycles of inquiry
School F (Middle School)	Students with disabilities consistently in danger of lower academic achievement	Instruction: specific to grade-level coherence	PDSA 1: Data dives conducted by teachers to complete inquiry cycles PDSA 2: Administer exit tickets to create grade-level coherence	Three self-contained classes implemented daily exit tickets	Abandon: Schoolwide student data tracking system

work, the ART teams helped the schools identify what they would adapt and sustain and what they would abandon.

Throughout the process, we maintained a dual focus on addressing the specific problem of practice and building leader and staff capacity for ongoing cycles of equity-focused improvement. When tensions arose between these goals, we generally prioritized capacity-building, viewing it as essential for sustainable change. This meant that we focused on the tool of improvement science and inquiry itself as opposed to our team navigating through individual problems of practice. Acknowledging that our support of each school was only designed to last at most 6 months, we decided that teaching each school leadership team to engage in this process and use their growing knowledge of equity-based initiatives to support their school in ways that addressed their unique challenges and opportunities was where our ultimate focus should be placed.

As a team, we maintained our commitment to this process of school support with a high level of fidelity, despite the newness of the process. In our weekly Friday team days, we shared points of struggle, weaknesses, victories, and questions. We used several protocols, including consultancies, team clearings (for morale-building), and data walks around our office. Our team meetings on Friday forced us to stay true to our stated process, make minor adjustments, and withstand pressure from both schools and central offices, who often wanted quick answers.

Study Phase

In January 2020, the team and I spent 2 weeks analyzing what we learned about our progress and our effectiveness in working with school leaders. We identified 4 key learnings that we used to adapt our practice in working with subsequent schools.

The Critical Importance of Context

Our first key finding was the importance of the school and community context to advance equity in the inquiry process. Each school's unique history, culture, and dynamics profoundly shaped how racial disproportionality manifested and what change strategies were viable. We learned that it was our job to create space for the expertise of the community and stakeholders to take center stage in navigating problem-solving and solution-testing.

For example, in School B, a high school with elevated suspension rates for Black male students, the contextual analysis revealed key factors, including recent leadership turnover, that created inconsistent discipline policies, lack of restorative practices training for staff, limited student voice in school decision-making, and heightened tensions around safety and discipline following a violent incident. This deep contextual understanding allowed the team to craft a change idea—implementing daily "huddles" with administrators, deans (primarily a discipline focused role in most NYC schools), and student leaders to proactively address potential conflicts—that addressed root causes in a way that fit the school's culture and readiness.

The Power of Collaborative Inquiry With Psychological Safety

Our second lesson was that adhering to the outlined collaborative inquiry process helped to maintain urgency in the inquiry cycle and provided psychological safety to advance equity. Across schools, we found that the structured yet flexible IS-CRT process created an exploratory environment for sometimes uncomfortable conversations about race, bias, and inequitable practices. The emphasis on understanding root causes of problems before identifying solutions helped depersonalize issues and focus on system factors to be changed or strengthened.

For instance, in School C, an elementary school where teachers' questioning practices reflected low expectations for Black and Brown students, the fishbone diagram process revealed the lack of culturally responsive curriculum and materials, limited teacher diversity, low assumptions about student capabilities, and an absence of protocols for higher-order questioning. This collaborative analysis created space for staff to name difficult truths about their practices without feeling attacked, building shared ownership of the problem and potential solutions.

Importantly, adhering to our collaborative process, even when it felt slow or uncomfortable, maintained momentum and urgency. Even at a deaccelerated pace, it prevented both paralysis in the face of complex challenges and the rush to implement ineffective quick fixes.

Willful Unlearning

We learned that our work required engaging leaders and their teams in willful unlearning and developing receptivity to new ways of thinking and intentional deconstruction of previously held beliefs to be able to engage in adaptive work (Tsang & Zahra, 2008). Across schools, we had to guide leaders to set aside ingrained habits and assumptions to fully engage in the improvement process. The new habits that we helped them learn were how to move from a stance of expertise to inquiry, challenge deficit narratives about students and families, recognize their biases and blind spots, embrace productive struggle, and learn from failure.

For example, the principal at School E initially resisted doing the root cause analysis. She felt that she already knew the problems and wanted to jump to solutions. However, by being held to the IS-CRT process, she learned how to uncover deeper issues—in this case, teacher beliefs about language acquisition and cultural responsiveness—and a much more impactful change idea. The principal herself acknowledged, "I had to unlearn my instinct to have all the answers. Once I embraced not knowing, it opened up so many new possibilities."

Centrality of Strategic Team Culture

Our fourth discovery concerned our own process, that our intentional approach to fostering our ART team culture was central to our ability to support schools effectively, especially to advance equity. The intensive norming we did as a team yielded significant benefits in our work with schools. Our culture-building work enabled us to model vulnerability and collaborative inquiry, demonstrating the very practices we were cultivating in school teams. We concluded that we became more able to navigate difficult conversations with skill and empathy, creating safe spaces for school leaders to engage in challenging equity work, and to maintain fidelity to our improvement process. Our team cohesion provided critical support for one another through challenges and setbacks, maintaining our resilience and effectiveness in the face of complex, demanding work, enabling us to be unified, adaptable, and empathetic as a team.

For instance, when the team supporting School F encountered resistance from the principal, the team members processed their frustrations in team meetings, receiving advice on navigating the relationship and finding creative ways to support teacher teams even without full principal buy-in. Our internal practices of distributing leadership, fostering critical friendship, and celebrating learning from failure directly informed how we showed up in schools.

Act Phase

Taken together, we concluded that our IS-CRT process was an effective approach for leadership and school development in continuous improvement and that our own team process was both effective in enabling us to do this work and beneficial for how we did the work.

Subsequently, the ART team and I expanded to serve additional schools, and in January 2020, we identified 12 schools in seven districts and began working with their principals. We used the same ART process and found similar initial results. Then in March, with the COVID outbreak, we shifted our work as all schools converted to virtual instruction. We continued with our approach to school support. By the end of that spring, we were actively engaged with the 12 schools, as well as three from the previous fall and two new other schools. Guided by our approach to critical continuous improvement, these schools navigated the difficulties of a global pandemic while maintaining a focus toward increasing equitable outcomes for their students.

RESULTS

Impact on the Problems

As shown in Table 8.2, several schools began to show early indicators of a positive impact on reducing racial disproportionality. School B achieved a 21% reduction in serious discipline incidents for Black male students, a significant step toward addressing disciplinary disparities. School D increased student achievement on culturally responsive assessments by 15%, suggesting improvements in equitable instructional practices. At School E, 90% of students created culturally sustaining visual representations of science vocabulary, indicating increased engagement and cultural relevance in science instruction.

Impact on Leaders

We observed significant shifts in leader mindsets and behaviors that were critical for continuous improvement, as reflected in survey and focus group data. In the first year of support, the six leaders generally described positive shifts in their ability not only to engage in continuous improvement, but also to do so in a way that sought equitable outcomes for their students. They reported gaining increased confidence in using data to advance equity and significantly greater comfort in having difficult conversations about race overall. As one principal reflected, "This process created room for us to have conversations we've needed to have for years. It wasn't always comfortable, but it felt necessary and productive in a way other PD never has."

Eventually, all six leaders demonstrated an enhanced ability to engage staff in collaborative inquiry, which represented a shift in school culture across the board. One leader took a bit longer, and did not fully buy into the continuous improvement process until we had to adjust to changes brought on by the COVID pandemic.

Impact on Schools

While the full impact of our work on the schools was difficult to ascertain, we saw promising improvements in continuous improvement capacity in the six schools. All the schools successfully completed at least one PDSA cycle, demonstrating their ability to engage in structured improvement processes.

Encouragingly, five of the six schools continued cycles of inquiry after our direct support ended, indicating a level of sustainability in the approach. Four schools took the initiative to expand their change idea to additional grade levels or departments, scaling up effective practices. In addition, three schools created internal improvement teams to sustain the work, institutionalizing the capacity for ongoing improvement.

While these results were preliminary, they suggest the potential of our approach to catalyze meaningful shifts in improvement practices and outcomes. The combination of structural changes, mindset shifts, and early impact indicators provides encouraging evidence for the efficacy of our equity-focused improvement science approach.

Impact on the Districts

Following the initial year of support, we scaled our support drastically to work with entire districts within the borough. Doing so required concurrent work with district leaders, who were responsible for evaluating the principals, to learn the improvement process as well. Given that the culture of hierarchy, compliance, and perfectionism was deeply ingrained in the system that we worked in, it was necessary to make the process educational for district leadership as well. As such, four district leaders requested that we expand our support to all schools in their community. By the 2020–2021 school year, we were serving over 100.

Impact on the ART Team

The ART team's pilot experience with six schools confirmed the validity of our approach by demonstrating the potential of combining improvement science tools with an explicit equity focus to support meaningful change in urban schools. We concluded that our approach allowed principals to engage more deeply with issues of racial inequity and disproportionality than did traditional compliance-focused support, by creating temporal space to work together, spending significant time in schools, and carving out dedicated room for improvement work amid competing demands. Our short cycles enabled us to address their urgency, while slowing down key processes.

Unfortunately, funding was subsequently discontinued, and with central district leadership changes, the ART team's work was disbanded.

LEADER REFLECTION

As a burgeoning leader like my colleagues, I learned several lessons forged in the proverbial fire. I entered the role of district leader with a profound sense of vulnerability and openness to learn and take risks.

Taking an Experimental Approach to Leading

While my approach to collaborative team design and school support, as described above, was rooted in research and literature, both information sources were new to me, as was how I chose to combine them. Incorporating a specific focus on equity throughout our focus and process was also experimental.

While, with time, I grew confident in my approach, I was initially less than steady-footed and was ready to be malleable as I learned and understood. In the first few months of my work in the Bronx, I simultaneously formed a new team and developed a work process, formed relationships with school and district leaders and a means of improving schools, and navigated a unique and cemented culture in the BCO. In some ways I was flying blind, with only what I had learned from my doctoral program at Fordham University, existing research, and my own experiences with what did not work to serve as guides in the process.

Engaging Strong Executive Support

I quickly learned that my work would have been exponentially more difficult and challenging on all fronts if I did not have the strong support of the Bronx executive superintendent. While her own management style was largely hands-off for my daily work, she strongly encouraged and protected how I explored and imagined what could be possible with the ART and pursuing equity. Her steadfast vision and affirmation provided me with the needed clearance and the confidence to continue to push and search for different paths toward shifting a system, particularly when encountering systemic and structural resistance at the district level and individual resistance from various leaders.

Creating Space for Challenging Equity Work

Perhaps most importantly, I learned to use my authority to work differently with schools. Most critical was being able to create a space for the expertise of each school community to bubble, or in some cases erupt, to the surface so that it could discover its actionable purpose.

I learned how to support schools and school leaders with an eye toward equity and respect for the knowledge and experiences that live in the context of each school community.

Ultimately, I learned the complex work of leading for equity in urban schools. While there are no quick fixes, intentional processes that center context, build capacity, and create space for transformation can catalyze meaningful change. By combining the disciplined inquiry of improvement science with the critical consciousness of CRT, I learned to support leaders in not just improving schools but reimagining them as sites of justice and liberation for all students.

QUESTIONS

1. How does the integration of critical race theory with improvement science create opportunities for addressing systemic inequities that might not be possible with either framework alone? Consider both the benefits and potential challenges of this hybrid approach.
2. This chapter emphasizes the importance of "willful unlearning" for school leaders. How might district and system leaders in your own context create conditions that support principals in this vulnerable process while maintaining accountability for improved outcomes?
3. This chapter describes multiple types of "space" for transformation—physical, temporal, psychological, intellectual, and cultural. Which of these spaces do you find most challenging to create in your context, and what specific strategies might help overcome those challenges?
4. How would the process outlined in the chapter look in your own district? Identify a problem of practice or area for growth in your district, begin to gather data (qualitative and quantitative), and complete your own fishbone diagram.

REFERENCES

Ahram, R., Fergus, E., & Noguera, P. (2011). Addressing racial/ethnic disproportionality in special education: Case studies of suburban school districts. *Teachers College Record, 113*(10), 2233–2266.

Bryant, D. (2020). *Context matters: Equitable school improvement is a work of ART* [Doctoral dissertation, Harvard University].

Bryk, A. S., Gomez, L. M., Grunow, A., & LeMahieu, P. G. (2015). *Learning to improve: How America's schools can get better at getting better.* Harvard Education Press.

Fergus, E. (2016). *Solving disproportionality and achieving equity: A leader's guide to using data to change hearts and minds.* Corwin Press.

Irby, D. J. (2021). *Stuck improving: Racial equity and school leadership.* Harvard Education Press.

Ladson-Billings, G., & Tate, W. F. (1995). Toward a critical race theory of education. *Teachers College Record, 97,* 47–68.

Muhammed, G. (2020). *Cultivating genius: An equity framework for culturally and historically responsive literacy.* Scholastic.

Tsang, E. W., & Zahra, S. A. (2008). Organizational unlearning. *Human Relations, 61*(10), 1435–1462.

CHAPTER 9

Leading Continuous Improvement

Cases and Findings

Margaret Terry Orr

The cases in this book provide in-depth portraits of eight leaders' ambitious efforts in using equity-focused improvement science practices to lead significant changes in schools. Focusing on key areas of curriculum, instruction, and student support, they transformed their practices using specific improvement strategies and developed their staff's capacity to engage in continuous improvement.

In reviewing the work of the eight leaders, it is evident that they simultaneously applied four leadership drivers for continuous improvement: (a) developing their own vision, mindset, and equity improvement disposition and practices; (b) engaging staff in learning to become more effective through risk-taking and reflective practice; (c) designing and implementing the technical aspects of their change efforts; and (d) fostering organizational structures and change processes to facilitate organizational change. Figure 9.1 shows these four leadership drivers as mutually reinforcing and continuously developing throughout the leaders' improvement efforts. How, and in what ways, the leaders enacted these is discussed below, highlighting both commonly used and unique strategies.

LEADER MINDSET

To begin, the leaders had to adopt their own improvement mindset, which encompassed a willingness to learn and change themselves and an improvement- and equity-based vision and dispositions.

A Willingness to Learn and Change

Equity-focused continuous improvement begins foremost with a leader's own mindset about organizational change. Using equity-focused improvement science practices, specifically, requires a different mindset from what

Figure 9.1. Leading Equity-Focused Improvement Science Efforts

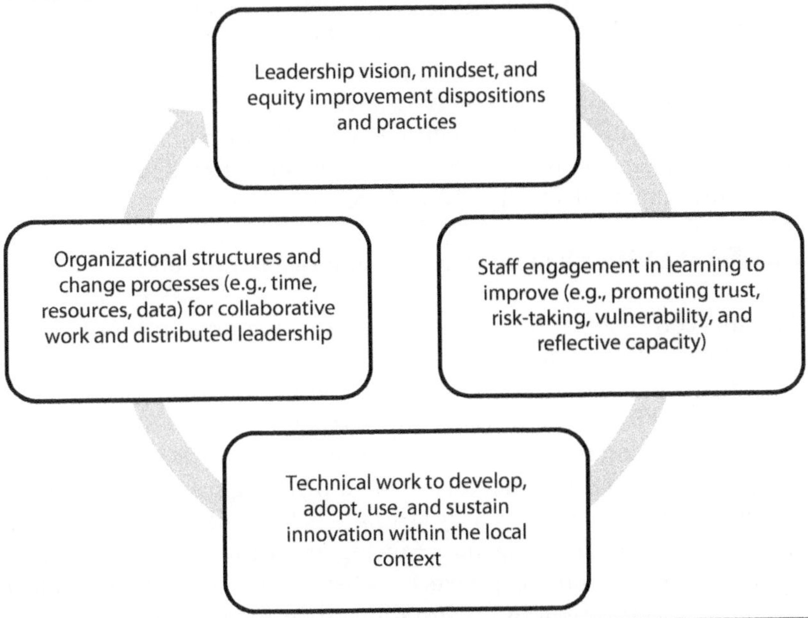

is typical for educational leaders. For example, in a study of six principals, Yurkofsky (2022) found that leaders' professional identities and beliefs about the usefulness of continuous improvement contributed to whether and how they used improvement practices or merely privileged compliance. Similarly, change theorists stress that successful organizational change requires an explicit shift in leadership mindset, particularly by adopting a learning orientation. Schein (2017) unpacks the dimensions of such a mindset, asserting that successful organizational change requires a leader's commitment to learning through problem-solving, a shared assumption that learning is worth investing in, the belief that others can and will learn, and the value of listening to and accepting help to build an organization's capacity to learn.

For many of these eight leaders, engaging in continuous improvement entailed such a mindset shift to lead change and to work with staff collaboratively. As several acknowledged in their reflections, leading an improvement science designed effort was new to them, challenging their prior assumptions about how to facilitate change. All, by virtue of their improvement approach, demonstrated a commitment to a learning and problem-solving orientation. Two leaders, Barnes and Fitzgerald, structured their inquiry work to learn about themselves, as they used this new approach to develop change solutions. Keogh admitted learning quickly that directing staff learning was ineffective; this realization caused him to shift to becoming more collaborative in working with staff. Joyner actively voiced her belief with her staff that they had the capacity to learn to work more effectively. Finally, DeFilippis purposefully experimented with a new change leadership approach, using his initiative to try out new research-based ideas about how to lead change more effectively and collaboratively.

Articulation of a Vision and Direction for Improvement Work

Having and communicating a vision is critical for organizational change. Kotter (1996) defines vision as "a picture of the future" and a rationale about "why people should strive to create that future" (p. 71). As he elaborated, a vision clarifies the direction for change, serves to motivate people to act, and aids alignment and coordination. All eight leaders established a vision and direction that they maintained throughout their improvement work. Their visions were driven by strongly held equity values and a commitment to increasing learning and reducing disparities among students' academic and social learning experiences. They made their visions explicit in the beginning and throughout, by sustaining their focus on problem-solving. Joyner captured her inclusive vision for school improvement in her use of travel metaphors, underscoring her belief that the staff could and would improve student learning together. Langley-Grey started her work with a staff exercise, using a protocol to guide them in developing a shared vision for their work.

Development of an Improver Disposition

Critical to the leadership orientation of the eight was having an improver disposition. By purposefully adopting an improvement science approach to problem-solving, the leaders committed to a specific way of thinking about and approaching problem-solving. This approach shares many of the attributes of adaptive leadership (Heifetz & Linsky, 2002) by maintaining a strong focus on a problem of practice, rather than a specific solution. Improvement science principles expand the meaning of this disposition by requiring a belief in the veracity of the process itself: that going slow (that is, spending time unpacking a problem, weighing possible solutions, and starting small to test them) would lead to better, sustainable solutions over time (Bryk et al., 2015). As is evident, all eight leaders committed to this process in launching their work. Their improver disposition proved to be essential in engaging others and pursuing solutions, regardless of the challenges, particularly COVID.

Assumption of the Lead Learner Role

Organizational change is about learning, and to be successful, a leader must adopt a learning orientation, becoming the lead learner throughout the change process (Schein, 2017). All eight leaders acted as the lead learner by modeling an inquiry orientation, compiling available quantitative data, sharing research literature, and listening to staff and students through empathy interviews. They made themselves and their learning explicit through their willingness to question existing systems and structures and the reasons why their focal problems existed or persisted, and by inviting others to do so as well. They modeled a learner stance by encouraging others to lead professional learning sessions, seeking staff feedback from meetings, discussing evidence openly with staff, and showing a willingness to adapt the solution and implementation process as needed. They stressed that their collaboration with staff was to learn, not evaluate. Finally, they made their risk-taking explicit by inviting their staff to try out a new approach and solutions and critiquing results with them. In her reflection, for example, Langley-Grey described how essential it was to model a learner stance herself in order to persuade staff to do so as well, thus risking trying out new practices.

Incorporation of an Equity Perspective

Engaging in continuous improvement in schools and districts is incomplete without concurrent attention to considerations of equity (Hinnant-Crawford et al., 2023). Improvement will fail without a deliberate focus on equity, because most root causes are tied to deficit thinking and structural inequities (Anderson et al., 2024). Attending to equity considerations entails explicitly looking for systemic inequities, questioning assumptions behind current practice to surface existing biases and race-based deficit perspectives, recognizing that disparities in student outcomes are attributable to inequities in the system itself, and committing to continual pursuit of the aim to adjust changes to improve current conditions (Hinnant-Crawford et al., 2023). Anderson et al. (2024) stress that the most critical points in incorporating an equity stance in continuous improvement work begin with creating and supporting a team throughout the process and incorporating equity and social justice in every stage of the improvement science process. Through reflective practice, leaders can ensure that their continual pursuit of this aim.

All eight leaders followed this guidance in purposefully attending to equity throughout the improvement process. They adopted an equity stance, beginning with their problem focus and its analysis, by questioning disparities in students' experiences. For some leaders, this focus began by examining why some students were making little to no academic progress (as in the cases of Barnes, Haas, and Langley-Grey) or felt a poor sense of belonging (as in Fitzgerald's case). Some pushed this examination by questioning the intersectionality of students' status and academic or social problems (such as Keogh's attention to the over identification of English Language Learners in special education and DeFilippis's focus on disproportionality in academically underperforming schools). Joyner focused on variations in outcomes by structuring a way for teachers to evaluate their instructional impact on high-, middle-, and low-performing students and thus increased instruction differentiation.

In some cases, developing an equity perspective and examining one's work was an essential part of the improvement work itself. Two leaders, Barnes and Langley-Grey, structured professional learning to enable staff to question their assumptions about current practice and surface existing biases and race-based deficit perspectives. They also exposed staff to culturally responsive instructional practice and materials, structuring opportunities for them to adapt their practice. In other cases, using an equity perspective was part of solution design. DeFilippis incorporated district-wide work on implicit bias and disproportionality to guide principals and their teams in evaluating disproportionality issues in their schools. Haas infused culturally relevant and contextually authentic math problems into the 7th- and 8th-grade math curricula as a core driver to promote student learning. Finally, for Barnes, the work entailed confronting her own assumptions, which in her case concerned the fragility of White women and their reaction to Black men.

ENGAGEMENT AND SUPPORT OF STAFF IN LEARNING TO IMPROVE THEIR PRACTICE

Organizational change begins with motivating others to change. Schein (2017) unpacks four processes that are essential to developing a motivation to change: providing disconfirming evidence that the organization or its processes are not accomplishing the goals; creating survival anxiety or the sense that an essential value is being compromised; mollifying learner anxiety; and creating psychological safety for risk-taking and learning. Mintrop (2016) stresses that engaging others in continuous improvement entails the psychological work of motivation, risk-taking, and courage for both leaders and their staff. Experts in improvement science recommend strengthening staff motivation and reducing anxiety by setting team norms and processes, promoting collaborative habits, and establishing collaborative routines (Anderson et al., 2023).

How these eight leaders motivated and engaged their staff throughout their improvement processes is detailed below, but they also took steps to attend to their psychological needs through several cross-cutting strategies.

They include fostering inclusion, addressing discomfort and unlearning, and promoting reflective practice and feedback.

Attention to Staff Psychological Needs and Fostering Inclusion

The eight leaders recognized the psychological demands that their continuous improvement work entailed and the need to begin early to develop staff's trust, demonstrate respect for their vulnerability and stress about the process, and promote risk-taking in trying out new strategies and solutions within the cyclical improvement process. Their primary means of developing trust and engagement was to be transparent about the goals, processes, and solutions being undertaken; and by seeking volunteers to participate in pilot efforts rather than requiring all staff to adopt new strategies first. They used collaborative processes through each phase of the work and promoted staff voice through direct participation in planning and enacting change and through feedback mechanisms.

Attention to Staff Discomfort and the Unlearning Process

The eight leaders were sensitive to emerging staff discomfort, particularly with the pace of change and competing issues, such as COVID, but without losing sight of their aims. Barnes, for example, lengthened the weeks for her staff's book study to enable deeper exploration of highly sensitive topics. Brown postponed whole-school inclusive culture work during faculty meetings while her staff grappled with COVID-related stress. Both Brown and Joyner helped their staff transition from old practices to new by using appreciative inquiry (Cooperrider & Whitney, 2005), reflecting on their core values and identifying their strengths and capacity to improve student learning.

Finally, some leaders deliberately structured support for critical unlearning by examining and reflecting on how existing practices and assumptions limited student learning. Without doing so, new learning would less likely take root and be sustained (Brook et al., 2016; Kim & Park, 2022). Supporting "unlearning" was key to DeFilippis's approach in working with school leaders to help them uncover how existing practices were leading to disproportionate effects on student experiences, such as student discipline. For other leaders, promoting unlearning was more subtle, embedded in helping staff learn how new practices yielded better outcomes than existing practices.

Promotion of Reflection and Provision of Feedback

To promote deep learning, the leaders structured opportunities for reflection and feedback (Mezirow, 1997). Several asked their staff to document their experiences as they tried out new practices. Fitzgerald had her staff write weekly reflections about their collaborative inquiry experiences, which she used to make adjustments to better support their work. Barnes scheduled time at the end of the improvement cycles to reflect with her leadership team about what worked, what was accomplished, and would-be future implications.

To help teachers and leaders learn to let go of old practices and try out new practices consistently, several leaders taught their staff, particularly in their pilot groups, how to give one another constructive feedback. Fitzgerald adopted a structured protocol for teacher pairs to give each other feedback and help them identify areas of success, potential growth, and opportunities for improvement. Barnes adopted a lesson study approach (Elliott, 2019), whereby teachers jointly designed a lesson and observed and critiqued one another using a jointly designed observation rubric.

THE TECHNICAL SIDE OF IMPROVEMENT

Much of the focus in organizational change theory centers on human relations and organizational dimensions. The technical aspects of a change or innovation are often underaddressed, yet they require developing strategies for the design, use, and sustainability of the change. A review of the eight leaders' work demonstrates their technical considerations in designing the interventions they adopted, the technical aspects of the improvement science process, and the technical structures and supports they created and used.

Design Work

Developing a solution for a problem of practice optimally entails design thinking (Brown, 2009). Design thinking encourages understanding a problem within its context, gaining insight from the user's perspective through empathy interviews with those most directly involved and the collection of other data, engagement in an ideation process, and, finally, creation of a solution design to test iteratively (Brown, 2009). The eight leaders followed many of these steps to develop testable solutions after first identifying their local problem and gathering qualitative and quantitative data to understand the user perspective.

Ideating solutions took many forms for the eight leaders, but they typically drew on four sources to inform them. First, they all examined the limitations or shortcomings of existing practice to determine gaps and opportunities for improvement. Second, they turned to research literature to identify how others tackled similar problems and gained ideas for their own designs. Third, some consulted with experts in their field, such as Brown's work with an Applied Behavioral Analyst consultant. Haas worked through a year with his school's 8th-grade teachers to refine their Integrate-Conceptualize-Adapt (ICA) instructional model, based on initial design features from his prior experiences. DeFilippis and Joyner worked with their leadership teams to design and refine a process for supporting multiple improvement science projects simultaneously (as their interventions) and then refined their processes further after an initial pilot. Barnes and Langley-Grey mapped out faculty learning experiences collaboratively with their leadership teams, similarly refining their experiences after the initial launch. Keogh worked with peer district leaders to map out a learning plan.

Consideration of Types of Innovations

The primary types of innovations or solutions that the leaders were testing were ultimately changes in teaching practices to improve student learning and engagement. The goal in all cases was to enable staff to develop instructional practices that would yield reliable results over time and be sustained as standard practice. As shown in Table 9.1, the eight leaders designed and tested a range of solutions, most for elementary or middle school students, half of which were in urban district settings. Three solutions were designed to modify and strengthen existing curriculum and instruction to better serve underperforming students in English Language Arts or math. Two used the improvement science process as the intervention in working with teachers or principals, who in turn designed their own solutions for problem-solving through short-cycle work to improve student learning and supports. Three leaders worked with their staff to adopt research-based solutions: morning meeting, a class for students with autism, and instructional supports for English as a New Language (ENL) students.

Adherence to Improvement Science Principles and Practices

The driver of the leaders' improvement work was the use of improvement science tools and procedures. All eight leaders carefully followed the six principles outlined by Bryk and colleagues (2015) to guide themselves and their staff. While following these six principles was a requirement of their dissertation in practice (Orr & Stosich, 2022), using them helped them to set direction, gain their staff's confidence in what they were undertaking collaboratively, and develop readiness for change.

As outlined in Bryk and colleagues' improvement science principles (2015), the leaders began by unpacking their problems and the contexts that shaped them. This step sharpened their understanding of the problem, challenged their own and others' assumptions, and, particularly for those who were new to their position, provided an opportunity to understand the system that contributed to the problem. Conducting empathy interviews with students or staff proved to be critical, and often novel for them, in

Table 9.1. Setting, Student Target, and Change Innovation for the Improvement Work of the Eight Leaders

Principal	Setting	School Level	Student Focus	Target Of Change	Change Innovation
Barnes	Urban	K–8 school	African American boys	All teachers, especially seven middle school literacy teachers	Incorporation of culturally responsive strategies into methods of teaching English Language Arts
Haas	Urban	Middle school	Grades 7 & 8, particularly underperforming students	Four 7th- and 8th-grade math teachers	Integrate-Conceptualize-Adapt (ICA) model
Fitzgerald	Suburban	Elementary school	K–5 students	Nine teachers	Morning meeting
Langley-Grey	Suburban	Elementary school	K–5 students	All teachers and staff, especially four K–1 teachers	Reading instruction infused with culturally responsive and trauma-informed practices
Brown	Suburban	Elementary school	Students with autism	Teachers and staff schoolwide, especially the new class teacher and staff and five special subject teachers	Class for students with autism
Keogh	Suburban	Elementary school	English Language Learners	Six teachers and two English as a New Language (ENL) specialists	Enhance Tier I instruction for ENLs, starting with vocabulary instruction
Joyner	Urban	Middle school	All students	All ELA and math teachers and two assistant principals	Improvement science in math and ELA
DeFilippis	Urban	K–12 schools	Targets differ among six schools	Six principals and their leadership teams from one borough	Improvement science practices to address disproportionality and academic problems

understanding their problems more deeply. Conversations with students, as Barnes, Fitzgerld, and Haas had, surfaced conditions about which these leaders had been unaware, and were useful to discuss with staff to frame solutions. In some cases, empathy interviews became a means of engaging staff in understanding a problem's complexity. For example, Langley-Grey had all staff interview one student each about their reading experiences and then used meeting time to guide analysis of what was learned.

Key to improvement science is slowing down the process to thoroughly investigate a problem and not jump quickly into solutions. The leaders used this key tenet to avoid under investigating their problems and to encourage their staff or leadership teams to spend time gathering and examining evidence, rather than making solution assumptions. Similarly, all the leaders created a fishbone diagram to unpack their problems' contributing factors and organize their system analysis. They often used their diagrams as a discussion device with staff to solicit input, communicate their understanding of the problem's context, and select a high-leverage area for intervention.

Similarly, they clarified and focused their improvement approach by proposing a theory of action and creating a driver diagram of proposed changes and means of achieving their aim. They all adopted the use of Plan-Do-Study-Act (PDSA) cycles to guide their work, adhering to the study and act phases, which are often overlooked in conventional change efforts. Most tracked two or more PDSA cycles for one intervention, making adjustments iteratively, or used PDSA cycles to track new strategies that their staff were trying and their own means of developing staff capacity. For example, Brown and Langley-Grey managed two or three different PDSA cycles, often concurrently, while Barnes and Fitzgerald tracked and reflected on the improvement process as their own explicit PDSA cycle. While all the leaders worked iteratively, making small improvements and adjustments as they went, several leaders—Brown, DeFilippis, Haas, and Joyner—built in time for lengthy study and act phases of their PDSA work, in order to review what they had learned, take stock, and relaunch. Finally, DeFilippis and Joyner's interventions were to have principals and staff, respectively, engage in short-cycle PDSAs, both to build their capacity for continuous improvement work and to test out changes in practice.

Available, User-Friendly Data

Improvement science work is highly dependent on having accessible and user-friendly data to investigate a problem of practice and track and monitor a solution. All eight leaders took steps to make existing data available to their staff in launching their improvement efforts—to call attention to a problem and provide staff with the opportunity to explore data further. Many of the leaders created tools and instruments to gather relevant data and support their staff's work: Barnes and Langley-Grey developed culturally responsive practice observation protocols for them and their staff to use in observing lessons. Brown worked with a consultant to develop a walkthrough observation tool for special area teachers and adopted New York State's Autism Program Quality Indicators to evaluate program quality. Haas tracked interim assessments and modified the state math assessment to measure year-to-year student gains during COVID, when state assessments were not administered.

Several leaders incorporated training in data use throughout their improvement process, designing data-sharing tools and instruments and showing how to collect and analyze student learning-related results using teacher made assessments. Langley-Grey trained her teachers on using Running Records consistently and analyzing the results to determine students' progress and differentiate learning experiences. Haas showed his staff how to compare student performance results between years and cohorts to evaluate their instructional practices and what students were learning. Both Keogh and Joyner took steps to help staff become comfortable with using data as aids in differentiating instructional practices, by creating worksheets for teachers to track the strategies they were trying and student responses.

Technical Structures and Supports

The primary technical challenge for continuous improvement is creating sufficient structures to support the work. For example, Tichnor-Wagner et al. (2017) found mixed reactions among design teams in two high school districts in using PDSA cycles to improve student outcomes. While valuing the cycles for continuous improvement, their respondents varied in their enthusiasm, capacity, and resources for using them, thereby impacting the results. Several staff members expressed frustration over the lack of supervisory support and paperwork demands, and they expressed opposition to measuring outcomes.

As will be explained in the next section, all eight leaders designed structures and processes to support the work, particularly to aid teachers' collaborative work and learning. On the technical side within these structures, the leaders routinized how they worked with staff by establishing norms, setting schedules, maintaining agendas and minutes, and designing data-sharing protocols and resources and reporting protocols.

Strategic Use of Time and Resources

Of all the resources that were critical to their improvement work, time was the most important—particularly the dedication of existing meeting times (grade-level team meetings and faculty meetings) and freeing up teachers and other staff to meet regularly. The eight leaders actively protected dedicated time for staff to engage in improvement work and spent considerable time planning how to use meeting times well. If they formed a team of teachers or staff to try out the improvement work and collaborate on implementation, as three leaders did, they provided instructional release time and protected these meeting times from competing demands (such as covering other classes).

Time was not the only resource that the leaders used for their improvement work. Some purchased books or provided articles for all staff to frame discussions about the problem or solution, particularly around culturally responsive practice. Some engaged consultants or district experts to help with the design work (Brown for an autism class, Keough for ELL instruction, and Joyner for improvement science practices). Such resources had both instrumental and symbolic value, reinforcing the importance of the work, providing a knowledge context, and underscoring the value of the staff as well as the ideas and strategies being used.

ENABLING AND SUPPORTIVE CHANGE SYSTEMS AND PROCESSES

Critical to continuous improvement is attending to the "how" of change by selecting secondary drivers that would activate the primary drivers in achieving the aim (Bryk et al., 2015). Together, both driver sets serve as a working theory of improvement that can be testable through the PDSA process. While the primary drivers (in this case the innovations being tried out) represent the "elements of the system that must change to accomplish the outcome" (Bennett & Provost, 2015, p. 40), the secondary drivers are the processes that create the change. They are the enabling and supportive systems and change processes that must be used or enacted for the intended improvement to occur.

Despite theory and research on effective change leadership and organizational practices, leaders typically employ hierarchical rather than inclusive approaches to working with others (Stosich, 2017). Similarly, in their research on the challenges to change in higher education institutions, Muluneh and Gedifew (2018) found that the most cited organizational change challenges were "poor communication strategies, problems related to facilitating changes and lack of followers' involvement in decisions" (p. 1261). As Mintrop (2018) explains further, educational leaders typically "use directive and control as their 'motivation' strategy and fill colleagues or subordinates with interminable professional development as a 'learning' strategy" (p. 116).

Experts in organizational change stress that actual change is about learning, and the leader's role is selecting an appropriate learning mechanism (Schein, 2017). Organizational change can fall short if a change mechanism is inappropriate or insufficient and does not foster both professional learning and internalization of new norms and practices. Without attention to the latter, staff may only superficially adopt a new change or revert to old behavior after attention to the change subsides. Schein outlines two basic mechanisms "by which we learn new behavior, beliefs, and values" (p. 330): use of role models with which we identify, and trial-and-error learning that tracks what works. Such approaches are critical because change is rarely just a technical adjustment; instead, it often requires a related shift in assumptions and beliefs about how things are done. Merely learning to imitate a new practice will not be sustainable without a related shift in underlying beliefs and assumptions.

For the eight leaders, enabling and supporting change processes consisted of shifts in their leadership approach, means of surfacing others' assumptions, developmental professional learning, adoption of trial-and-error learning, and redesigned means of how faculty collaborate for continuous improvement. Threaded throughout their change processes was a desire to shift organizational culture and capacity into continued data-informed learning and growth. The leaders' theory of improvement simply was this: If leaders and staff worked collaboratively on problem-solving and solution-testing for one problem, they would gain the skills, capacity and dispositions for both present and future problems.

A Change Leadership Approach

The eight leaders in this book recognized that their improvement work would require specific and often new leadership practices and approaches. First and foremost, they actively engaged important tenets of organizational change (Kotter, 1996; Schein, 2017), which emphasized the leader's role in clarifying the need for change and staff's contribution to the current problem state. To that end, they purposefully adopted key structures and processes to facilitate continuous improvement through equity-focused improvement science. They set agendas and direction for improvement, shifted to a collaborative approach, and distributed leadership by sharing responsibility with others.

They also adopted an adaptive approach to solving persistent problems of practice. Implicit in leading continuous improvement is adaptive leadership. Such leadership involves developing and maintaining a sustained focus on a problem, taking a developmental, inclusive approach to engaging others in sticking with the problem, structuring improvement work, and trying out solutions to fit local contexts—all while building a culture of trust and reflective practice (Bryk et al., 2015; Heifetz & Linsky, 2002; Mehta et al., 2022). At the heart of such an adaptive approach is the ability to be flexible, sometimes consciously so. Barnes, for example, reflected on how she had to learn to become flexible and enable others to take the lead, and what she learned from this experience.

The Surfacing of Assumptions

In all eight cases, as part of their improvement process, the leaders explicitly helped others surface and address underlying beliefs and assumptions that were contributing to the problems of practice and existing solutions. Barnes, for example, rather than providing supplemental literacy instruction for low-performing Black boys, focused instead on engaging teachers in learning about their implicit bias and adopting culturally responsive instructional practices for them. Keogh and Langley-Grey challenged assumptions about which students and which instructional content were teachers' responsibilities. DeFilippis and his team helped principals and their leadership teams adopt an equity perspective to tackle disproportionality-related problems in their schools. All eight leaders challenged the strongly held beliefs that adjusting instructional practices would not yield better student outcomes by using short-cycle PDSA cycles to test new practices and compare results over time for outcome differences.

Developmental Learning

To activate the primary drivers for improvement and achieve their aim, while simultaneously developing their staff capacity to continuously improve, the eight leaders looked for ways to support their staff's professional learning about the practices and assumptions that their new innovations required. Kegan et al. (2014) advocate that leaders adopt "deliberately developmental" approaches for their organizational improvement efforts. The authors stress that such processes focus on the change process itself, not just on outcomes; incorporate psychological safety; take steps to see the ways that staff and leaders are stuck; and provide regular opportunities to move past limiting patterns of thinking and acting (Kegan et al., 2014). To do this, the eight leaders were faced with choices about how to engage their staff in learning in ways that fostered growth and development of each individual staff member, whose needs and orientation to learn and change may differ.

Darling-Hammond et al. (2017), in their review of relevant research, identified seven features that are most typically present in highly effective professional development. These features are that professional development "is content focused, incorporates active learning utilizing adult learning theory, supports collaboration, typically in job-embedded contexts, uses models and modeling of effective practice, provides coaching and expert support, offers opportunities for feedback and reflection, is of sustained duration" (p. 2). Similarly, Kegan et al. (2014) advocated that leaders adopt development processes that include gaining an understanding of the problem and reasons change is needed; and focusing on the change process itself, not just on outcomes. This includes incorporating psychological safety, taking steps to see the ways staff and leaders are stuck, and providing regular opportunities to move past limiting patterns of thinking and acting (Kegan et al., 2014). Effective adult learning principles (Drago-Severson et al., 2013), stress that adult learning also be reflective, job-embedded, and differentiated. The eight leaders recognized that their proposed changes and innovative practices required structuring learning that would have these developmental attributes by using structured professional learning and modeling practice for observation and critique.

Structured Professional Learning

The leaders often reorganized faculty or grade-level time for professional learning. Langley-Grey provided yearlong professional learning for all staff on culturally responsive practice and trauma-informed care as a portion of each monthly faculty meeting. Brown planned a series of professional learning on inclusion for her faculty meetings to support implementation of a class for students with autism. Barnes used the school's dedicated professional learning time to engage all staff in a 10-week book study on culturally responsive practices.

Modeling

The eight leaders used various forms of modeling for learning and reinforcing change: modeling new practices themselves and developing the staff's capacity to model for one another. They recognized the importance of using role models within their schools to engage other staff both in their approach to change and to the change itself. Several leaders modeled innovation-related practices with their staff. By co-teaching throughout the year, Haas modeled the efficacy of their new instruction approach. Barnes and Langley-Grey modeled culturally responsive practices within faculty meetings.

Not all modeling concerned best practices. Instead, in several cases, teachers demonstrated or shared newly learned practices with one another for critique and feedback. Barnes and Langley-Grey had their pilot groups of teachers design a model lesson for one to teach and others to observe and critique. Fitzgerald had teachers work in pairs to teach and support each other on strategies in using morning meeting practices.

Trial-and-Error Learning

Improvement science principles, by design, lean into trial-and-error learning as a powerful means for organizational change. These principles rely upon explicit, evidence-based testing of targeted solutions and evidence-based evaluation to track what works and under what conditions over several iterations to adjust the solutions until they yield reliable results

(Bryk et al., 2015). All eight leaders used the PDSA cycles of improvement explicitly, collecting evidence along the way about implementation experiences and challenges, adapting their change innovations and approaches as needed, and tracking how well they were making progress toward their ultimate aim.

They all engaged their staff in this trial-and-error learning for their innovations by using the PDSA cycle steps explicitly, sharing and discussing the results as they proceeded, and involving staff in determining adaptation as needed. A few engaged their staff explicitly in trial-and-error learning about various dimensions of the improvement process itself, taking time to evaluate evidence about how well the process worked and how it could be improved. Often, this led to discussions about how the process should become a standard work process for how staff learn together and tackle other curricular and instructional priorities.

A key part of trial-and-error learning is adopting standards of evaluation that are aligned with the new values and expectations (Schein, 2017). Several leaders adopted or created new observation rubrics to explicitly measure the new expectations, often with their pilot group staff or leadership teams, as part of making the proposed changes clear and identifiable. Brown and her staff adopted the New York State's Autism Program Quality Indicators to evaluate program quality.

Collaborative Inquiry Processes

A commonly used secondary driver to foster organizational learning and change is organizing improvement work within professional learning communities or communities of practice (DuFour & DuFour, 2012; Wenger, 1998). These approaches are rooted in participatory action research (Kemmis et al., 2019) as innovative ways to improve practice through participation and democracy in the inquiry process (Bray et al., 2000).

Essential to change leadership is a commitment to collaboration with staff and others, sharing responsibilities and distributing leadership. The aim of such collaboration is to engage educators as learners in all phases of the change process: to understand the nature and severity of the need to change, to create new practices as part of the change, and to reinforce new practices to support continuation (Schein, 2017).

All eight leaders adopted collaborative processes to facilitate their inquiry and improvement work. They wanted to support their staff in learning to work together to use data to improve practice, and they relied on collaborative inquiry processes to provide structure for the process. They also saw collaboration as a way to improve the way their staff worked with one another to increase student learning; and they shifted them to become more active inquirers about how their practice could improve student experiences—in ways that might be sustainable over time.

As shown in Table 9.2, the leaders adopted one or more collaborative learning processes: collaborating with a leadership team, redesigning their grade-level teams (GLTs) as professional learning communities, and forming pilot teams as communities of practice. Many leaders developed their leadership teams into communities of practice, working collaboratively as they deliberated about the problem, solution approach and means of engaging staff. They also reflected with the teams about what they learned and how to strengthen improvement.

Four leaders shifted their GLTs to work collaboratively as professional learning communities by training them to study their practice together often within PDSA inquiry cycles. Their aim was to shift the teams' focus from information-sharing to problem-solving and professional learning, starting with their work on the problem of practice.

Most leaders started small by piloting both a new way of working on practice and the innovations they were testing. Thus, they began their most intensive work with a small group of volunteers who worked as a community of practice. Within these groups, the leaders typically took a participant stance to further democratize the process and foster trust and risk- taking, often throughout the school year. They capitalized on the volunteers' readiness to learn and improve and generating motivation and interest among other staff as they learned about the pilot group's improvement experiences.

Promotion of Coherent Change

To create systemwide coherence in their change work, the leaders took steps to layer their change efforts, with attention to both the pilot work and organization learning. Three leaders used multiple meeting forums to create

Table 9.2. Collaborative Inquiry Processes

Leader	Collaboration with a Leadership Team or Facilitators	Redesigned GLT Meetings	Support for a Pilot Group for Intensive Practice
Barnes	X		X
Haas		X	X
Fitzgerald			X
Langley-Grey	X	X	X
Brown	X	X	
Keogh			X
Joyner	X	X	
DeFilippis	X		X

coherence around the professional learning and improvement work underway. Langley-Grey simultaneously worked with a pilot group of teachers, her grade-level teams, and monthly faculty meetings to pursue the work to improve reading instruction for their students, with attention to culturally responsive and trauma-informed practice. Barnes and Brown layered the improvement work sequentially; Barnes started with schoolwide learning about culturally responsive practice before engaging a group of 7th-grade ELA teachers in trying out the new practices as an inquiry group. Brown first created a viable class for students with autism and then advanced to working with special area teachers to support the new students, then working outward to transform the school as a whole.

Reinforcement of the Change

Any new change is vulnerable to decay without "refreezing" to stabilize new beliefs and practices and reinforce them with actual results (Schein, 2017). Most of the eight leaders engaged in their improvement processes continuously throughout the school year, reinforcing what was being learned with ongoing formative and eventual summative results. Several were able to persist and scale up their change processes to other grades or schools, which had a further reinforcing effect. The new processes became normalized as: "the way we do things around here." Haas's approach coupled scaling up from the 8th grade to the 7th grade, while reducing support for the 8th-grade teachers to reinforce new practices. Keogh and Langley-Grey were approached by staff with requests to expand the improvement approach into other problem areas. Others, however, were not able to scale up or help sustain new practices because of leadership change or their own job change. Even then, as Joyner learned after leaving her principalship, some staff tried to sustain the new learning by reaching out to her for support and guidance from afar.

ACHIEVEMENT OF THE AIM

Throughout their improvement work, the eight leaders whose change work is reported in this volume strove to improve student learning and engagement through a variety of innovations. All refocused the way that they and their staff worked together in problem-solving and solution- testing. The final results of their joint efforts were quite positive, yielding improved instructional practices and student supports, including a new program for students with autism. Even more important were the changes they fostered in their schools and districts, collaboratively creating data-informed cultures in which staff and leaders supported one another to try new practices and improve existing practices.

At its core, continuous improvement requires changing organizational culture, shifting to an organizational learning stance and an improvement mindset, creating a stable and supportive learning culture for safe risk-taking and experimentation, and embracing an adaptive orientation and learning loop (Anderson et al., 2023). These organizational culture shifts were the most significant accomplishments of the eight leaders.

REFERENCES

Anderson, E., Cunningham, K. M. W., & Eddy-Spicer, D. H. (2024). *Leading continuous improvement in schools.* Routledge.

Anderson, E., Cunningham, K. M. W., & Richardson, J. W. (2023). Sustaining continuous school improvement: A framework for transformative organizations. In E. Anderson & S. D. Hayes (Eds.), *Continuous improvement* (pp. 145–167). Information Age Publishing.

Bennett, B., & Provost, L. (2015). What's YOUR theory. *Quality Progress, 48*(7), 36–43.

Bray, J., Lee, J., Smith, L., & Yorks, L. (2000). *Collaborative inquiry in practice.* Sage.

Brook, C., Pedler, M., Abbott, C., & Burgoyne, J. (2016). On stopping doing those things that are not getting us to where we want to be: Unlearning, wicked problems and critical action learning. *Human Relations, 69*(2), 369–389. https://doi.org/10.1177/0018726715586243

Brown, T. (2009). *Change by design.* HarperCollins.

Bryk, A. S., Gomez, L., Grunow, A., & LeMahieu, P. (2015). *Learning to improve: How America's schools can get better at getting better.* Harvard Education Press.

Cooperrider, D., & Whitney, D. (2005). *Appreciative inquiry: A positive revolution in change.* Berrett-Koehler Publishers.

Darling-Hammond, L., Hyler, M. E., & Gardner, M. (2017). *Effective teacher professional development.* Learning Policy Institute.

Drago-Severson, E., Blum-Destefano, J., & Asghar, A. (2013). Learning and leading for growth: Preparing leaders to support adult development in our schools. *Journal of school leadership, 23*(6), 932–968.

DuFour, R., & DuFour, R. B. (2012). *Essentials for principals: The school leader's guide to professional learning communities at work.* Solution Tree Press.

Elliott, J. (2019). What is lesson study? *European Journal of Education, 54*(2), 175–188. https://doi.org/10.1111/ejed.12339

Heifetz, R., & Linsky, M. (2002). *Leadership on the line: Staying alive through the dangers of leading.* Harvard Business School Press.

Hinnant-Crawford, B., Lett, E. L., & Cromatie, S. (2023). ImproveCrit: Using critical race theory to guide continuous improvement. In E. Anderson & S. D. Hayes (Eds.), *Continuous improvement: A leadership process for school improvement* (pp. 105–124). Information Age Publishing.

Kegan, R., Lahey, L., Fleming, A., & Miller, A. (2014). Making business personal. *Harvard Business Review.* https://hbr.org/2014/04/making-business-personal

Kim, E. J., & Park, S. (2022). Unlearning in the workplace: Antecedents and outcomes. *Human Resource Development Quarterly, 33*(3), 273–296. https://doi.org/10.1002/hrdq.21457

Kemmis, S., McTaggart, R., & Nixon, R. (2019). Critical participatory action research. In O. Zuber-Skerritt & L. Wood (Eds.), *Action learning and action research: Genres and approaches*, (pp. 179–192). Emerald Publishing Limited. https://doi.org/10.1108/978-1-78769-537-520191016

Kotter, J. P. (1996). *Leading change*. Harvard Business School Press.

Mehta, J. D., Yurkofsky, M., & Frumin, K. (2022). Linking continuous improvement and adaptive leadership. *Educational Leadership, 79*(6), 36–41.

Mezirow, J. (1997). Transformative learning: Theory to practice. *New Directions for Adult and Continuing Education, 1997*(74), 5–12.

Mintrop, R. (2016). *Design-based improvement: A practical guide for educational leaders*. Harvard Education Press.

Muluneh, G. S., & Gedifew, M. T. (2018). Leading changes through adaptive design. *Journal of Organizational Change Management, 31*(6), 1249–1270. https://doi.org/10.1108/JOCM-10-2017-0379

Orr, M. T., & Stosich, E. L. (2022). Designing the EdD for transformative change. In E. Anderson & S. Hayes (Eds.), *Continuous improvement: A leadership process for school improvement* (pp. 429–450). Information Age Publishing.

Schein, E. H. (2017). *Organizational culture and leadership*. Wiley.

Stosich, E. L. (2017). Leading in a time of ambitious reform: Principals in high-poverty urban elementary schools frame the challenge of the Common Core State Standards. *Elementary School Journal, 117*(4), 539–565. https://doi.org/10.1086/691585

Tichnor-Wagner, A., Wachen, J., Cannata, M., & Cohen-Vogel, L. (2017). Continuous improvement in the public school context: Understanding how educators respond to plan-do-study-act cycles. *Journal for Educational Change, 18*, 465–494. https://doi.org/https://doi.org/DOI 10.1007/s10833-017-9301-4

Wenger, E. (1998). *Communities of practice: Learning, meaning and identity*. Cambridge University Press.

Yurkofsky, M. (2022). From compliance to improvement: How school leaders make sense of institutional and technical demands when implementing a continuous improvement process. *Educational Administration Quarterly, 58*(2), 300–346. https://doi.org/10.1177/0013161X211053597

Index

The letter *f* or *t* after a page number refers to a figure or table, respectively.

About the Editor and Contributors

Margaret Terry Orr is a professor at Fordham University and EdD program director and chair of its Division of Educational Leadership, Administration and Policy. For over 40 years, she has researched and published numerous books and articles on leadership preparation approaches, the influence of preparation on leader practice, and a variety of innovative school and district reform initiatives. She received the Edwin M. Bridges Award for Significant Contributions to the Preparation and Development of School Leaders (University Council for Educational Adminstration, 2015) and the David G. Imig Distinguished Service Award (Carnegie Project on Education Doctorate, 2024). Her current research focuses on rigorous performance assessment research and development in educational leadership, nationally and internationally. She is committed to inquiry-oriented educational leadership and using equity-focused improvement science to more effectively address intractable problems in schools and other organizations. She currently lives in Westchester County, NY, and enjoys spending time with her four sons on Fire Island.

Rosalyn S. Barnes is a spiritual leader and scholarly practitioner. She is passionate about developing and empowering others to show up in authenticity. She is gifted in teaching, mentoring, transforming organizations, and developing leaders. She served as a dedicated principal for 12 years. Her mentorships include ministers, principals, entrepreneurs, and doctoral candidates. In 2021, she was nationally recognized by the Carnegie Project on Education Doctorate and was awarded the dissertation of the year for her equity-focused study on Black boys and literacy. After retiring from public education, she founded Faith and Resilience, LLC, a company dedicated to building foundations and reviving faith-based, K–12 schools and community-based organizations. As a professional development provider, author, and content creator, she continues to transform the lives of individuals and organizations. Dr. Barnes will often say, "This is the greatest work I'll ever do, inspire greatness and make an impact in the lives of others."

Tashia Brown is a lifelong educator with 26 years of experience in the public sector. After teaching for 7 years at the elementary level, she had a strong passion and desire to make a difference for all students on a larger scale, in particular students who have been historically marginalized. Dr. Brown pursued educational leadership, serving as an assistant principal for 4 years before serving as an elementary school principal for 16 years, which is her current role. As a school leader, Dr. Brown remains steadfast in cultivating school communities where all children have equal access to an excellent education, one that empowers them to fulfill their potential and live out their hopes and dreams.

Kris DeFilippis is an educator, researcher, author, and activist whose work centers critical inquiry to advance equity and antiracism, shift organizational culture, and focus on contextual strategic planning. Currently, Kris serves as clinical faculty and program director for Educational Leadership at New York University's Steinhardt School of Culture, Education, and Human Development. Previously, as an executive director/assistant superintendent in the New York City Department of Education, Dr. DeFilippis coached district and school leadership and faculty to apply critical and context-specific improvement science to reduce disproportionality, complete root cause analyses, strategically explore goals, and align multitiered systems of support to district goals and STEM implementation. In addition to district leadership, he has served public education systems in varying contexts in roles including custodian, teacher's aide, coach, teacher, department chairperson, and building administrator.

Trisha Fitzgerald earned her doctoral degree in educational leadership, administration, and policy from Fordham University in 2021. With a career spanning 29 years in education, she has served in various roles, including classroom teacher, elementary principal, and currently as executive director for human resources and leadership, Pelham Union Free School District. Dr. Fitzgerald is also an adjunct professor at Fordham University, where she has taught at the doctoral level, teaching courses focused on leading a learning organization and leading instructional improvement. Dr. Fitzgerald's research interests center on social-emotional learning, particularly the sense of belonging, and adult learning, reflecting her commitment to fostering inclusive and supportive environments for students and educators alike. Her work bridges theory and practice, emphasizing the importance of cultivating strong relationships and continuous learning within educational communities.

Josef Haas is a former middle school vice principal and math teacher with a deep commitment to education and leadership. During his tenure as vice principal, he earned his doctorate in education from Fordham University, focusing on teacher coaching and organizational improvement. As a teacher, Dr. Haas was known for his ability to simplify mathematical concepts, engaging students and fostering a love for learning. In his leadership role, he worked to enhance curriculum development, support teachers, and build a positive school culture. Although he is no longer working in education, his career was marked by a dedication to student success, educational equity, and professional development. Dr. Haas is passionate about leveraging data and technology to improve learning environments and is now applying his skills and knowledge to new ventures outside the classroom, where he continues to advocate for lifelong learning and personal growth.

Gail Joyner is a 35-year educator who has worked diligently throughout her career to "challenge the status quo." After 13 years as an English teacher (grades 7–12), she became an assistant principal for 2 years. For the last 20 years she has served as a principal in two high schools and a Pre-K–8 school and is currently serving as an assistant superintendent. In her capacity as a building and district leader, she utilized Plan-Do-Study-Act cycles as a vehicle for continuous improvement. She supported teams in the development of consistent processes and practices around data. This approach provided targeted tiered systems of support to students. Her transformational leadership has allowed her to impact student achievement outcomes while empowering students and staff to meet and exceed the standard. She remains committed to coaching and supporting teachers and administrators through engaging in high-quality professional learning.

Christopher Keogh is a curriculum leader and educator in New York, with expertise spanning educational technology, school building, and district leadership. He has spearheaded initiatives to align instructional programs with state standards and district policies, emphasizing equity, academic rigor, and a holistic approach to student success. Driven by a belief in education as a transformative force, Dr. Keogh is passionate about supporting young people as they discover their voices and potential. His work focuses on fostering continuous improvement in schools, particularly through the development of multitiered systems of support. His doctoral research explored effective Tier I instructional practices for multilingual learners, reflecting his commitment to inclusive and asset-based education. With a focus on student learning and innovative instructional strategies, Dr. Keogh remains dedicated to advancing educational excellence and equity.

Shaundrika Langley-Grey is a passionate educator, leader, and advocate who believes in the power of connection, courage, and equity to transform education. With over 2 decades of experience, including serving as a building and district administrator for a team of dedicated professionals, she has made it her mission to create spaces where students, educators, and communities feel seen, valued, and empowered. As a university instructor, she teaches graduate-level courses in counseling and special education, inspiring the next generation to lead with compassion and purpose. Her work focuses on bridging gaps in mental health access, fostering inclusivity, and guiding leaders to embrace vulnerability and innovation as tools for change. Dr. Langley-Grey is deeply committed to building systems that honor every story and voice. She lives with her husband and children and continues to find joy in helping others rise.